IRAN'S MINISTRY OF INTELLIGENCE

CONCISE HISTORIES
OF INTELLIGENCE
SERIES

Series Editors
Christopher Moran, Mark Phythian, and Mark Stout

The Concise Histories of Intelligence series provides students, scholars, and general readers with accessible guides to the most important and impactful intelligence services of the past and present. The books in the series span a wide range of national contexts, facilitating comparative analysis. Each title addresses the origins and history of a service, its range of activities, its leadership, its place in its country's intelligence and political system, and its role in the country's domestic and foreign security endeavors.

Other Titles in the Series

Pakistan's ISI: A Concise History of the Inter-Services Intelligence Directorate
Julian Richards

The Russian FSB: A Concise History of the Federal Security Service
Kevin P. Riehle

IRAN'S MINISTRY OF INTELLIGENCE

A CONCISE HISTORY

STEVEN R. WARD

Georgetown University Press / Washington, DC

The publisher is not responsible for third-party websites or their content. URL links were active at time of publication.

Library of Congress Cataloging-in-Publication Data

Names: Ward, Steven R., author.
Title: Iran's Ministry of Intelligence : a concise history / Steven R. Ward.
Description: Washington, DC : Georgetown University Press, 2024. | Series: Concise histories of intelligence | Includes bibliographical references and index.
Identifiers: LCCN 2024011608 (print) | LCCN 2024011609 (ebook) | ISBN 9781647125110 (hardcover) | ISBN 9781647125103 (paperback) | ISBN 9781647125127 (ebook)
Subjects: LCSH: Iran. Vizārat-i Iṭṭilāʿāt va Amnīyat-i Kishvar—History. | Intelligence service—Iran—History.
Classification: LCC JQ1785.A55 I683 2024 (print) | LCC JQ1785.A55 (ebook) | DDC 327.1255009—dc23/eng/20240408
LC record available at https://lccn.loc.gov/2024011608
LC ebook record available at https://lccn.loc.gov/2024011609

∞ This paper meets the requirements of ANSI/NISO Z39.48-1992 (Permanence of Paper).

25 24   9 8 7 6 5 4 3 2 First printing

Printed in the United States of America

Cover design by Jeremy John Parker
Interior design by Paul Hotvedt

Contents

Illustrations

Figures

Text Boxes

Chronology of Important Iranian Intelligence and National Security Events

1978

January: Protests against Shah Mohammad Reza Pahlavi's rule grow into a mass popular movement called the Iranian or Islamic Revolution. The shah's intelligence service, Sazman-e Ettalaat Va Amniat-e Kashvar (SAVAK; Organization for Intelligence and National Security), underestimates role of exiled Grand Ayatollah Ruhollah Khomeini and Iran's Shia clergy.

June: In an attempt to placate protestors, the shah fires the head of SAVAK and later has him arrested.

1979

January: The shah departs Iran after naming Shahpour Bakhtiar the regency government's prime minister. Bakhtiar disbands SAVAK.

February: Khomeini returns to Iran and establishes a provisional government. Revolutionary tribunals prosecute and execute numerous former high-ranking SAVAK officials.

March: A popular referendum approves establishment of the Islamic Republic of Iran. During the spring and early summer, the new government employs former SAVAK personnel to revive counterintelligence and other operations.

April: The government announces formation of the Islamic Revolutionary Guard Corps (IRGC).

November: Students storm the US embassy in Tehran, take fifty-two Americans hostage, and demand Washington extradite the ex-shah, then receiving medical treatment in the United States, to Iran for trial. The provisional government resigns and is replaced by the interim Revolutionary Council.

December: A national referendum approves a constitution that establishes the position of supreme leader, which Khomeini assumes.

December: In the Islamic Republic's first known external assassination operation, alleged Iranian operatives kill Shahriar Shafiq, the former shah's nephew, in France.

1980

January: Iranians elect Abolhassan Banisadr the Islamic Republic's first president, but the prime minister chosen by the legislature retains most executive powers.

July: The prime minister's intelligence bureau helps uncover and stop the Nuzhih plot, a planned military coup to remove Khomeini and his government. The former shah dies in Egypt.

July: In Iran's first significant lethal operation in the United States, alleged Iranian operative Dawud Salahuddin, an American Muslim convert, kills former Iranian diplomat and Iran Freedom Foundation president Ali Akbar Tabatabai in Maryland before fleeing to Tehran.

September: Iraqi military invasion initiates eight-year-long Iran-Iraq War.

1981

January: Iran releases US hostages after 444 days of captivity.

June: President and future supreme leader Ali Khamenei seriously wounded in failed assassination attempt. The next day an alleged Mujahedin-e Khalq (MEK; People's Holy Warriors) member bombs the Islamic Republican Party (IRP) headquarters, killing seventy-four senior officials, sparking an expanded crackdown on the MEK and other opposition political parties.

1983

August: The Majles (legislature) passes a law to establish the Ministry of Intelligence.

1984

August: The Ministry of Intelligence (known in the West by the abbreviation MOIS) formally begins operations, with Mohammad Reyshahri as first minister.

1988

July: Iran accepts United Nations Security Council Resolution 598, which ends the Iran-Iraq War when a cease-fire takes effect in August.

July–December: The MOIS participates in the execution of thousands of prisoners, primarily MEK dissidents.

1989

January: The IRGC begins its yearlong consolidation of its external operations units into the Islamic Revolutionary Guard Corps–Qods Force (IRGC-QF).

April: Iran revises its constitution to eliminate the office of prime minister and place all executive authority in the office of the president.

June: Khomeini dies, and Khamenei becomes supreme leader.

August: New president Ali Akbar Hashemi Rafsanjani replaces Reyshahri with Ali Fallahian.

1991

August: Alleged MOIS operatives assassinate Shahpour Bakhtiar in France.

1992

March: Islamic Jihad, a terrorist organization linked to Iran, conducts a suicide bombing against the Israeli embassy in Buenos Aires, killing twenty and injuring 252.

September: MOIS operatives kill officials of the Kurdish Democratic Party of Iran at a restaurant in Berlin.

1994

July: A Hezbollah operative with Iranian logistic support bombs the Argentine-Israelite Mutual Association building, killing ninety-five and injuring two hundred.

1997

August: President Mohammad Khatami appoints Qorbanali Dorri-Najafabadi to be intelligence minister.

October: The US Department of State places the MEK on its list of foreign terrorist organizations, citing the group's killing of six Americans in Iran in the 1970s and an attempted attack against the Iranian mission to the United Nations in New York City in 1992.

1998

November: Khatami forms a committee under former MOIS deputy minister Said Hajjarian to investigate the deaths of five Iranian dissidents, crimes popularly known as the Chain Murders.

1999

January: The MOIS announces the arrest of nearly a dozen MOIS and IRGC intelligence officers in connection with the Chain Murders.

February: Dorri-Najafabadi resigns and is replaced by Ali Yunesi.

June: MOIS officer Said Emami, the suspected Chain Murders ringleader, allegedly commits suicide in prison while awaiting trial.

July: Iranian security forces quash massive nationwide student protests incited by the closure of a reformist newspaper after it published MOIS information.

2000

March: An unknown assailant shoots and paralyzes Hajjarian, who had become increasingly active in reformist politics.

November: The regime prosecutes and eventually imprisons journalist Akbar Ganji for claiming that regime officials, including Fallahian and future MOIS head Gholam Hoseyn Mohseni-Ejei, were behind a series of political murders committed from 1980 to 1989.

2001

January: An Iranian military court sentences three former MOIS officers to death and twelve others to life imprisonment for their involvement in the Chain Murders. Iran's Supreme Court later orders a retrial that commutes the death sentences to prison terms and acquits three defendants.

2003

July: Iranian officials admit that Canadian photographer Zahra Kazemi died from blows suffered while in MOIS custody. An Iranian court later exonerates the accused officer.

2004

December: Yunesi announces arrest of ten Iranians on charges of spying for the United States and Israel.

2005

August: President Mahmud Ahmadinejad appoints Mohseni-Ejei to lead the MOIS.

2009

June–August: Iranian security forces respond violently and detain thousands during massive nationwide protests, popularly known as the Green Movement, that erupted following Ahmadinejad's disputed reelection victory.

August: Ahmadinejad replaces Mohseni-Ejei with Heydar Moslehi.

November: Using existing IRGC intelligence units, Iran establishes an expanded IRGC Intelligence Organization (IRGC-IO) under a cleric, Hossein Taeb.

December: In one of Iran's first cyberattacks against US interests, the Iranian Cyber Army hacks and defaces major social media home pages in response to Green Movement protests.

2010

January: The MOIS accuses sixty international organizations of inciting protests and waging a "soft war" against Iran.

February: The MOIS captures Abdulmalik Rigi, leader of the Sunni Baluch rebel group Jundallah (Army of God). The regime quickly prosecutes and hangs Rigi.

September: Iran's Atomic Energy Organization reports facilities were infected by a sophisticated computer worm named Stuxnet.

2011

January: The MOIS disrupts an alleged Israeli spy ring accused of orchestrating the assassination of a nuclear scientist in 2010.

April: President Ahmadinejad pressures Moslehi to step down, but Khamenei forces the minister's reinstatement.

May: The MOIS arrests thirty people allegedly involved in a purported Central Intelligence Agency (CIA) spy network run through US embassies in the United Arab Emirates, Turkey, and Malaysia.

2012

February–December: In retaliation for the assassinations of Iranian scientists, IRGC-QF operatives attempt a series of attacks against Israeli diplomats and US and British nationals in India, Georgia, Thailand, Turkey, Azerbaijan, Bulgaria, Kenya, and Nigeria.

March: US officials confirm that the MEK received funds from the Israeli intelligence organization ha-Mossad le-Modiin ule-Tafkidim Meyuhadim (Mossad; Institute for Intelligence and Special Operations) and carried out assassinations of Iranian nuclear scientists.

April: The MOIS announces the arrests of members of an alleged terrorist group with links to Israel operating in Iran.

September: The State Department removes the MEK from its list of foreign terrorist organizations.

2013

April: Bosnia expels two Iranian diplomats for espionage and links to terrorism after receiving Israeli information that the two were MOIS officers.

August: President Hassan Rouhani appoints Mahmud Alavi minister of intelligence.

2015

July: Iran and the permanent five members of the United Nations Security Council (the United States, the United Kingdom, France, China, and Russia) plus Germany finalize an agreement, the Joint Comprehensive Plan of Action (JCPOA), that places additional constraints on Iran's nuclear program in exchange for the lifting of nuclear-related sanctions.

December: In the Netherlands, an MOIS-directed assailant kills Mohammad Reza Kolahi Samadi, an MEK member sentenced to death in absentia for his involvement in the 1981 IRP headquarters bombing.

2017

June: The MOIS and other security forces kill or capture Islamic State of Iraq and al-Sham (ISIS) terrorists involved in the murder of eighteen Iranians and the wounding of more than fifty during assaults on Iran's parliament and Ayatollah Khomeini's mausoleum in Tehran.

November: In the Netherlands, an MOIS-linked assailant kills Ahmad Mola Nissi, a leader of the Arab Struggle Movement for the Liberation of Ahwaz (ASMLA).

2018

June: Germany arrests MOIS officer Asadollah Asadi for leading a plot to bomb an MEK-affiliated rally in Paris.

September: The MOIS arrests twenty-two people allegedly linked to an attack on a military parade in Ahvaz and claims to have evidence identifying Saudi Arabia as sponsoring the attack.

October: Danish intelligence disrupts an MOIS assassination plot against Habib Jabor, the leader of ASMLA in Copenhagen, by arresting a Norwegian citizen of Iranian descent caught surveilling Jabor's home.

November: US-Iranian tension increases following President Donald Trump's May 2018 decision to leave the JCPOA agreement and reinstate sanctions against Iran that target the country's oil, financial, and shipping industries.

December: Albania, which hosts a large group of MEK refugees, expels all Iranian diplomats, including the ambassador, following allegations that they had violated their diplomatic status and threatened national security.

2019

January: In the aftermath of the 2015 and 2017 killings of ASMLA leaders in the Netherlands and the unsuccessful 2018 plots in Denmark and France, the European Union imposes sanctions on Iran.

January: An Israeli court convicts a former Israeli energy and infrastructure minister of spying for the MOIS.

April: The US State Department designates the IRGC a foreign terrorist organization. Iran denounces the decision, and the Majles approves a bill casting the United States Central Command, which controls US military forces in the Middle East, as a terrorist organization.

June: The MOIS claims to have uncovered an alleged CIA cyber network of 290 spies working inside and outside Iran.

2020

January: A US drone strike kills IRGC-QF commander Maj. Gen. Qassem Soleimani near Baghdad International Airport. Iran retaliates with a missile barrage against a US air base in Iraq and accidentally shoots down Ukrainian International Airlines Flight 752 as it takes off from Tehran.

June–July: Iran suffers a series of industrial disasters and cyber sabotage at a missile production facility, the Natanz nuclear facility, and petrochemical plants in Khuzestan. Other incidents include fires in Tehran and damage to seven ships in the port of Bushehr.

August: An unknown assailant kills al-Qaeda's second-in-command, Abdullah Ahmad Abdullah (aka Abu Muhammad al-Masri), along with his daughter in Tehran.

November: The MOIS claims its warnings were ignored after alleged Israeli-directed assailants use a remote-controlled machine gun to ambush and kill Mohsen Fakhrizadeh, a defense ministry research director and a key figure in Iran's nuclear program.

2021

July: The US Federal Bureau of Investigation (FBI) foils an Iranian intelligence plot to abduct Iranian American activist Masih Alinejad in New York. In September the US Department of the Treasury sanctions four Iranian operatives involved in the plot.

August: Former judiciary chief Ebrahim Raisi becomes Iran's eighth president and appoints Esmail Khatib minister of intelligence. Khamenei appoints former MOIS head Mohseni-Ejei Iran's chief justice.

2022

January: The White House warns Iran against threatening US citizens as the State Department extends diplomatic security details for former Trump administration officials.

February: An allegedly Israeli large-scale drone attack destroys an Iranian storage facility for unmanned aerial vehicles after Israel announces "Octopus Doctrine" to exhaust Iran with a range of military, diplomatic, cyber, and other actions.

March: An IRGC missile unit attacks an alleged Mossad base in Iraq.

April–July: The MOIS claims disruption of multiple Mossad-directed cells planning assassinations and sabotage.

May: Assailants in Tehran kill IRGC colonel Sayyad Khodai, allegedly an IRGC-QF deputy commander involved in planning abductions and assassinations.

June: IRGC brigadier general Mohammad Kazemi replaces Hossein Taeb as IRGC-IO chief. Khatib and Kazemi pledge improved cooperation.

September: Albania severs diplomatic relations with Tehran and expels Iranian diplomats over an alleged Iranian-sponsored cyberattack in July that targeted public services, state records, and government intranet communications.

September: Nationwide antigovernment protests begin following the death in custody of a twenty-two-year-old Kurdish Iranian woman, Mahsa Amini, who had been detained by Iran's morality police for improper dress.

September: The United States sanctions the MOIS and intelligence minister Khatib for cyber-enabled activities against the United States and its allies.

October: ISIS attacks the Shah Cheragh shrine in Shiraz, the group's first terrorist operation inside Iran since 2018, reportedly killing fifteen people and injuring at least forty.

December: Protests and strikes continue across Iran more than three months after Mahsa Amini's death as the regime conducts its first executions connected to the demonstrations.

2023

January: The MOIS announces arrests of alleged members of an MEK network purportedly involved in promoting domestic unrest in late 2022.

February: The MOIS announces arrests of alleged Israeli-directed saboteurs behind a late January drone attack on a military production facility in Esfahan.

September: After Iran releases five Americans in exchange for five Iranians held by the United States, Washington sanctions the MOIS and former president Ahmadinejad for enabling the wrongful detention of US citizens.

October: The Palestinian militant group Hamas attacks Israel from Gaza, initiating a conflict joined by other Iranian-supported militant groups in Lebanon, Syria, Iraq, and Yemen belonging to the "Axis of Resistance."

October–December: Attacks by Axis of Resistance groups on Red Sea shipping and US bases in Iraq and Syria threaten to widen the war and increase US-Iran tensions.

December: The United States sanctions alleged MOIS officers for recruiting individuals in the United States for surveillance and potential lethal operations targeting current and former US government officials.

Note: This chronology was drawn from the series of chronologies published over four decades by the Middle East Institute's *Middle East Journal*, from the United States Institute of Peace's website Iran Primer, various American newspapers, and *Outlaw Regime: A Chronicle of Iran's Destructive Activities*, published in 2018 by the US Department of State's Iran Action Group.

Preface

This history examines the Ministry of Intelligence of the Islamic Republic of Iran, a critical arm of that government's domestic and external security apparatus. It addresses the ministry's origins and development, its support to the governing system, and its once paramount but now diminishing role in Iran's broad intelligence community, with sufficient context on Iranian political and security developments to explain the factors shaping the ministry. While other Iranian security services are discussed as needed in examining the Ministry of Intelligence's roles and missions, the ministry itself is the central focus of this book in order to facilitate comparative analysis with other countries' primary intelligence services. Such an analysis is challenging because, by any standard of modern intelligence organizations, Iran's intelligence community is extremely opaque. In addition, the security apparatus has overlapping responsibilities that complicate the tasks of separating and analyzing the ministry's operational roles, methods, and procedures. In short, the Ministry of Intelligence presents many challenges to researchers trying to understand its development, performance, and culture.

Nonetheless, the ministry remains an important subject of study. Its domestic security role and overseas activities are key features of the Islamic Republic of Iran's efforts, as the US intelligence community has consistently concluded, to erode American influence, entrench its own, and project power in the Middle East while minimizing threats to regime stability.[1] Iran's government sees itself locked in a struggle with the United States and its allies, whom Tehran perceives as intent on undermining its regime. In 2018 Supreme Leader Ayatollah Ali Khamenei highlighted this long-standing rivalry when he told Ministry of Intelligence staff that Iran confronted "a huge intelligence war" that required an offensive response.[2] To this end, the ministry and other elements of Iran's intelligence community over the past decade have been linked to assassination and kidnapping plots in the United States, Europe, the Middle East, and South Asia and remain committed to developing networks of informants and agents of influence inside the United States.[3]

To protect the regime, Iran's Ministry of Intelligence is a key player in suppressing domestic dissent, combating antigovernment groups, and defending against foreign espionage, subversion, and sabotage. Its organizational culture emphasizes protection of national identity and solidarity by combating perceived foreign attempts to promote unrest and sedition. Tehran has an expansive definition of internal threats, however, and this includes the activities of independent journalists, human rights advocates, labor unions, and even environmentalists.[4] The ministry uses similar national security justifications for a range of external operations that prioritize targeting expatriate Iranian critics of the regime over the collection of foreign political, military, and economic information.

Why This Book?

This introductory overview attempts to update and improve on the paucity of available English-language works on Iran's Ministry of Intelligence to promote an understanding of its history and actions. It is intended primarily for upper-level undergraduate and graduate students, intelligence and foreign policy professionals, and general readers. As of this writing, the most detailed, frequently cited, and somewhat flawed work is a 2012 Library of Congress report, *Iran's Ministry of Intelligence and Security: A Profile*.[5] This history aspires to provide a more contemporary and better-sourced account, drawing, in part, on my familiarity with the Islamic Republic gained from my nearly thirty years of service as a CIA intelligence analyst. I devoted most of my career to Iranian security issues and in recent years have consulted on Iran for the National Intelligence Council and US Central Command.

Primary sources on the Ministry of Intelligence are limited. This history relies on Iranian and Western newspaper articles that, because they record contemporaneous accounts and direct statements by relevant Iranian and other officials, represent some of the best information sources available. Those selected appear to have stood the test of time in terms of their accuracy and reliability despite a dearth of corroborating information. This history also uses various secondary sources selected because their authors have shown an in-depth understanding of Iran or have provided reasoned analysis of the subject matter. I have tried to make my Iranian sources cited in the endnotes transparent to the reader. In addition, cited Persian-language and related news sources are listed in the bibliography with a brief description of their background and, as appropriate, political orientation.

Where possible and with the help of a Persian-speaking research assistant, I have gathered and used translations of public Iranian government documents and statements. Iran, however, treats virtually all information about its intelligence apparatus as classified. Our research included examination of Iranian repositories such as the Majlis Research Center and the Islamic Revolution Document Center. Still, we were able to find only a few sources that provided some previously unknown details about the ministry or added value in understanding the ministry's self-image. There almost certainly is more work to be done here for histories that go beyond the introductory goals of this volume.

Like the Library of Congress profile, this examination uses materials produced by Iranian dissidents and other close observers of Iran, including American and Israeli scholars, who are openly opposed to the Islamic Republic. In these cases, I generally have limited my use to statements of fact rather than repetition of the authors' analyses. I used a similar approach with official government statements by Iran, the United States, Israel, and other countries by repeating their stated views to show where they stand rather than to validate the accuracy of their positions. All sides in the rivalry use official pronouncements to overstate allegations and denigrate their opponents. I have tried to account for any biases, including my own, to make this presentation as objective as possible, and I signal where caution is needed with words such as "alleged," "claimed," "purported," and so on.

The chapters that follow address basic questions about the ministry's origins and its development amid war and the multiple genuine internal and external security threats the Islamic Republic faces in its geopolitical rivalries with Israel, Saudi Arabia, the United States, and others. The text also examines the ministry's leaders, their relationships with other senior Iranian officials, and the impact of their tenures on the ministry. One chapter is devoted to outlining the ministry's organization, available demographic details, and basic information on its recruitment and training of officers. It also discusses the ministry's organizational culture and its view of intelligence ethics. Another part of the history examines the ministry's operations and tradecraft, using its observed intelligence successes and failures over nearly four decades. It then addresses the ministry's role in Iran's intelligence community and its engagement with foreign intelligence services and nonstate actors. Finally, before providing an analysis of the ministry's future development, the text explores how the ministry represents itself in the media and contrasts this briefly with the regime's representation of its other primary intelligence organization to illustrate how the ministry distinguishes itself and how it might change in the coming years.

The MOIS Abbreviation and Transliteration Matters

As explained in chapter 1, this Iranian organization is properly called Vezarat-e Ettelaat Jomhuri-ye Eslami-ye Iran (Ministry of Intelligence of the Islamic Republic of Iran). During and since my CIA career, the Iranian service's name has been regularly translated as the Ministry of Intelligence and Security, and use of the English abbreviation MOIS had become a widespread practice. Some translations rendered *Ettelaat* as "Information," its general meaning in Persian, rather than "Intelligence," which, given the context—information used for policymaking, national security planning, and operations—was the more accurate conversion. I occasionally came across Western works that referred to the Vezarat-e Ettelaat va Amniyat-e Keshvar (Ministry of Intelligence and National Security) and used the acronym VEVAK. During my research for this book, however, I was made aware of the fact that the Iranians had never used either of these Western appellations and that, in Iran, the ministry uses the Farsi acronym VAJA. I was unable to discover the source of this discrepancy, but readers should be aware of the multiple permutations of the ministry's name in the West, especially when developing search terms for future research. For consistency, this text will follow the example of the US government and use MOIS as the abbreviated form.

I do not speak or read Persian and have relied on translations of Persian-language sources. Readers should be aware that the transliteration of Persian words and names varies from source to source. To avoid confusion, I have kept spellings consistent throughout the text even when they are different in the cited sources. Finally, for simplicity, I have not used diacritical marks with Persian and Arabic words and phrases.

Acknowledgments

This book would not have been possible without the assistance of Bahman Tavili, a native Persian speaker and a graduate of Azad University in Tehran, Ohio State University, and the Georgetown University Security Studies Program. An experienced researcher in open-source data collection, analysis, and translation, he was incredibly helpful in finding and translating Iranian government documents and press articles, reviewing the text, and sharing valuable insights that helped me think through issues and improve the assessments in this history. For reviewing the draft manuscript and helping to improve its accuracy and clarity, I want to thank friends and former colleagues Daniel Byman, a Georgetown University School of Foreign Service professor, a member of the US State Department's International Security Advisory Board, and a former director of Georgetown's Security Studies Program and Center for Security Studies; former National Security Council official Kenneth Pollack, a senior fellow specializing in Middle Eastern political-military affairs at the American Enterprise Institute; and John Sotos, a widely respected and now retired US government senior analyst on Iran's government and politics. Finally, I must express my appreciation to Don Jacobs and his associates at Georgetown University Press for their assistance in the final editing and publishing process.

All statements of fact, opinion, or analysis expressed are those of the author and do not reflect the official positions or views of the US government. Nothing in the contents should be construed as asserting or implying US government authentication of information or endorsement of the author's views. To the extent any mistakes have made their way into the text, I am solely responsible for such errors.

Notes

1. For recent assessments, see Office of the Director of National Intelligence (ODNI), *Annual Threat Assessment of the US Intelligence Community* (Washington, DC: ODNI, February 6, 2023), 17–19, https://www.dni.gov/index.php/newsroom/repor ts-publications/reports-publications-2023/3676-2023-annual-threat-assessment-of -the-u-s-intelligence-community; ODNI, *Annual Threat Assessment of the US Intelligence Community* (Washington, DC: ODNI, February 7, 2022), 14, https://www.hs dl.org/c/ 2022-annual-threat-assessment-released/; and US Congress, Senate Armed Services Committee, *Worldwide Threats*, 117th Cong., 1st sess., April 29, 2021 (testimony of Avril Haines, director of national intelligence), n.p., https://plus.cq.com / doc/testimony-6207090.
2. "Iran's Supreme Leader Warns of 'Huge Intelligence War,'" BBC Monitoring Middle East [khamenei.ir in Persian], April 18, 2018, ProQuest (when available, original sources cited by BBC Monitoring are listed in brackets); Scott Peterson, "Why Europe Is Again a Battlefield for Iran's Internal Wars," *Christian Science Monitor*, May 1, 2019, https://www.csmonitor.com/World/Middle-East/2019/0501/Why-Europe-is -again-a-battlefield-for-Iran-s-internal-wars.
3. US Congress, *Worldwide Threats*; ODNI, *Annual Threat Assessment* (2022), 14.
4. Hannah Sommerville, "Transnational Repression: How Iran Haunts and Kills Its Critics around the World," IranWire, November 18, 2021, https://iranwire.com/en/fe atures/10803.
5. The initial version of this report was pulled for revisions after being criticized for its sourcing. The subsequent version, while generally solid, still relies on some uncorroborated claims and now dated information. Library of Congress, Federal Research Division, *Iran's Ministry of Intelligence and Security: A Profile* (Washington, DC: Library of Congress, December 2012). On the sourcing controversy, see Justin Elliott, "How a Government Report Spread a Questionable Claim about Iran," ProPublica, January 14, 2013, https://www.propublica.org/article/ government-study-iran-30000-intel ligence-ministry; and "Widely Cited Government Study on Iranian Spies 'Pulled for Revisions,'" ProPublica, January 22, 2013, https://www.propublica.org/article /widely-cited-government-study-on-iranian-spies-pulled-for-revisions.

Abbreviations

AEI	American Enterprise Institute
AFGS	Armed Forces General Staff
AMIA	Asociación Mutual Israelita Argentina (Argentine-Israelite Mutual Association)
APT	advanced persistent threat
ASMLA	Arab Struggle Movement for the Liberation of Ahwaz
CIA	Central Intelligence Agency
FBI	Federal Bureau of Investigation
HUMINT	human intelligence
ICC	Intelligence Coordination Council
IRC	Islamic Revolution Council
IRGC	Islamic Revolutionary Guard Corps
IRGC-IO	Islamic Revolutionary Guard Corps–Intelligence Organization
IRGC-QF	Islamic Revolutionary Guard Corps–Qods Force
IRIB	Islamic Republic of Iran Broadcasting
IRNA	Islamic Republic News Agency
IRP	Islamic Republican Party
ISIS	Islamic State of Iraq and al-Sham
ISIS-K	Islamic State of Iraq and al-Sham-Khorasan
ISNA	Iranian Students News Agency
JCPOA	Joint Comprehensive Plan of Action

KDPI	Kurdistan Democratic Party of Iran
LEC	Law Enforcement Command
LEF	Law Enforcement Force
MODAFL	Ministry of Defense and Armed Forces Logistics
MOIS	Ministry of Intelligence
MEK	Mujahedin-e Khalq
MIR	Mujahedin of the Islamic Revolution
ODNI	Office of the Director of National Intelligence
SAVAK	Organization for Intelligence and National Security
SAVAMA	Organization of Intelligence and National Security of Iran
SCC	Special Court for Clergy
SIGINT	signals intelligence
SIS	Secret Intelligence Service
SNSC	Supreme National Security Council
SVR	Foreign Intelligence Service
UINS	University of Intelligence and National Security
USIP	United States Institute of Peace

1

Foundation

The Ministry of Intelligence of the Islamic Republic of Iran (known in the West by the abbreviation MOIS) is Iran's primary intelligence service and coordinating head of the regime's intelligence community. Over the course of its four decades of existence, the ministry has confronted competent and dangerous terrorist and dissident groups, damaging foreign espionage, serious domestic unrest, and an ongoing shadow war with Israel. MOIS activities have served as critical campaigns in a long-standing intelligence war waged between Iran and its rivals, including the United States. As described in later chapters, the ministry's more recent efforts to protect the Iranian regime have added to tensions at home and in the region.

Established in 1984, the Ministry of Intelligence grew out of the 1978–79 revolution that deposed the reigning monarch, the shah of Iran. The MOIS absorbed remnants of the shah's disbanded intelligence service along with some of its police state tactics. It also was staffed by Islamic revolutionaries who brought their loyalty to Iran's clerical leadership, familiarity with clandestine political opposition, and concerns about counterrevolution and foreign intervention. In addition, the ministry inherited some of the revolution's political divisions and differing approaches to law and civil rights that still impact national security policymaking in Iran. A brief review of the shah's intelligence services and the establishment of the Islamic Republic provides important context for understanding the ministry's origins and its foundation.

The Shah's Intelligence Services and the Iranian Revolution

In ruling Iran from 1941 to 1979, Shah Mohammad Reza Pahlavi relied heavily on a number of domestic intelligence organizations to monitor and eliminate threats to the monarchy and his increasingly autocratic rule. Following a failed assassination attempt in early 1949, the shah declared martial law, outlawed the communist Tudeh (Masses) Party, and strong-armed the parliament into giving him power over it and the media. With assistance from the US Army, the shah in the early 1950s established a military intelligence bureau under Teymour Bakhtiar to root out communists, contain other militant threats to the throne, and, over time, repress all political opposition. One of the first significant challenges, however, came not from the communists but from Prime Minister Mohammad Mossadeq, a popular nationalist and antiroyalist politician.

Mossadeq wanted to expand the power of elected leaders and, to achieve this, saw a need to reduce the shah's control of the military, the main arm of the monarchy's security apparatus. By 1951 the prime minister had gained widespread domestic popularity and international renown by nationalizing Iran's oil industry and removing it from British control. Encouraged by his popular standing, Mossadeq in 1952 tried to transfer the shah's role in appointing the minister of war and the military's chief of staff to the prime minister's office. When the shah rejected this effort, Mossadeq resigned and created a political crisis that led to his reinstatement and the shah's acquiescence to most of his demands.

The monarch countered Mossadeq in August 1953 by using the Iranian military—helped by the British Secret Intelligence Service (SIS) and, more significantly, by the involvement of the US Central Intelligence Agency (CIA)—to remove the prime minister. Bakhtiar's military intelligence bureau then spent the next year arresting hundreds of Mossadeq's most vocal supporters.[1] With assistance from a small CIA training mission, the shah in 1957 expanded Bakhtiar's operation, designating it the Sazman-e Ettelaat Va Amniat-e Kashvar (Organization for Intelligence and National Security). Popularly known by its Persian acronym SAVAK, the new organization focused on protecting the shah's rule and worked to overcome the poor coordination that had plagued the separate intelligence units of the armed forces, the Gendarmerie (an internal security force that protected borders and rural areas), and a national urban police force, the Shahrbani.[2]

Ambitious to make Iran a major regional power, the shah during the 1960s and early 1970s strengthened his alliance with the United States. An increased US role in supporting the growing Iranian military helped to protect the monarchy against the Soviet Union and the region's pro-Soviet Arab regimes and revolutionary movements. The shah also tried to orient Iran toward the West, imposing modernization programs to improve Iranian industry, trade, and education that impacted various Iranian interest groups. These economic and social reforms, the presence of tens of thousands of Americans supporting the Iranian military and involved in Iran's economy, and the shah's increasingly autocratic rule created an array of political enemies. The most active opponents included groups of secular leftists, communists, and Marxists as well as Islamic militants led by clerics of the Shia sect of Islam followed by most Iranians. By 1964 Grand Ayatollah Ruhollah Khomeini became the most prominent clerical opponent to imperial policies,[3] championing widespread views that the policies were antireligious. He also voiced opposition to an unpopular status-of-forces agreement with the United States he described as a surrender of Iran's sovereignty and honor.

When Khomeini's opposition fostered popular unrest, the shah exiled him in November 1964, causing the ayatollah to depart for Turkey before eventually settling in Iraq. The monarch also expanded SAVAK, which grew to as many as five thousand employees, with thousands of paid informers.[4] Military personnel ran the service, which operated under the prime minister's office but answered only to the shah. SAVAK developed investigative methods to monitor all types of political activity as well as journalists, literary figures, and academics. Its informers kept universities, labor unions, and peasant farmer organizations under constant surveillance.[5] The service also gained sweeping powers to censor media, control passports, and screen candidates for jobs in government and education. SAVAK officers posted in embassies scrutinized Iranians living and studying abroad. As the 1960s ended, SAVAK was monitoring almost every facet of Iranian public life.[6]

The shah continued to expand SAVAK and other elements of his police state and allowed increasingly harsh methods of operation.[7] SAVAK gained the authority to arrest suspected dissidents, hold them indefinitely, and subject detainees to severe interrogations. It also developed a fearsome reputation for intimidation, disappearances, and extrajudicial killings. Human rights groups documented that, despite a nominal royal ban, beatings, whippings, electric shocks, and other tortures were standard operating procedure in SAVAK prisons. New security organizations included the Imperial Iranian Inspectorate to watch the military, municipal police department intelligence divisions for the local monitoring of dissidence, and the Special Bureau. This latter unit was a clandestine organization led by Gen. Hosein Fardust, the shah's childhood friend and a former SAVAK deputy director, that spied on SAVAK, other government agencies, and Iran's political elite.

By the mid-1970s SAVAK had filled Tehran's Evin Prison, the main facility for political opponents, and other new prisons throughout the country. SAVAK had become a state within a state as it interfered with the armed forces, the press, universities, telecommunications, the postal service, and even manufacturers and retailers.[8] In the monarchy's waning years, most Iranians learned to avoid talking about politics because SAVAK tactics included having informers make disparaging comments about the shah to get others to reveal their thoughts. The informers also sowed mistrust by planting rumors that genuine activists were SAVAK agents.[9] After the 1979 revolution, the new regime published a pamphlet based on captured documents that revealed the scope of SAVAK activities in the late 1970s and placed its personnel strength at fifteen thousand full-time officers, with thousands of informants.[10]

Opposition to the shah grew more violent in the 1970s with the rising militancy of leftist and Islamist groups spurred by growing economic problems and the shah's refusal to enact meaningful political reforms.[11] Two of the major secular components of the revolution were the National Front, a long-standing political coalition established by Mosaddeq in 1949, and its more popular offshoot, the Freedom Movement, led by Mehdi Bazargan, a French-educated engineer who had served in Mosaddeq's cabinet. Formed in the early 1960s, the Freedom Movement sought to combine features of European-style socialism, modern technology, and the more progressive aspects of Islam and Iran's culture to promote social justice.[12] In 1965 more radical Freedom Movement members formed a guerrilla organization that came to be called the Mujahedin-e Khalq (MEK; People's Holy Warriors), a Marxist-Islamist faction that built a substantial following before and during the revolution. The MEK, joined by similar Marxist and Islamist groups patterned on foreign leftist guerrilla movements, waged insurgent warfare with fighters trained in Palestinian militants' camps in Lebanon. Because the United States was one of the shah's primary backers, the anti-Western MEK targeted American interests, attacking the Iranian-American Society, the US Information Agency's office, and the offices and personnel of American corporations. In 1973 the group assassinated the deputy chief of the US military mission to Iran.[13]

SAVAK was eventually able to contain the guerrillas by conducting virtually unrestrained operations against them. Stymied by the monarchy's repression, the armed groups went further underground, built their memberships, and readied themselves to return to action when circumstances permitted. Despite its successful counterguerrilla operations, however, SAVAK failed to penetrate the MEK and similar secular revolutionary networks. During this period, Islamic revolutionaries in underground groups spread throughout the country and increasingly shifted away from their leftist roots toward Khomeini's more conservative views. General Fardust later suggested that the service had no talent for countering subversion because it focused on cultivating a fearsome image to deter opposition and unrest.[14]

SAVAK repression affected many and alarmed even more Iranians, contributing to the grievances that in 1978 erupted into the Iranian Revolution. This genuine people's revolt against government oppression, corruption, economic inequality, and foreign policies involved many political factions, including the MEK, other secular leftists and communists, and Khomeini's many followers. The exiled ayatollah used his religious authority and charisma to give the mass antishah demonstrations cohesion and common purpose. Emerging as the movement's leader, first in Iraq and then from Paris, Khomeini used SAVAK injustices as one of the themes all Iranians understood to build support for overthrowing the monarchy.[15]

The revolution began in January 1978 and spread quickly as the monarchy's initially violent response to demonstrations fed a series of protests and incidents throughout Iran that the shah and his security services were unable to contain. The shah was then suffering from lymphomatous cancer, an illness he kept secret from government officials. The ailing monarch vacillated between strong, repressive responses and appeasement to end the increasingly popular demonstrations, which were being joined by multiple segments of the Iranian people. In late summer, in an effort to accommodate moderate elements of the revolution to help him remain in power, the shah removed the head of SAVAK, Gen. Nematollah Nassiri, and fired nearly three dozen senior SAVAK officers, severely demoralizing the security services. At the end of September, the government arrested Nassiri and other SAVAK officers in another unsuccessful attempt to mollify the protestors.[16]

Unable to appease the revolutionaries and unwilling to order more violent measures to try to save his reign, the increasingly ill shah at the start of 1979 announced his intent to go into exile. Before departing in mid-January 1979, the shah installed Shahpour Bakhtiar, a liberal elder statesman, as prime minister. Bakhtiar, however, had no support among the leaders of Iran's armed forces and security services and lacked ties to the secular and religious leaders of the revolution. General Fardust, meanwhile, had sided with the revolutionaries and was working to keep Iran's security services neutral in the contest between the people and Bakhtiar's regency administration.[17] The general subsequently claimed that because he could see that the monarchy was too corrupt to weather the revolution, he decided to place himself at Khomeini's mercy.[18]

Khomeini's Divided Government

From Paris, Khomeini had tasked the clerics and other supporters around him to begin preparations for governing Iran after the revolution succeeded. Mehdi Bazargan of the Freedom Movement had flown to France to declare support for Khomeini and make an alliance with Khomeini's movement. As a result, the Freedom Movement leader gained a seat on the clandestine Islamic Revolution Council (IRC), which Khomeini had designated the highest revolutionary authority in Iran until he returned to the country.[19] Khomeini allowed Bazargan, a Western-educated Islamic modernist, and other similarly inclined revolutionaries to believe that he would be content to move to the background once the revolution was won.[20] Some of Khomeini's supporters, however, had infiltrated Bazargan's circle and spied on him, suggesting that Khomeini's clerical deputies were already planning on containing the Freedom Movement leader's power and influence.[21]

After the shah left the country, Khomeini returned to Iran on February 1, 1979. In a gesture of respect, many of Iran's Shia greeted the grand ayatollah as an imam, an honorific that was usually reserved for describing the divinely appointed Shia leaders of the faith's early history. After the armed forces declared their neutrality in the political contest, the revolutionaries routed Bakhtiar's government and the shah's remaining security services over the next week and a half, a period now celebrated as the Ten Days of Dawn. During this time multiple militant groups entered and ransacked SAVAK's buildings. They took documents to protect themselves or use against others until members of Khomeini's bodyguard stopped the pillaging and secured the facilities and their contents, according to a review of a history of SAVAK's demise published in 2013 by the regime's Islamic Revolution Document Center.[22] The relatively rapid collapse of the Pahlavi dynasty, however, caught many of the revolutionaries—the secular democrats, the Marxists, other leftists, and the various Islamic groups—ill prepared to advance their political ambitions.

During this time, Khomeini appointed Bazargan the prime minister of a new provisional government as the Islamist, liberal, and leftist elements of the revolution immediately began to compete over implementing their differing visions of governance. The liberal lay nationalists appointed to administer the provisional government under Bazargan favored a democratic republic with an Islamic aspect. The ayatollah and his disciples in the IRC, who had more power and influence throughout the country, were intent on establishing a government based on Khomeini's theory of *velayat-e faqih* (the guardianship of the jurisconsult). The concept promoted rule by an expert in Islamic law with the political acumen to lead an Islamic society. Called *vali-ye faqih* (guardian jurisconsult), this ruler was intended to be a widely followed Shia ayatollah such as Khomeini had become.

Amid the early postrevolutionary period's turmoil and with supporters to help set up a shadow government, Khomeini soon emerged as Iran's paramount leader. He moved quickly on public referendums to declare Iran an Islamic republic and initiate the preparation of a constitution written by clerical supporters of velayat-e faqih. Khomeini also established a revolutionary tribunal system to oversee the ad hoc courts set up throughout the country to try enemies of the revolution. These courts provided a start for many future intelligence leaders as they worked to punish the shah's officials and eliminate potential rivals to the clerics' power.[23]

As expected, the proposed constitution enshrined the velayat-e faqih concept when it was approved in late 1979. The new constitution heavily favored Khomeini's theocracy over democratic governance. For the republican part, it provided direct elections of a president and a unicameral legislature, known as the Majles (Assembly, short for Islamic Consultative Assembly). The constitution included institutional checks and balances, such as having posts for prime minister and president, and opportunities for diverse political discourse and decision-making. It also set the stage for discussions about the future intelligence service's subordination to Iran's elected officials or other power centers.

On the Islamic side, the constitution created the position of a powerful supreme leader who had to be a *marja-ye taqlid* (source of emulation), a standing usually achieved only by grand ayatollahs. As with the concept of velayat-e faqih, Khomeini was one of the few Shia clerics qualified under the constitution to become leader.[24] Chosen to serve an unlimited term of office by an elected Assembly of Experts dominated by clerics, the supreme leader (or simply the leader) is the commander in chief of the armed forces. He also appoints the chief justice, who heads the judiciary, and the prosecutor general, a post similar to the US attorney general. In addition, the leader appoints six clerics to the twelve-man Guardian Council, which can veto legislation it deems inconsistent with Islamic law and approves candidates for public office with information provided by the regime's intelligence services.[25]

Selected as supreme leader, Khomeini strengthened his position by taking advantage of the unavoidable friction created by the establishment of an executive branch split between a president and prime minister. When the president and prime minister belonged to different factions, as occurred from 1981 to 1989, Khomeini played a mediating role that made the opposing groups more reliant on him. Factional disputes, however, were not limited to the elected institutions.[26] The politically active clerics who supported Khomeini were divided between the Islamic Republican Party (IRP), the theological community in Qom (a Shia holy city and center of religious studies), and a less influential group of moderate clergymen. Formed by Khomeini's top lieutenants from the IRC to execute his theocratic vision, the IRP dominated the government but did not fully control the executive and legislature. The Qom community dominated the judiciary, controlled many local clerical posts, and was responsible for indoctrinating the security services.[27] Khomeini often had to arbitrate between officials in the unelected parts of the regime who differed over pursuing ideologically pure versus more pragmatic approaches to Iran's problems.[28]

Another important aspect of the 1979 constitution was its attempt to institutionalize and apply Khomeini's revolutionary view of Islam to foreign and security policies, which shaped the roles of the evolving intelligence and security apparatus. The preamble stated that with regard to international relations, Iran would work with other Islamic movements to pave the way for global Islamic unity and perpetuate the struggle to liberate the deprived and oppressed throughout the world.[29] Article 3 required a foreign policy based on Islamic criteria, with a fraternal commitment to all Muslims and unsparing support to the oppressed of the world.[30] Article 152 specifically called for defending the rights of all Muslims, while Article 154, after directing the avoidance of interference in other countries' internal affairs, dictated support to the "just struggles" of the oppressed.[31] These articles, in practice, justified MOIS and Iranian Revolutionary Guard Corps (IRGC) external operations and their work with various revolutionary movements.

It is common for countries to have ideology play a role in security and foreign policies, and state ideology throughout Iran's history had been mixed with national interests, geopolitical realities, and an attendant pragmatism.[32] The institutionalization of revolutionary Islamism, however, increased its policy role during the first decade following the shah's downfall. Over time, the Islamic Republic, constrained by various economic, military, and political weaknesses, would become more pragmatic and flexible by giving increased emphasis to national interests. Ideology would continue to play an important role, however, in framing policy parameters and guidance for the security services even as Tehran practiced realpolitik to ensure regime survival and meet the other immediate needs of the emerging ruling establishment, which would become more commonly known as the *nezam* (system).[33]

Early Intelligence Activities

The collapse of Iran's intelligence and civil law enforcement agencies at the end of the revolution spawned nongovernment popular organizations that tried to fill the gap on behalf of the new regime. During and after the revolution, *komitehs* (committees) arose across the country in mosques, youth centers, and captured police stations and set up revolutionary tribunals. During 1979 these tribunals executed at least eighty-three former SAVAK officers, including General Nassiri, for their role in interrogations, torture, assassinations, and other crimes.[34] The komitehs also worked to suppress perceived counterrevolutionary threats while enforcing their version of law on other Iranians. Meanwhile, other young revolutionaries had taken over military intelligence units, judging them to be the best place to identify and investigate potential counterrevolutionaries and coup plotters as well as uncover perpetrators of shah-era crimes for transfer to the revolutionary tribunals.[35]

Khomeini allowed these activities to continue because of concerns over police force loyalty, military coup attempts, and foreign interference. He eventually ordered the komitehs to be organized and subordinated to the government and then given police duties and related information-gathering activities.[36] Khomeini also exploited prescient steps he had taken in exile, when he cultivated relationships with SAVAK officers in anticipation of the need for a national intelligence service to combat threats to an incoming revolutionary regime.[37] Apparently encouraged by these contacts, as soon as the provisional government began, senior intelligence officers approached it to reestablish the counterespionage directorate and save its archive of information, according to the review of the regime's SAVAK history.[38] The review indicated that Barzagan's government accepted the offer, keeping more than 90 percent of the counterintelligence directorate working for the prime minister's office through at least the middle of 1980.

To manage these and other SAVAK officers who had offered their services, Bazargan set up an intelligence bureau within his office at the urging of Mohammad-Ali Rajai, a revolutionary who later served as prime minister and Iran's second president.[39] The regime entrusted Ebrahim Yazdi, deputy prime minister for revolutionary affairs, and the prime minister's son, Abdul Ali Bazargan, with managing the affairs of the remaining SAVAK organizations, including the directorates for internal security and overseas operations.[40] The bureau soon found itself sharing intelligence duties with the komitehs, military intelligence units, and a new revolutionary security organization, the IRGC.[41]

Khomeini and other senior leaders determined before returning to Iran that they would need a security force based on the armed revolutionary groups to protect their new government and its revolutionary ideals.[42] On April 22, 1979, amid ongoing clashes between Islamic and leftist groups, Khomeini issued a decree formally creating the IRGC, which he made subordinate to himself; a coordination council composed of representatives of the IRC and, to a lesser degree, the provisional government; and a new IRGC command council. To perform its security mission, the IRGC created elements that became a counterpart to Bazargan's intelligence bureau and collected intelligence on internal and external opponents of the Islamic Republic. The IRGC later assumed the external role of exporting the revolution to project Iran's power and influence. While IRGC personnel handled most of the recruitment, training, and support of Shia revolutionary groups throughout the region, the CIA judged that the initial Iranian bureaucracy for exporting the revolution consisted of the IRGC, the Ministry of Foreign Affairs, and the prime minister's office.[43]

The IRGC joined the komitehs in purging and supplanting many of the shah's remaining military, security, and law enforcement officials and was used to offset the Artesh, Iran's regular armed forces, which the revolutionaries suspected of continued loyalty to the former monarch. The two revolutionary organizations also confronted the numerous leftist, Marxist, and ethnic armed groups opposed to Khomeini's movement and the new government.[44] The IRGC soon created an intelligence unit focused on rebellious ethnic minority groups and the regime's legal but more militant political opposition, such as the MEK. Similarly, the komitehs and the remaining local law enforcement organizations established their own intelligence sections to spy on neighbors and potential opponents of the nezam. To check the new revolutionary forces' power, the regime gave them overlapping responsibilities. In addition,

Khomeini assigned personal representatives to the security services as well as to government ministries and provincial governments to ensure adherence to velayat-e faqih and loyalty to the leader.[45]

After the constitution's approval in December 1979, the prime minister gained most of the regime's executive power. Among the office's powers was the ability to appoint a cabinet of ministers to run the government. These posts included the interior and defense ministers with the former responsible for law enforcement agencies and komitehs, while the latter administered the armed forces' intelligence organizations. The prime minister retained the intelligence bureau, which then sought to coordinate the actions of the various security services' intelligence organizations.

According to the regime's SAVAK history, the relationship between the provisional government and the large numbers of SAVAK counterintelligence personnel working for it through its first year created rumors about the formation of a new organization similar to the shah's intelligence service. By mid-1980 Western media was citing exiled Iranian dissidents and US intelligence officials as sources for identifying this new service as the Sazman-e Ettelaat va Amniat-e Melli Iran (SAVAMA; Organization of Intelligence and National Security of Iran) and for claims that it was headed by Fardust.[46] The former general acknowledged in his memoirs that some government officials consulted him about the formation of a SAVAK-like intelligence organization.[47] In an undated interview broadcast just weeks before his death in April 1987, however, Fardust denied working for a postrevolution security service.[48]

The regime rejected these claims about the existence of SAVAMA. The SAVAK history reportedly suggests that opponents of the government, especially those related to former prime minister Bakhtiar, were behind the allegations, which Western intelligence services appear to have accepted.[49] Former intelligence bureau officials do not refer to SAVAMA in discussing their work in published interviews. Still, SAVAMA remains a term used by some sources to describe the body behind Iranian intelligence operations that apparently were conducted out of the prime minister's office from 1979 to 1984.

According to Said Hajjarian, one of the founders of the MOIS, the regime eventually created a division of labor between the prime minister's office and the IRGC, with the former responsible for foreign intelligence and counterintelligence and the latter responsible for domestic security.[50] During the regime's early years, the intelligence bureau focused on finding and eliminating threats from Tehran's many internal and external opponents rather than collecting foreign intelligence information. The US government and expatriate oppositionists speculated that Iran maintained SAVAK personnel stationed overseas and that these officers primarily monitored exiled Iranians.[51] Overall, absorbing SAVAK provided important continuity in intelligence operations during the early 1980s and contributed to some of the initial Iranian intelligence successes.[52]

These early accomplishments, from Iran's perspective, included the assassination of regime opponents abroad. In May 1979 the head judge of the revolutionary tribunals issued death sentences in absentia for the deposed shah, Bakhtiar, and a number of other royal family members and high-level officials. The first overseas assassination occurred in December when unknown assailants murdered the shah's nephew, Shahriar Shafiq, in Paris. French authorities linked the killing of this Iranian naval officer, who allegedly was planning an amphibious invasion of Iran at the time, to an earlier trip to France by Fardust.[53]

During this period, Bazargan's premiership ended abruptly when he and his cabinet resigned following the militant takeover of the US embassy in Tehran on November 4, 1979. The capture of US diplomatic personnel by a group of pro-Khomeini radicals calling themselves the Muslim Student Followers of the Imam's Line began a 444-day hostage crisis that ended in January 1981. The incident and Washington's responses, including a failed rescue attempt in April 1980, ignited a surge in anti-Americanism and antisecularism that strengthened the religious conservatives and heightened concerns about Western espionage and efforts to undermine the new Islamic Republic.

Iran's security services exposed as many as six minor coup threats in the first half of 1980, some of which had connections with the shah's former officials outside the country and added to regime concerns about the exiled opposition and domestic opponents. In July Iranian intelligence units uncovered the Nuzhih coup plot, a large and advanced conspiracy to kill Khomeini and overthrow the government by military officers and other shah loyalists that Iran believed had been supported by exiles associated with Bakhtiar.[54] In the plot's immediate aftermath in August, assassins tried but failed to kill the former prime minister in Paris. That same month, shortly after Fardust allegedly visited the United States, Dawud Salahuddin (né David Belfield), an American convert to Islam, killed vocal regime critic Ali Akbar Tabatabai in Maryland before fleeing to Tehran.[55]

When Mohammad-Ali Rajai became prime minister in August 1980, he nominated Khosrow Tehrani to head the intelligence bureau. A young revolutionary who had been imprisoned for three years by the shah's government, Tehrani served on the IRC's leadership council after the revolution.[56] Upon taking his new position, Tehrani hired members of the Muslim Student Followers of the Imam's Line and the Mujahedin of the Islamic Revolution (MIR), a coalition of seven armed Islamic groups. The MIR consisted, in part, of former MEK members who opposed Marxism and the secular left and who later provided some of the IRGC's early leaders.[57] Hajjarian was among these new hires and claimed experience in interrogating US military personnel captured during the US embassy takeover as well as participants in the Nuzhih coup plot.[58]

In September 1980 Iraqi dictator Saddam Hussein ordered his military to attack Iran, initiating the eight-year-long Iran-Iraq War. Over time, the war heightened divisions between the elected and unelected parts of the government and the regime and its political opponents. As it had with the hostage crisis, the leaders of the Islamic Republic used the Iraqi invasion to help consolidate their power domestically. Tehran quickly mobilized Iranians to defend the country and successfully foiled Baghdad's plans for a short and decisive offensive campaign. Iran's first elected president, a layman and Islamic leftist named Abolhassan Banisadr, had taken over in early 1980 from the interim Revolutionary Council that replaced Bazargan's provisional government. Named acting commander in chief of the armed forces by Khomeini, Banisadr and the IRGC repeatedly clashed over war strategy during the conflict's opening stages.[59] The president also found himself regularly constrained by the IRP and allied factions as they fought over the scope of his executive powers and those of the regime's unelected institutions and security services.

By 1981, in response to the clerics' tightening grip on power, domestic political opponents instigated serious and sometimes violent political unrest that the security services struggled to contain. This violence reached a peak in mid-1981 a week after the Majles impeached Banisadr and removed him from office for challenging the clerics' role in government. On June 28, 1981, militants bombed the IRP headquarters, killing seventy-four senior elected and clerical leaders, including Ayatollah Mohammad Beheshti, Iran's chief justice and Khomeini's most senior lieutenant. The next day Banisadr and MEK leader Masoud Rajavi, whose group was later blamed for the bombing, fled the country. Rajavi eventually moved his organization to Baghdad in 1986 where it aligned with Iraq against the Islamic Republic.[60]

Establishing the Ministry

The IRP headquarters bombing was followed on August 30, 1981, with another bombing that killed Prime Minister Mohammad-Javad Bahonar, President Mohammad-Ali Rajai, and the Shahrbani commander, Brig. Gen. Hushang Vahid-Dastjerdi. According to Hajjarian, the assassinations, bombings, and armed tensions of the early 1980s influenced the regime's decision to establish an intelligence ministry.[61] A 2020 MOIS-produced documentary, *Medal-e-Gomnami* (Anonymous medal), repeated the claim, suggesting that an October 1982 MEK truck bombing of Tehran's main square, which killed more than eighty and injured approximately seven hundred, convinced the government that it needed an organization with extensive intelligence and security responsibilities to prevent such incidents.[62] This seems reasonable because, according to a 2012 interview of one of his contemporaries, the then prime minister Mir-Hoseyn Musavi had found using the intelligence bureau as a de facto intelligence coordinator to be complicated by the overlapping responsibilities of Iran's numerous security and intelligence organizations.[63] The same source stated that Hajjarian first suggested the creation of a ministry of intelligence to address these coordination problems.

First proposed in late 1982, the scheme to concentrate the intelligence activities of the IRGC, komitehs, and prime minister's office in a single entity raised two primary issues for the regime.[64] The first focused on whether it should be a ministry subordinate to the prime minister and accountable to the legislature or established as an independent organization outside the cabinet and nominally above politics and oversight pressures.[65] Tehrani and Hajjarian recommended an executive branch ministry that would be subject to scrutiny and accountability by elected officials, which would help avoid abuses of power.[66] Apparently viewing such oversight as potentially too constraining, IRGC leaders and conservative politicians generally opposed centralizing intelligence activities within a single ministry, arguing that multiple organizations reduced vulnerabilities.[67] Advocates for a ministry warned that dispersed activities among multiple organizations would create conflicts and offsetting weaknesses. Other arguments centered on whether a future intelligence agency should be subordinate to the IRGC, the judiciary, or the supreme leader rather than the executive and legislative branches.[68] According to Hajjarian, fear of a powerful and possibly uncontrollable intelligence organization contributed to the compromise on creating the new Ministry of Intelligence.[69] Another future MOIS leader similarly suggested that the regime organized the ministry under the executive and legislative branches in part to avoid the "bitter experience" with SAVAK.[70]

The second issue involved long-standing worries by officials in the prime minister's intelligence bureau about the moral complexities of intelligence operations and the need for a competent authority to handle these matters. Perhaps wary of clerical concerns, they wondered, according to one bureau official, if it was permissible for an intelligence ministry to break religious law to protect the regime.[71] For example, could intelligence officers look into bedrooms as part of a surveillance operation? According to the same source, the officials turned for advice to Mohammad Reyshahri, the head of the revolutionary military tribunals. Reyshahri was a *mujtahid*, a cleric with expertise on religious law, and had experience with the investigative procedures used to support the prosecutions of shah-era officers and suspected regime opponents in the military.

With Reyshahri's advice, the prime minister's office finalized the proposal and sent it to Khomeini for his approval. The final version included a requirement for the minister to be a mujtahid and for the minister's appointment to be contingent on the leader's endorsement.[72] This change ensured that the minister was ultimately subordinate to the leader. Along with propositions to avoid the creation of another abusive intelligence service, the requirement for a minister who would be responsive to the leader apparently secured sufficient support among the conservative clerics for creating a ministry accountable to the legislature.

The Majles passed the legislation that created the Ministry of Intelligence on August 18, 1983.[73] Article 1 tasks the ministry with obtaining and processing foreign intelligence information, protecting intelligence information, and conducting counterintelligence operations to prevent domestic and foreign conspiracies against the Islamic Revolution and the Islamic Republic of Iran. Military intelligence remained the responsibility of the armed forces, but the Artesh, the IRGC, and other parts of government were required to coordinate activities with and provide requested information to the new Ministry of Intelligence.

Article 2 established an Intelligence Coordination Council (ICC) composed of the intelligence, interior, and foreign ministers; the prosecutor general; the heads of the IRGC and Artesh intelligence units; and the heads of the IRGC, Artesh, and law enforcement forces intelligence protection organizations ("protection" referring to organizational security and some counterintelligence duties). Article 5 set limits on IRGC internal security activities until the new Ministry of Intelligence was ready to begin operations, while the subsequent four articles established the duties of military and law enforcement intelligence and protection organizations.

The ministry's specific duties, as described in Article 10, include the collection of information and its production, analysis, evaluation, and classification. It also is tasked with the discovery of conspiracies, subversion, espionage, and sabotage against the independence, security, territorial integrity, and governing system of the Islamic Republic of Iran. Other specific duties include the protection of ministry information, documents, records, facilities, and personnel along with related training and assistance to other organizations and institutions. In addition, the ministry has the duty to provide intelligence services to other parts of the government and conduct intelligence sharing and cooperation with qualified countries as determined by the cabinet. Article 12 is a key part of the law because it forbids employees of the ministry, intelligence protection organizations, and other intelligence units from participating in any political party, organization, or group. A separate law stipulated the requirement for the minister, as included in the approved proposal, to be a cleric with the rank of mujtahid.[74]

The establishment of the new ministry required the transfer of most of the IRGC intelligence units' resources in late 1983 and 1984. This transfer occurred at a time when regime leaders were concerned about the Revolutionary Guard's power and independence, possibly forming the foundation for the subsequent institutional hostility between the service and the ministry.[75] According to Hajjarian, the other intelligence organizations were slow to comply with the new Ministry of Intelligence bill. He noted that the Revolutionary Guard, which at the time had the largest intelligence structure, was especially resistant. Guard leaders argued that the IRGC needed and constitutionally should have its own intelligence organization, offering to share intelligence with the new ministry as needed.[76]

The Ministry of Intelligence of the Islamic Republic of Iran was officially established in August 1984. The Majles confirmed Mohammad Reyshahri as the first minister of intelligence. The new service was staffed by former SAVAK, intelligence bureau, IRGC, komiteh, and other revolutionary personnel. Like its predecessor, the MOIS approached intelligence less as the collection and analysis of foreign secrets than as investigative work to protect the revolution by countering seditious domestic threats and foreign espionage. Nonetheless, with its inheritance of SAVAK's police state tactics and experience in clandestine political dissidence, the new ministry was well prepared to deal with the array of security threats facing the young Islamic Republic. Like in other regime organizations, a supreme leader's representative assigned to the ministry provided oversight to ensure its loyalty, ideological conformity, and commitment to protecting the nezam.

Reyshahri complained about the initial weakness of the ministry's legal authorities in the establishment law.[77] He specifically wanted powers for obtaining information similar to the judiciary's search and arrest warrants and the armed forces' authority for temporary detention. The MOIS initially had no facilities other than the central building of the SAVAK compound, part of which the regime converted into a document center that allowed the new ministry to retain SAVAK's documents.[78] Some of the ministry's funding, meanwhile, relied on a number of affiliated businesses to generate income to supplement its budget.[79]

As the MOIS began operations, the IRGC intelligence unit, as allowed by the establishment law, adopted a more operational military intelligence focus in support of the war against Iraq that temporarily reduced its internal security role. After the war with Iraq ended in August 1988, however, the IRGC resumed its involvement in non-military-related security and intelligence missions, such as repressing domestic dissidents and assassinating external regime opponents.[80] In 1991 the regime merged the remaining komitehs with the Gendarmerie and Shahrbani to create the Law Enforcement Force (LEF) under the Interior Ministry. Although the IRGC remained the ultimate guarantor of the regime's survival, the regime had the new LEF take the lead in policing most internal security threats and made it part of Iran's intelligence community.[81]

The new law made no change to IRGC external operations, which after 1983 continued to provide support to terrorist and other militant organizations in the effort to export the revolution. In 1989 the Revolutionary Guard merged four organizations into the Islamic Revolutionary Guard Corps–Qods (Jerusalem) Force (IRGC-QF), a combination special operations force, clandestine intelligence organization, and covert action arm, to centralize extraterritorial operations. In addition to training and logistic support to revolutionary groups in the region, the IRGC-QF conducted intelligence-collection and counterintelligence activities as part of its external operations.[82] As discussed in later chapters, MOIS officers, especially those based in embassies, regularly supported IRGC-QF activities.

Within a few years, Iran made additional changes to consolidate the ministry's position as the central actor in internal security, counterespionage, and intelligence collection. In April 1989 constitutional reforms removed one source of tension from the government's administration of intelligence by abolishing the prime minister's office. The president assumed all executive authority, including the ability to select, with the leader's approval, the intelligence minister. Nonetheless, the regime's lines of control and influence over intelligence activities remained complex (see box 1.1). Reyshahri, a regime insider with close connections to Khomeini's inner circle, would solidify loyalty to the leader and a strong religious orientation as key elements of MOIS identity and culture during his term. As examined in the next chapter, the evolution of the ministry's missions and outlook would be shaped significantly by

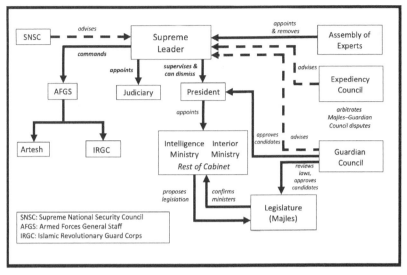

Figure 1.1. Regime lines of intelligence-related control, checks, and balances. Adapted from Kenneth Katzman, *Iran: Politics, Gulf Security, and U.S. Policy*, CRS Report RL 32048 (Washington, DC: Congressional Research Service, 2016), 53; and Defense Intelligence Agency, *Iran Military Power: Ensuring Regime Survival and Security Regional Dominance* (Washington, DC: DIA, 2019), 27, https://www.dia.mil/Portals/110/Images /News/Military_Powers_Publications/Iran_Military_Power_LR.pdf.

the experiences of its leaders, Iran's fractious politics, and persistent foreign threats.

Notes

1. For details on these events, see Stephen Kinzer, *All the Shah's Men: An American Coup and the Roots of Middle East Terror* (Hoboken, NJ: John Wiley & Sons, 2003); and Mark J. Gasiorowski, *Mohammad Mosaddeq and the 1953 Coup in Iran* (Syracuse, NY: Syracuse University Press, 2004).
2. Steven R. Ward, *Immortal: A Military History of Iran and Its Armed Forces* (Washington, DC: Georgetown University Press, 2009), 191.
3. The ranking of and relationships between Shia clergy is a complex matter beyond the scope of this introduction, but some familiarity with the broad structure is helpful for understanding these and later developments in the history of the MOIS. Shia clergy are trained to interpret and expand on religious law and, based on their postseminary studies and writings, are accorded ranks that provide them greater influence and responsibilities. *Mujtahid* is the first rank for a cleric who is recognized

Box 1.1. Regime Lines of Control, Checks, and Balances

Iran's government is a fusion of unelected, clerical-dominated policy-making bodies and elected institutions responsible for routine governance that sets the framework for intelligence and security activities:

- Supreme leader: Directs Iran's domestic, foreign, and security policies; serves as armed forces commander in chief; appoints senior military leaders, chief justice (judiciary head), prosecutor general, and lower court judges; and approves intelligence operations.
- President: Highest elected official but subordinate to the supreme leader. Performs executive functions, including cabinet appointments; provides policy guidance to ministries and agencies; and prepares government budget.
- Supreme National Security Council: Consists of at least eleven members: the president (chair), the Majles speaker, the chief justice, the Armed Forces General Staff chief, the IRGC commander, the Artesh commander, the ministers of intelligence, foreign affairs, and the interior, two leader representatives, and, as appropriate, other policy officials. Develops national security policies for the leader's approval and is managed by the SNSC secretary appointed by the leader.
- Majles: Unicameral parliament of 290 seats confirms cabinet selections, drafts and passes legislation, appropriates funds, ratifies treaties and similar agreements, and provides limited oversight of intelligence and security matters.
- Assembly of Experts: Elected eighty-eight-member body that chooses—and can remove—the supreme leader, can amend constitution, and nominally provides oversight of the leader's activities.
- Guardian Council: Consists of six leader-appointed clerics and six judiciary-selected and Majles-confirmed lawyers. Reviews—and can reject—legislation to ensure conformity with Islamic law. Approves candidates and certifies election results.
- Expediency Council: Created in 1988 to resolve legislative disputes between the Majles and the Guardian Council, this forty-two-member council appointed by the leader can remove legislative powers and provides oversight of president and cabinet. It also serves as policy advisory body to the supreme leader.
- Armed Forces General Staff: Uses leader's guidance to set military policy and strategic guidance for the IRGC and the Artesh.

as capable of interpreting Islamic sources. The rank of ayatollah is bestowed on the most respected senior mujtahids with demonstrated scholarship. Grand ayatollah (*ayatollah ozma*) is the highest rank ascribed to a senior Shia cleric and is applied to those with a large following of Shia faithful.

4. John Ghazvinian, *America and Iran: A History, 1720 to the Present* (New York: Alfred A. Knopf, 2021), 237.

5. Library of Congress, *Iran's Ministry of Intelligence and Security*, 6.

6. Ghazvinian, *America and Iran*, 237–39.

7. Ghazvinian, 237–39, 256–57; James Buchan, *Days of God: The Revolution in Iran and Its Consequences* (New York: Simon & Schuster, 2012), 217.

8. Buchan, 117.

9. Ghazvinian, *America and Iran*, 257.

10. Library of Congress, *Iran's Ministry of Intelligence and Security*, 6.

11. For a brief examination of this period, see Ward, *Immortal*, 211–13.

12. Nikki R. Keddie, *Roots of Revolution: An Interpretive History of Modern Iran* (New Haven, CT: Yale University Press, 1981), 213–14.

13. This discussion is derived from Ervand Abrahamian, *The Iranian Mojahedin* (New Haven, CT: Yale University Press, 1989), 84–85, 100–101, 105; and Ervand Abrahamian, "The Guerrilla Movement in Iran, 1963–1977," *Middle East Review* 86 (March/April 1980), http://www.merip.org/mer/mer86/guerrilla-movement-iran-1963-1977.

14. Buchan, *Days of God*, 117.

15. Ghazvinian, *America and Iran*, 278.

16. Ward, *Immortal*, 214.

17. Michael Axworthy, *Revolutionary Iran: A History of the Islamic Republic* (New York: Oxford University Press, 2013), 7.

18. Ervand Abrahamian, *Tortured Confessions: Prisons and Public Recantations in Modern Iran* (Berkeley: University of California Press, 1999), 161.

19. Buchan, *Days of God*, 184.

20. Axworthy, *Revolutionary Iran*, 144.

21. Andrew Scott Cooper, *The Fall of Heaven: The Pahlavis and the Final Days of Imperial Iran* (New York: Henry Holt, 2016), 244.

22. The Islamic Revolution Document Center grew out of the initial effort to collect and protect SAVAK files. "What Happened to SAVAK after the Revolution?" Tarikh Irani, March 7, 2013, http://tarikhirani.ir/fa/news/4080/انقلاب-از-پس-ساواک-سرنوشت چه‌شد--.

23. Ervand Abrahamian, *A History of Modern Iran* (Cambridge: Cambridge University Press, 2008), 162–63.

24. After Khomeini's death in 1989, Iran revised its constitution to remove this requirement and clear the way for the regime's preferred candidate to become supreme leader.

25. Abrahamian, *History of Modern Iran*, 163–64.

26. Wilfried Buchta, *Who Rules Iran? The Structure of Power in the Islamic Republic* (Washington, DC: Washington Institute for Near East Policy, 2000), 22.

27. CIA Directorate of Intelligence, *Iran: A Handbook*, Reference Aid NESA 82-10167, May 1982, 27, https://www.cia.gov/readingroom/document/cia-rdp83b00232r000100110002-8.

28. Buchta, *Who Rules Iran?*, 22.
29. Rouhollah K. Ramazani, "Constitution of the Islamic Republic of Iran," *Middle East Journal* 34, no. 2 (Spring 1980): 185, JSTOR. See also "Iran (Islamic Republic of) 1979 (rev. 1989)," in *Constitute: The World's Constitutions to Read, Search, and Compare*, ed. Zachary Elkins, Tom Ginsburg, and James Melton, https://www.con stituteproject.org/constitution/Iran_1989?.
30. Ramazani, "Constitution of the Islamic Republic of Iran," 189.
31. Ramazani, 202.
32. On the historical balance between ideology and pragmatism in Iran, see Rouhollah K. Ramazani, "Ideology and Pragmatism in Iran's Foreign Policy," *Middle East Journal* 58, no. 4 (Autumn 2004): 549–59.
33. For an examination of the balance between ideology and other considerations, see Walter Posch, "Ideology and Strategy in the Middle East: The Case of Iran," *Survival* 59, no. 5 (October/November 2017): 69–98.
34. Amnesty International provided the report on the number of executions. See Michael Getler, "Khomeini Is Reported to Have a SAVAK of His Own," *Washington Post*, June 7, 1980.
35. "Saeed Hajarian Tells about Hashemi's Lack of Trust in Him and His Friends / Remembers Being in the Second Department of the Army, the Ministry of Intelligence, Interrogating the Agents of the Nojeh Coup . . . ," Khabar Online, August 26, 2012, https://www.khabaronline.ir/news/237993/سعیدحجاریان-از-بی-اعتمادی-هاشمی به-او-و-دوستانش-می-گوید-خاطره, translated in "Iran News Round Up," American Enterprise Institute (AEI) Critical Threats Project, September 4, 2012, https://www.cr iticalthreats.org/briefs/iran-news-round-up/iran-news-round-up-september-4-2012 -1 (hereafter cited as September 2012 Hajjarian interview).
36. September 2012 Hajjarian interview.
37. Donald M. Utchel, "The Parallel Security Apparatus: Examining the Cases of Baathist Iraq, Syria, and Iran" (PhD diss., University of Nevada, Las Vegas, 2019, ProQuest), 218.
38. "What Happened to SAVAK?"
39. Said Shariati, "Said Hajjarian on the Formation of the Intelligence Ministry," *Shargh Daily*, October 13, 2019, https://www.sharghdaily.com/790869/3-اخبار-بخش وزارت-اطلاعات-چگونه-پا-گرفت.
40. Alain Rodier, "Iranian Intelligence Services," French Intelligence Research Center, News Note no. 200, January 2010, https://cf2r.org/actualite/les-services-de-rense ignement-iraniens/; "What Happened to SAVAK?"; Shariati, "Said Hajjarian on Formation."
41. Shariati, "Said Hajjarian on Formation."
42. Afshon Ostovar, *Vanguard of the Imam: Religion, Politics, and Iran's Revolutionary Guards* (New York: Oxford University Press, 2016), 43–44.
43. CIA Directorate of Intelligence, *Iran: Recruitment and Training of Foreign Terrorists*, Terrorism Review GI TR 84-011, May 24, 1984, 7–8, https://www.cia.gov/rea dingroom/docs/CIA-RDP85-01095R000100050002-8.pdf.
44. Shaul Bakhash, *The Reign of the Ayatollahs: Iran and the Islamic Revolution* (London: I. B. Tauris, 1985), 67; Sepehr Zabih, *The Iranian Military in Revolution and War* (London: Routledge, 1988), 209–10; James M. Markham, "In Iran, Fears of a Revolution within a Revolution," *New York Times*, February 16, 1979; James M.

Markham, "Marxist-Leninist Guerrilla Group Is a Potent Force in the New Iran," *New York Times*, February 15, 1979.

45. Ward, *Immortal*, 230.
46. Michael Isikoff and Bob Gettlin, "Iranian Police Link to Tabatabai Murder Probed," *Washington Star*, August 9, 1980, https://www.cia.gov/readingroom/document/cia -rdp90-00552r000606550002-9; Getler, "Khomeini Is Reported."
47. "What Happened to SAVAK?"
48. Abrahamian, *Tortured Confessions*, 159–61.
49. "What Happened to SAVAK?"
50. September 2012 Hajjarian Interview. See also "What Happened to SAVAK?"
51. Getler, "Khomeini Is Reported."
52. Axworthy, *Revolutionary Iran*, 342.
53. "Paris Killing Linked to Iran Police Aide: Lawyer Ties Slaying of the Shah's Nephew to a Trip by General," *New York Times*, December 9, 1979.
54. See Mark J. Gasiorowski, "The Nuzhih Plot and Iranian Politics," *International Journal of Middle East Studies* 34 (2002): 649–60; and Ward, *Immortal*, 238–40.
55. US Congress, House Homeland Security Subcommittee on Counterterrorism and Intelligence and Subcommittee on Oversight, Investigations, and Management, "Iranian Terror Operations on American Soil," 112th Cong., 1st sess., October 26, 2011 (Matthew Levitt statement), https://www.govinfo.gov/content/pkg/CHRG -112hhrg73741/html/CHRG-112hhrg73741.htm; Robert Pear, "Khomeini Security Chief Reportedly Seen in U.S," *New York Times*, August 15, 1980.
56. "What Happened to SAVAK?"
57. "What Happened to SAVAK?" On the Mujahedin of the Islamic Revolution, see Ostovar, *Vanguard of the Imam*, 49–54.
58. September 2012 Hajjarian interview. See also "What Happened to SAVAK?"
59. On these factional politics, see Mohammad Ayatollai Tabaar, "Factional Politics in the Iran-Iraq War," *Journal of Strategic Studies* 42, nos. 3–4 (June 2019): 484–87, EBSCO.
60. On the development of the MEK and its relationship with Iraq, see Abrahamian, *Iranian Mojahedin*; and Ronen A. Cohen, *The Rise and Fall of the Mojhahedin Khalq, 1987–1997* (Brighton, UK: Sussex Academic Press, 2009).
61. "37 Years Ago the General Assembly Approved the Formation of the Ministry of Intelligence. How Did the Ministry of Information Operate?" Islamic Republic News Agency, October 13, 2019, https://www.irna.ir/news/83514723/وزارت-اطلاع ات-چگونه-پا-گرفت. See also Zeynab Rajaee, "A Review of the Formation of the Min-istry of Information," Mehr News, May 14, 2022, https://www.mehrnews.com/ne ws/5480909/مروری-بر-نحوه-شکل-گیری-وزارت-اطلاعات-توصیه-امام-به-ری-شهری.
62. Ministry of Intelligence of Islamic Republic of Iran, *Medal-e-Gomnami* [Anony-mous medal], 2020, https://www.youtube.com/watch?v=KdnBvHVM68k; "60 Die in Teheran as Bomb Blast Rips Downtown Square," *New York Times*, October 3, 1982.
63. Mojtaba Hoseyni, "The Unsaid Words of Shariatmadari from Reyshahri after 34 Years," Mashregh News, December 26, 2012, https://www.mashreghnews.ir/news /181153/.
64. CIA Directorate of Intelligence, *Iran: A Handbook*, 28.

65. Hoseyni, "Unsaid Words of Shariatmadari."

66. Shariati, "Said Hajjarian on Formation."

67. Shariati.

68. "37 Years Ago."

69. "37 Years Ago."

70. Rajaee, "Review of the Formation."

71. Hoseyni, "Unsaid Words of Shariatmadari."

72. Hoseyni.

73. Islamic Consultative Assembly, "Law Establishing the Ministry of Intelligence of the Islamic Republic," August 18, 1983, https://rc.majlis.ir/fa/law/show/90795, hereafter cited as 1983 Ministry of Intelligence Establishment Law; "Establishment Law of the Ministry of Intelligence of the Islamic Republic," Guardian Council Research Institute, n.d., http://nazarat.shora-rc.ir/Forms/frmShenasname.aspx?id=v2MPT3GqwB8=&TN=l7tLyhyOobj0SooAFUE3m68PnpG7mruN.

74. "History of the Ministry of Intelligence," Jamaran, July 24, 2003, https://www.jamaran.news/اطلاعات-وزارت-تاریخچه-28992/12-اخبار-بخش; Buchta, *Who Rules Iran?*, 165–66.

75. CIA Directorate of Intelligence, *Iran: Growing Prospects for Instability*, Intelligence Assessment NESA 84-10285, October 1984, 9, https://www.cia.gov/readingroom/document/cia-rdp85t00314r000300090005-6.

76. Shariati, "Said Hajjarian on Formation."

77. Shariati.

78. Shariati; "What Happened to SAVAK?"

79. "Why Was the Economic Activity of the Ministry of Information Closed?" Tabnak, September 22, 2012, https://www.tabnak.ir/fa/news/277718/وزارت-اقتصادي-فعاليت-چرا اطلاعات-تعطيل-شد.

80. Raz Zimmt, "The Intelligence Organization of the IRGC: A Major Iranian Intelligence Apparatus," Meir Amit Intelligence and Terrorism Information Center, November 5, 2020, https://www.terrorism-info.org.il/en/the-intelligence-organization-of-the-irgc-a-major-iranian-intelligence-apparatus, 9.

81. Sunil Dasgupta, "Internal Security and Military Reorganization: The Rise of Paramilitaries in Developing Societies" (PhD diss., University of Illinois at Urbana-Champaign, 2003), 271, ProQuest.

82. Ali Alfoneh, "The Evolution of Iran's Qods Force since 1979," Washington Institute for Near East Policy, PolicyWatch no. 3,495, June 3, 2021, https://www.washingtoninstitute.org/policy-analysis/evolution-irans-qods-force-1979.

2

Leaders

Eight clerics have served as Iran's intelligence minister between 1984 and 2023. As described in the following sections, although all supported the nezam, they have reflected the political divisions within the Islamic Republic. Six of the eight have been from the conservative factions, while two were associated with reformist and pragmatist factions. Four intelligence ministers were graduates of the Haqqani Seminary, which emphasized training clerics to have an understanding of current events and science and produced numerous hard-line conservative regime officials. Some of the ministers had extensive experience as judges and prosecutors. Most have remained powerful members of the regime through their subsequent government positions and political activities.

Mohammad Reyshahri (August 1984–August 1989)

Iran's first minister of intelligence, Mohammad Reyshahri, came to prominence during the Islamic Revolution's aftermath and helped to establish the ministry. He then guided it during a period of war, challenges from within Iran's clerical establishment, and persistent threats from exiled regime opponents. Reyshahri was born in 1946 and received his initial clerical training in Qom. His political activities began in June 1963 during the religious protests that erupted following Khomeini's public criticism of the shah's reform policies and the US status-of-forces

وزارت اطلاعات
جمهوری اسلامی ایران

Figure 2.1. Ministry of Intelligence seal

agreement. Reyshahri then fled to Iraq and continued his studies in Najaf, another Shia holy city and learning center. SAVAK imprisoned him
for a few years after he returned to Iran. With the revolution's victory,
he rose quickly within the power structure of the new Islamic Republic.[1]

Reyshahri became a revolutionary court judge and dealt with officials
of the shah's government accused of crimes against the people. He then
was elevated to head the revolutionary military tribunals, where he over-
saw the trials of service members and supervised the investigation into
the failed 1980 Nuzhih coup plot. He also tried members of the outlawed
Tudeh Party and clerics who opposed velayat-e faqih.[2] According to one
of his colleagues, prior to the creation of the MOIS, Reyshahri taught a
course on "intelligence morality."[3]

As one of the ministry's founders, Reyshahri developed its early policies, practices, and culture.[4] At its inception, the MOIS confronted internal opposition to the regime and threats emanating from the ongoing
Iran-Iraq War. An examination of the service's activities during this period suggests that the mujtahid minister emphasized gathering evidence

for prosecutions rather than intelligence for policymaking. Reyshahri also appears to have followed the establishment law in promoting a nominal culture of moral behavior, devotion to duty, and political neutrality to avoid creating an organization that abused its power.[5] Yet, as discussed below, he also supported brutal and sometimes lethal extrajudicial techniques in performance of the ministry's missions.

Starting in 1987, Reyshahri supervised a new judicial body, the Special Court for Clergy (SCC).[6] Established to discipline dissident clerics, the SCC had its origins in the prosecution of Mehdi Hashemi, a critical juncture in securing the ministry's relationship with Khomeini and his successor. Hashemi was the brother-in-law of Khomeini's designated heir, Grand Ayatollah Hoseyn-Ali Montazeri. An antishah revolutionary, Hashemi had a reputation for violent extremism and had been imprisoned by SAVAK for alleged murders. After the revolution, he joined the IRGC and became a member of its Command Council and director of its external operations unit, the International Division, a forerunner of the contemporary clandestine special operations unit IRGC–Qods Force. In May 1986, however, the regime arrested Hashemi and forty associates for various alleged crimes, including leaking information to a Lebanese newspaper about government contacts with Washington to trade Americans held hostage in Lebanon for badly needed arms to fight Iraq.[7] The regime was determined to punish him for undermining the policy initiative and embarrassing the senior officials behind it.[8]

Khomeini assigned the case to Reyshahri, who later claimed that Hashemi's influential patrons made interrogations difficult, according to historian Ervand Abrahamian.[9] Still, MOIS officers extracted a confession from the young firebrand, which was aired on national television. Montazeri complained that the accusations were unfair and tried to stop the establishment of the SCC to prevent his brother-in-law from being tried outside the normal appeals system. Charged with waging war on God, inciting sedition, and similar crimes, Hashemi pleaded guilty and asked for forgiveness. Instead, he was executed before the verdict was publicly announced, an action Reyshahri admitted was rushed to preempt Montazeri's intervention.[10] The minister's actions set a precedent for MOIS support to the leader in disciplining potential political challenges from within the nezam.

During Reyshahri's tenure, the MOIS was involved in another

episode that further divided Montazeri from Khomeini. In 1988 Iran suffered a series of military and political setbacks, including multiple Iraqi military offensives that devastated Iranian ground forces and Iraqi missile attacks on Iranian cities. Just weeks before Tehran accepted the cease-fire that ended the conflict, the Iraqis allowed the MEK's military wing, the National Liberation Army, to attack into Iran.[11] IRGC and Iranian army units decisively defeated the MEK forces, but Khomeini responded by issuing a fatwa (religious edict) condemning to execution thousands of mostly MEK prisoners seen as unrelenting in their opposition to the regime.[12]

Over the course of the subsequent two months, the MOIS and IRGC participated in the killing of as many as five thousand prisoners. According to Amnesty International and other groups, a four-member committee established to execute the leader's orders, popularly known as the "death commission," included Mostafa Purmohammadi, the head of the MOIS counterintelligence directorate and its representative to Evin Prison, and Ebrahim Raisi, a future chief justice and president.[13] Although known as a radical, anti-Western cleric, Montazeri condemned the executions, calling them the biggest crime in the Islamic Republic's history. This new discord between Khomeini and Montazeri eventually forced the latter ayatollah to relinquish his role as designated successor in March 1989.[14] A few months later, in June 1989, Khomeini died without an heir. A succession crisis was averted when the Assembly of Experts modified the constitution to allow Ali Khamenei, a conservative anti-American cleric then serving as president, to become supreme leader despite not having achieved the rank of ayatollah.

After serving as intelligence minister, Reyshahri remained an influential regime insider. Khamenei named him Iran's prosecutor general in August 1989, his position for two years. From January 1990 to December 1998, the former minister was the SCC prosecutor general. In this posting he put on trial clerics who questioned the new leader's religious qualifications. Later, the SCC and the MOIS ordered officials in Qom to close seminaries maintained by donations to grand ayatollahs critical of the regime.[15]

Reyshahri was politically active, running unsuccessfully for president in 1989 and 1997. He also established a short-lived political party that favored egalitarian social and economic policies but supported harsh repression of dissent and a strong commitment to velayat-e faqih. The cleric sat on the Assembly of Experts from 1991 to 2006 and from 2016 to 2022 while serving concurrently on the Expediency Council from 1997 to 2012.[16] Reyshahri later became the chief custodian of the Abdol Azim al-Hasani Shrine in Rey, south of Tehran, and died in March 2022.

Ali Fallahian (August 1989–August 1997)

Following the 1989 constitutional reforms, newly elected president Ali Akbar Hashemi Rafsanjani nominated Ali Fallahian to become Iran's second intelligence minister. Fallahian's tenure occurred during a period of sporadic postwar domestic political turmoil and accelerated regime efforts to eliminate exiled oppositionists. Born in 1949, Fallahian received his clerical education at the Haqqani Seminary in Qom. Before the revolution, SAVAK imprisoned him for his vocal opposition to the monarchy. From 1982 to 1985 Fallahian commanded Iran's remaining komitehs, which were gradually disbanding. He also was a member of the Islamic Republican Party, which was then led by President Khamenei, Majles speaker Rafsanjani, and other close Khomeini confidants. Fallahian was among the founders of the MOIS and served as Reyshahri's principal deputy. In addition to his MOIS duties, he was chosen as one of the prosecutors for the Mehdi Hashemi trial and then served as the SCC prosecutor general from June 1987 to January 1990.[17]

Under Fallahian, the ministry participated in regime efforts to deter potential challenges from dissident minority groups and to complete the postrevolution project of eliminating the regime's remaining political opponents. In particular, the early 1990s were marked by a number of high-profile assassinations attributed to his ministry along with MOIS participation in overseas terrorist attacks against Israeli interests. These actions included the 1989 murders of Abdulrahman Qassemlou, leader of the Kurdistan Democratic Party of Iran (KDPI), and Bahman Javadi, a leader of Komala, the Kurdish communist party, in Austria; the 1990 killing of Kazem Rajavi, brother of the MEK leader, in Switzerland; and the 1990 murder of Cyrus Elahi, a member of the opposition monarchist group Flag of Freedom, in France.[18]

Fallahian was accused of direct involvement in one of the most notorious killings, the 1991 assassination in France of Shahpour Bakhtiar, then the leader of the National Movement of Iranian Resistance.[19] Under a death sentence for more than a decade, the former prime minister had lost his chief assistant in an unsolved murder in April. Nonetheless, on August 6, three Iranian men were able to get invited into his home, pass through security, and then stab Bakhtiar and his secretary with knives taken from the kitchen. The trio departed the home and passed by security before their crime was noticed.

French authorities managed to capture or have extradited some of the conspirators and put them on trial for murder. Two of the defendants had direct MOIS ties, and one, Ali Vakili Rad, was a senior MOIS officer who had been attached to the Qods Force at the time of the killings. Investigators also developed information that the MOIS was involved in the recruitment of the plot's conspirators in the late 1980s. In particular, Fallahian, while Reyshahri's deputy, made several direct phone calls to at least one potential recruit to encourage his participation. The trial acquitted one defendant, sentenced another to ten years, and condemned Rad along with six men tried in absentia to life in prison. Fallahian made a veiled confession in an August 1992 interview aired on Iranian state television, saying, "We track them [political opponents] outside the country, too. . . . Last year, we succeeded in striking fundamental blows to their top members."[20]

At the time, Iran's exiled opposition posed a minor but real threat to the regime's interests. For example, in April 1992, MEK teams conducted simultaneous assaults on Iranian diplomatic missions in New York, Canada, Germany, France, the United Kingdom, Switzerland, the Netherlands, Denmark, Sweden, and Norway, which possibly contributed to the regime's willingness to continue targeting its external opponents.[21] In addition, Qassemlou's 1989 assassination sparked a series of clashes over the next few years between KDPI fighters and Iranian troops in the western Kurdish region of Iran. In response, MOIS assets in September 1992 killed Dr. Sadeq Sharafkandi, Qassemlou's successor as KDPI head, and three aides in Berlin. The assassinations became known as the "Mykonos Murders" after the name of the Greek restaurant where the killings occurred. In March 1996 a German court issued an arrest warrant for Fallahian and, in April 1997, found that Khamenei and Rafsanjani also were complicit in the murders.[22]

The United States and other countries later claimed that Fallahian had participated in the decision-making on one of the most infamous Iranian-supported terrorist operations while he was intelligence minister.[23] Iran regularly worked with Hezbollah, the Lebanese Shia militant group founded and supported by the IRGC, to conduct lethal operations overseas. Formed in 1982 in response to the Israeli invasion of Lebanon, Hezbollah and its terrorist arm, the Islamic Jihad Organization, were involved in numerous anti-US terrorist attacks, including the 1983 and 1984 suicide truck bombings in Beirut of the US embassy, its annex, and the US Marine Corps barracks. In July 1994 Islamic Jihad bombed the Asociación Mutual Israelita Argentina (AMIA; Argentine-Israelite Mutual Association), killing ninety-five and injuring two hundred. The FBI concluded in 1998 that Iranian intelligence officials were involved in this attack, and in 2006 Argentine authorities issued an international arrest warrant for Fallahian for his role in approving it. In mid-2022 the Israeli intelligence service Mossad (Institute) shared an internal study with the *New York Times* that concluded Iran had approved, funded, and supplied training and equipment for the 1994 AMIA attack and a 1992 bombing of the Israeli embassy in Buenos Aires. Mossad judged, however, that, contrary to long-standing allegations, MOIS officers had not had an on-the-ground operational role in either action in Argentina.[24]

Fallahian's desire to strike blows against the nezam's opponents was undiminished despite the international attention from the Mykonos Murders and AMIA bombing. As revealed during his successor's term, Fallahian was a key part of a hard-line conservative effort in the mid to late 1990s to silence domestic critics. After leaving the ministry in 1997, he made a few unsuccessful forays into politics, including a failed presidential campaign in 2001.[25] Fallahian served on the Assembly of Experts (1999–2016), but his criminal reputation at home and abroad seemed to limit his access to other significant regime roles. Nonetheless, Khamenei later publicly congratulated Fallahian for his "great achievements in combating and uprooting the enemies of Islam, inside and outside the country."[26]

Qorbanali Dorri-Najafabadi (August 1997–February 1999)

When he became the third MOIS head, Qorbanali Dorri-Najafabadi was an influential political actor in Iran. His tenure was cut short, however, by crimes erupting from the regime's violent overreaction to domestic dissent. The cleric, born in 1945, was educated at the Haqqani Seminary and, after the revolution, headed a komiteh in Arak. He joined the IRP and by 1983 had become a member of its central council. Dorri-Najafabadi won election to the first Majles and remained in the legislature from 1980 to 1988 and from 1992 to 1997. In 1988, he supervised Grand Ayatollah Montazeri's office before Khamenei in 1990 named him the leader's representative to Iran's secular universities. He was elected to the Assembly of Experts in 1991 and joined the Expediency Council in 1997, where he continued to serve through 2023.[27]

Dorri-Najafabadi's selection as minister by Mohammad Khatami, a reform-minded cleric who unexpectedly won the presidency in 1997, underlined the ministry's importance in the regime's ongoing political struggles. Rejecting Khamenei's favored candidate, Iranians had shown strong popular support for the Khatami-led reformist faction's stance that Islam could accommodate political modernization. Khatami also suggested that popular desires for political and social reforms could be addressed through elections and Iran's existing constitutional provisions. Khamenei, however, foisted Dorri-Najafabadi on Khatami as a compromise nominee for intelligence minister after allegedly rejecting fifteen other candidates.[28] Despite the cleric's past service and Haqqani Seminary background, conservative elites, perhaps suspicious of the minister's association with the then disgraced Ayatollah Montazeri, seemed to consider Dorri-Najafabadi a relatively liberal and pragmatic minister.[29] Meanwhile, more militant ministry elements, experienced in working outside official channels, had already started operations to suppress reform-minded regime critics.[30]

The Chain Murders

A few months after the first anniversary of Dorri-Najafabadi's confirmation as minister, a series of extrajudicial slayings, popularly called the "Chain Murders," created a scandal that led to his resignation.[31] In late November and early December 1998, five dissident intellectuals were killed or disappeared. Investigations into the crimes, also known as the "Serial Murders," later pointed to numerous other similar mysterious deaths over preceding years. The brutal stabbings of married opposition political leaders Dariush and Parvaneh Foruhar, in particular, triggered popular demands for an inquiry that the regime was unable to resist.[32] Khatami appointed a special investigating committee to examine the possible role of Iran's intelligence and security services in the murders. The committee consisted of former MOIS deputy ministers Said Hajjarian and Ali Rabii along with Ali Yunesi, a mujtahid who had headed Iran's military courts.[33]

The investigation gained momentum after incriminating audio recordings of the events at the Foruhars' home and of the conspirators' mobile phone conversations collected by MOIS technical surveillance personnel were leaked by a ministry staffer to Hajjarian.[34] The recordings revealed that during the assassins' confrontation with the Foruhars one of the killers called Mostafa Purmohammadi, then the head of MOIS internal security operations, to discuss the unplanned murder of Parveneh Foruhar. During the call, the assassin mentioned Dorri-Najafabadi by name, stating that his order was "only to kill the man."[35] The committee apparently developed little information on the other murders but instead uncovered more damning evidence of a clandestine campaign to kill critics of the regime's authoritarian policies.

The investigators reported the existence of three secret committees that allegedly planned and carried out the assassinations of regime opponents going back to Fallahian's tenure as minister. The three committees' members came from the MOIS, IRGC intelligence, and the Office of the Supreme Leader.[36] According to the investigators, Fallahian coordinated the execution of the committees' plans, which started with lists of Iranians to be killed followed by the release of defamatory press reports about the targets as pro-Western opponents of velayat-e faqih and Iran. Fallahian then acquired fatwas from loyal high-ranking clerics to justify the murders by declaring the targeted individuals to be apostates and enemies of God.[37]

Once the fatwas were given, planning for the assassinations began. The investigative committee detected eighteen fatwas legitimizing the assassination of regime opponents and intellectuals seeking more cultural freedoms.[38] The uncovered target lists included Shirin Ebadi, a future Nobel laureate who was part of the legal team supporting the investigation. She later suggested that the conspirators had used multiple methods of killing to keep investigators from connecting the murders as well as to avoid international attention such as Iran had received from the 1988 dissident executions.[39]

Faced with the evidence developed by the president's committee, on January 4, 1999, the ministry issued an unprecedented statement acknowledging that rogue officers had committed the crimes. On January 20, however, the regime had the president's committee issue a statement to exonerate the MOIS and IRGC for their officers' actions by verifying that the assassins had acted on their own initiative.[40] Aided by Khamenei's efforts to downplay the scandal and warnings to Khatami's supporters against seeking the minister's resignation, Dorri-Najafabadi briefly held on to his post. The president, however, directed MOIS officials to refuse orders from Dorri-Najafabadi and excluded him from cabinet and SNSC meetings. Khamenei eventually relented, and Dorri-Najafabadi resigned on February 9, citing pressure from internal and external enemies who, he claimed, hoped to weaken the security forces by damaging their reputation.[41]

Sensitive to public sentiment, Khamenei allowed the investigations and eventual prosecutions to continue.[42] Dorri-Najafabadi's successor soon claimed that, while no MOIS deputy ministers were involved, the regime had arrested a "number of directors-general."[43] Iranian officials subsequently presented twenty-two MOIS and other internal security service employees for trial. Officials charged Said Emami, a senior MOIS officer, with running a rogue death squad and placed him in custody with nine other officers. The regime later claimed months after the fact that Emami had committed suicide in prison. Iranian courts eventually sentenced three MOIS officers to death and imprisoned twelve others for murder.[44] In 2003, however, Iran's Supreme Court reduced two of the death sentences to life imprisonment.[45]

After his resignation, Dorri-Najafabadi became the head of Iran's administrative court, where he served until August 2004. Khamenei then named him Iran's prosecutor general, a post he held until August 2009. During widespread popular protests over the disputed 2009 presidential election, he participated in a judiciary committee to investigate charges about postelection mistreatment of detainees with Ebrahim Raisi, then the judiciary's principal deputy, and Purmohammadi, who had left the MOIS to lead the State Inspectorate Organization, which supervised Iran's executive departments, the military, and other state-run institutions.[46]

Ali Yunesi (February 1999–August 2005)

Khamenei allegedly forced Ali Yunesi on Khatami as intelligence minister, but, at least initially, the new minister seemed to satisfy Iran's rival political factions because his impeccable revolutionary background offset his role in the investigation of the Chain Murders.[47] Born in 1955, Yunesi studied at the Haqqani Seminary and received degrees in judicial law and political science. Like many revolutionaries, Yunesi went to Lebanon for guerrilla training with the Palestine Liberation Organization and was imprisoned by the shah's government in the 1970s. After the revolution, he worked in intelligence, became a Reyshahri protégé, and in 1984 was named head of the military's judicial organization.[48]

From 1988 to 1990 Yunesi served as the capital city's prosecutor general. Critics claimed that in this high-profile post the cleric was responsible for the trials and executions of more than one hundred Iranian dissidents. Yunesi dismissed this charge as defamatory despite being a judge and prosecutor during a period of intense repression of regime opponents.[49] In 1989 Khamenei made Yunesi his representative to the army's intelligence branch. The leader subsequently placed him in charge of the judiciary's military courts, which also were responsible for crimes committed by MOIS personnel.[50]

After his confirmation, Yunesi announced that reforms within the ministry were "inevitable" and swore loyalty to the "policies of the government and the president."[51] By this time, Yunesi had aligned with Khatami's political faction, and the MOIS chief took more liberal positions than might have been expected given his background. He later told an IRGC-affiliated newspaper that he did not accept the hard-line "political logic" of the Haqqani Seminary's founders.[52] The ministry's shift from a conservative to a more pragmatic orientation was strengthened by Khatami's success in getting Khamenei's approval for the installation of Ali Rabii as Yunesi's principal deputy.[53]

The new minister pushed ahead with efforts to identify and arrest the so-called rogue elements within the MOIS. He conveyed to his officials that they were not allowed to take the law into their own hands and purportedly purged the ministry of those involved in the dissident killings.[54] Yunesi later claimed that under his leadership the MOIS reduced its harsh methods and instead sought to guide people to support the government and resist foreign entreaties to work against the regime. His reforms included efforts to keep the ministry politically neutral, better assist the foreign ministry, and expand relations with friendly countries. The MOIS similarly became more involved in economic activities to prevent rather than help prosecute corruption.[55]

Among Iran's establishment conservatives, mistrust of and opposition to MOIS policies grew.[56] From the start of Yunesi's tenure, Iran faced intense domestic political battles as conservatives sought to reverse the reformists' electoral gains. In July 1999, after the government closed a reformist newspaper for publishing MOIS information about controlling the press, student protests in Tehran were met by an assault on a dormitory from conservative vigilantes and security forces. The attack precipitated some of the largest antigovernment protests since the revolution. A group of twenty-four senior IRGC officers, dissatisfied with the president's response, sent a letter to Khatami that effectively threatened a military coup unless his administration took stronger action to crush the protests.[57]

Yunesi's MOIS also confronted an ongoing MEK campaign of violence against the government during the first few years of his tenure. After the Iran-Iraq War, the main MEK organization remained based in Iraq and launched sporadic attacks against Iran and its interests. From 1993 to 1998, the group conducted bombings inside Iran against oil pipelines near Abadan, the Imam Reza Shrine in Mashhad, and Tehran's revolutionary court building. Starting in June 1998 and accelerating through early 2000, MEK teams used mortars to attack IRGC bases near the border with Iraq, defense industry centers, and the presidential complex and the Armed Forces General Staff (AFGS) and IRGC headquarters in Tehran. During this same period, MEK assassins tried but failed to kill Ali Razini, the head of the capital's judiciary and a judge in the 1988 "death commission" trials. Another MEK attack targeted but failed to kill former IRGC senior commander Mohsen Rafiq-Dust.

MEK assassins then succeeded in taking the life of AFGS deputy commander Maj. Gen. Ali Sayad Shirazi, a popular war hero who had commanded Artesh ground forces during the conflict with Iraq.[58]

Tension between Iran and the United States also grew steadily during the early 2000s. Bilateral relations had improved marginally from 1997 to 2001 as Khatami sought to open Iran to the West. After the September 2001 terrorist attacks on the United States, Khatami's administration, among other offers of support, aided US efforts to create a new Afghan government to replace the Taliban regime. The George W. Bush administration, however, continued to view Iran as a terrorist-supporting state with a suspected nuclear weapons program. A period of mutual heightened distrust and hostility began in January 2002 when Israel disrupted an IRGC attempt to smuggle arms to Palestinian militants and President Bush described the Islamic Republic as part of an "axis of evil" with Iraq and North Korea.

The United States' initial military successes in Afghanistan and Iraq appeared to unnerve Iran's leadership, and by mid-2003 senior Iranian officials began to warn of US attempts to pressure the regime using psychological warfare and interference in Iran's internal affairs.[59] Iran cast perceived Western psychological and information operations as *jang-e narm* (soft war) and included popular Western culture and diaspora Iranian programming available on satellite television and the Internet as major components of the threat. By 2004 the MOIS was joining other security services in countering soft war by arresting Iranian bloggers and Internet-based writers, seeking to silence them and intimidate others with charges of aiding hostile governments and opposition groups, endangering national security, and insulting Iran's leaders.[60] Meanwhile, Tehran turned to the Qods Force to prevent feared US military actions against Iran by supporting insurgents in Iraq and Afghanistan to entangle American forces in those countries.[61] According to US Defense Department claims, Iranian support to Iraqi Shia insurgents contributed to the deaths of at least 603 US service members in Iraq, roughly 17 percent of all US personnel deaths in that country from 2003 to 2011.[62]

During the last two years of Yunesi's tenure, the United States and the European Union placed increased diplomatic and economic pressure on Tehran over its nuclear program. Negotiations led by France, Germany, and the United Kingdom to stop suspected Iranian nuclear

weapons development achieved some limited successes before founder-
ing as Khatami's administration came to an end.[63] Pressed by sanctions
and Western criticism of the regime's human rights violations, Tehran
became increasingly concerned about the threat of foreign-inspired economic unrest and sedition, which led the MOIS to clamp down further
on domestic critics.

Nonetheless, Iran's hard-line conservatives responded to the perceived inadequacy of Yunesi's approach to domestic threats by expanding existing and creating new intelligence bodies. As discussed in more
detail in chapter 5, Khamenei and like-minded members of the nezam
wanted to bolster intelligence organs that were not subject to executive
or legislative oversight.[64] The IRGC intelligence branch and the Qods
Force, in particular, expanded operations in competition with the MOIS
throughout Yunesi's tenure.

After leaving the ministry at the end of the Khatami administration,
Yunesi became an intelligence and security adviser to the judiciary.
Other than this apparently brief sinecure, Yunesi, unlike his predecessors, was not selected to serve on the Assembly of Experts and Expediency Council. Instead, he remained close to more pragmatic political
leaders, such as Rafsanjani and Hassan Rouhani, Rafsanjani's longtime
associate and a former SNSC secretary (1989–2005). Yunesi became
Rouhani's deputy for legal and jurisprudential research at the Center
for Strategic Research, a leading Iranian national security think tank
established by Rafsanjani. When Rouhani became president in 2013, the
former intelligence minister served as an adviser on ethnic and religious
minorities affairs.[65]

Gholam-Hoseyn Mohseni-Ejei (August 2005–July 2009)

In 2005 the populist conservative mayor of Tehran, Mahmud Ahmadinejad, won the presidency and appointed hard-line cleric Gholam Hoseyn
Mohseni-Ejei the fifth minister of intelligence. During a period of rising
popular discontent aggravated by Western economic sanctions, Mohseni-Ejei's tenure would be marked by harsh measures to suppress protests
and ongoing counter–soft war operations targeting Iranian users of the
expanding world of digital technologies and social media applications.
Born in 1956, he became a cleric at the age of seventeen after studying

theology at the Haqqani and Qom Seminaries. Mohseni-Ejei later received a master's degree in international law from Islamic Azad University in Tehran. In 1984 he joined the new Intelligence Ministry, where he was placed in charge of vetting potential employees. A year later Mohseni-Ejei was named the judiciary's representative to the MOIS, a position he held through 1988 and again from 1991 to 1994 after a brief stint as the head of Tehran's Economic Affairs Court. He served as an SCC prosecutor from 1995 to 1998 and then was promoted to the court's prosecutor general post, where he stayed until becoming intelligence minister. Mohseni-Ejei concurrently headed an investigative court for civil servants (1998–2002) and served as a member of the regime's Press Supervisory Board (2002–5). In addition, he taught courses in the MOIS and revolutionary courts training departments.[66]

Mohseni-Ejei's court appointments made him a leading player in the conflicts between the judiciary and reformist politicians, activists, and journalists during Khatami's presidency. One of his first important cases involved the August 1981 bombing of the prime minister's office, during which he targeted future reformist politicians, such as Mohsen Sazegara, one of the IRGC's founders, and Khosrow Tehrani, an official of the prime minister's intelligence bureau credited with advocating the creation of an intelligence ministry.[67] In 1998 Mohseni-Ejei was the presiding judge for the trial of Gholam-Hoseyn Karbaschi, a former Tehran mayor and key organizer of Khatami's 1997 election victory. The regime apparently was trying to use this and related trials involving like-minded politicians, organizers, and financiers to cripple the reformists before upcoming Majles elections. Similarly, when Mohseni-Ejei headed the SCC, it imprisoned several reformist clerics, including Abdollah Nuri, an outspoken and popular newspaper publisher and former interior minister who was publicly critical of the regime's conservatives.[68] The Chain Murders investigations suggested that Mohseni-Ejei, while the judiciary's representative to the MOIS, was involved in the 1998 disappearance of Iranian dissident Pirouz Davani.[69]

After becoming intelligence minister in August 2005, Mohseni-Ejei spearheaded a regime campaign against domestic political activists, academics, and journalists to prevent feared attempts to overturn the regime in the aftermath of the so-called democratic color revolutions in Georgia, Ukraine, and Lebanon of the mid-2000s.[70] He described the "enemy's new policy" as using economic pressure and propaganda to divide Iranians from their government and warned that the MOIS would confront anyone working to subvert the nezam.[71] The ministry also targeted several dual nationals for sedition, including US think tank scholar Haleh Esfandiari, journalist Roxana Saberi, and others.[72] All were released in a few months after the regime apparently determined that they had served their purpose as purported proof of Tehran's accusation that the United States was trying to promote sedition and as a warning to Iranians to avoid antiregime activities.

The Green Movement

The MOIS came under increased criticism for a lack of effectiveness in preventing and stopping the nationwide protests that followed the disputed June 2009 presidential election. When Purmohammadi, then installed as minister of the interior, announced shortly after the polls closed that President Ahmadinejad had won reelection, the other candidates immediately alleged a fraudulent vote count. Demonstrators soon began some of the largest protests seen in Tehran and other Iranian cities since those in 1979 and 1999. Called the Green Movement, the protestors sought to reverse the election results in favor of former prime minister Mir-Hoseyn Musavi and his more progressive platform. The protests continued for weeks despite a violent regime security force response and increased MOIS arrests of opposition leaders. Over the course of the subsequent six months, thousands of Green Movement protestors were detained amid reports of widespread prisoner abuse. Unsatisfied, Ahmadinejad accused the ministry of failing in its duties and even suggested that MOIS personnel had engineered the unrest to undermine his administration.[73]

In July 2009 Ahmadinejad dismissed Mohseni-Ejei as intelligence minister, ostensibly over these failures. The president, however, was primarily punishing him for joining other establishment conservatives and senior clerics in objecting to the appointment of a controversial administration official as first vice president, who administered the executive branch and became acting president if the incumbent were incapacitated.[74] Ahmadinejad also fired the MOIS deputy ministers for counterintelligence, technical services, protection, and legislative affairs. After another senior deputy minister refused to serve as acting minister,

Ahmadinejad temporarily took on the role and endured widespread criticism until he nominated and won approval for Mohseni-Ejei's replacement.[75]

Immediately following his dismissal, the one-term intelligence minister became heavily involved in the trials of Green Movement demonstrators as Iran's prosecutor general. He also served on a special investigative committee to examine abuse allegations against prison officials that, despite substantial evidence to the contrary, pronounced the charges unfounded.[76] Appointed to the Expediency Council in 2007, the former minister remained there through 2023. On August 20, 2014, Mohseni-Ejei became an assistant to the chief justice and was promoted to deputy after Ebrahim Raisi was named judiciary head in December 2018. Following Raisi's election as president in 2021, Khamenei appointed Mohseni-Ejei Iran's new chief justice and judiciary head.[77]

Heydar Moslehi (September 2009–August 2013)

As the Green Movement protests continued through late summer of 2009, President Ahmadinejad turned to Heydar Moslehi, a trusted cleric with close IRGC ties and a history of promoting regime dogma, to serve as intelligence minister. Moslehi, born in 1957, received his religious training in Qom.[78] He later acquired a master's in theology from the Imam Khomeini Educational and Research Institute, an influential institution that rejects democracy and promotes an especially hard-line interpretation of velayat-e faqih. Notably, in light of Moslehi's later experiences as MOIS head, it also trained clerics in the humanities to "deal with deviant and eclectic ideas."[79] In early 1979 Moslehi joined a komiteh, where his work apparently gained the notice of clerics close to Khomeini.[80]

Moslehi then became strongly associated with the Revolutionary Guard. When the Iran-Iraq War began, Khomeini appointed Moslehi his representative to two major IRGC headquarters, where the young cleric remained until the conflict ended. In 1989 he became Khamenei's representative to the IRGC ground forces, which was followed by the same ideological-political assignment to the Basij, a paramilitary reserve with internal security and law enforcement duties performed by branches throughout the country and within state-run educational, labor, and other organizations. Moslehi capped his work with the Revolutionary Guard by serving as the leader's representative to the IRGC Air Force through 2006.[81]

Following Ahmadinejad's 2005 election, the president made Moslehi his adviser on clerical affairs. In mid-2006 Moslehi resigned this post, and Khamenei appointed him head of the Pious Endowments and Charity Affairs Organization, one of many religious foundations in Iran that are basically large conglomerates with real estate and industrial holdings. The regime generally chooses favored conservatives as heads of these organizations to better serve the nezam's political and economic interests, providing some measure of Moslehi's political relationships.[82] Before and after the war, Moslehi was a lecturer on ideology and culture at Iran's various intelligence organizations. He also managed five cultural political journals and helped to produce political guidebooks for the IRGC and Basij.[83]

Moslehi took the MOIS helm as the conservative elite marginalized the reformist opposition. Following the regime's line, Moslehi described the Green Movement as a type of sedition with "its own special complexity" relative to the past seditions of Banisadr, the MEK, and Montazeri.[84] The nezam also faced increasing divisions between Khamenei's and Ahmadinejad's supporters. During the president's second term, conservative establishment figures and media outlets began to refer to Ahmadinejad and his closest aides as a "deviant current" that held unorthodox views on Islam and emphasized Iranian nationalism over revolutionary principles.[85] Moslehi, meanwhile, resisted the president's attempts to make the ministry more responsive to the administration's political needs. The minister claimed he told Ahmadinejad before taking the job that as a cleric he had to accept the leader's guidance over that of a layman president.[86]

This tension erupted in April 2011 when the president fired Moslehi, purportedly for wiretapping the office of Ahmadinejad's chief of staff. Khamenei overruled the decision and ordered Moslehi to resume his position. For the remainder of his presidency, Ahmadinejad repeatedly challenged Khamenei and the ministry by accusing conservative allies of the leader of corruption and other misdeeds.[87] These disputes probably reinforced Khamenei's desire to bolster the IRGC's role in intelligence because of its subordination to him as commander in chief.[88]

From 2010 to 2013 the MOIS confronted foreign attacks against Iran's nuclear program. In January 2010 the first in a two-year-long series of assassinations of Iranian nuclear scientists occurred in Tehran that the regime blamed on Israel, with alleged CIA and British SIS complicity. In September Iran's primary uranium enrichment facility suffered major damage from the Stuxnet "worm," a computer malware attack.[89] As discussed in chapter 4, the cyber campaign against Iran continued, and the regime's security services, including the MOIS, responded with offensive cyber operations against Israel, Saudi Arabia, and the United States.

Moslehi reported in April 2012 that his ministry had broken an Israeli spy ring and in June claimed the arrest of MEK members allegedly involved in the scientists' assassinations.[90] The MOIS, however, apparently had no or only a minor supporting role in a series of Qods Force–directed retaliatory attacks in 2012 against Israeli diplomats and US and British nationals in India, Georgia, Thailand, Turkey, Azerbaijan, Bulgaria, Kenya, and Nigeria. Most of the attacks were disrupted or caused few injuries, but a July 2012 attack on a Bulgarian bus carrying Israeli tourists killed five Israelis and injured thirty-two.[91]

Moslehi's ministry achieved a significant victory against separatists in February 2010 when it captured Abdulmalik Rigi, the leader of the Sunni Baluch terrorist organization Jundallah (Army of God). The regime believed that Saudi Arabia and the other Gulf Arabs, with US and British collusion, supported Jundallah.[92] The group had conducted a series of high-profile bombings from 2008 to 2010 that killed 154 people, including six senior IRGC commanders, and injured more than three hundred.[93] Working with Iran's military, the MOIS arranged to have a plane Rigi was taking from Dubai to Kyrgyzstan diverted to an Iranian airfield. An Iranian court tried, convicted, and executed Rigi for his role in the bombings.[94]

As Moslehi ended his tenure as minister in August 2013, political turmoil and, in some areas, Shia-Sunni tensions were increasing across the region. Iranian leaders initially had welcomed the 2011 Arab Spring political protests, which they portrayed as an Islamic awakening inspired by Iran's revolution and as a setback for US-friendly leaders in the region. The regime, however, soon found itself trying to save its ally, Syrian dictator Bashar al-Assad, from domestic rebellions by that country's Sunni Arabs and Kurds. While the Qods Force took the lead in operations in Syria, MOIS officers participated in Iran's efforts to sustain the Syrian regime.[95] After leaving the cabinet in August 2013, Moslehi became an adviser to the head of the Imam Khomeini Relief Foundation, another major endowment that aids the poor in Iran and Muslim communities throughout the world.[96]

Mahmud Alavi (August 2013–August 2021)

Mahmud Alavi, Iran's seventh MOIS leader, tried to soften the ministry's reputation domestically but found his approach undermined by competition from IRGC intelligence operations, a surge in terrorist and foreign service violence, and popular unrest spurred by US-led economic pressure. Alavi was born in Iran in 1954 but spent his early years in Najaf, and while the source of his initial clerical education is unclear, he received a master's degree in theology and a doctorate in Islamic law from Ferdowsi University, a prestigious public university in Mashhad.[97] After the revolution, Alavi won election to the Majles, where he served four terms (1981–88 and 1992–2000).

In 1989 President Rafsanjani appointed Alavi the deputy of public relations and propaganda of the Ministry of Defense and Armed Forces Logistics (MODAFL), a post he occupied until 1991.[98] This office was part of MODAFL's Political-Ideological Organization, which, as its name implies, is responsible for the oversight and conduct of political indoctrination at the ministry. Khamenei in 2000 made Alavi the head of the Artesh political-ideological bureau, a position he held through 2009. Alavi then was elected to the Assembly of Experts, where he continued to serve through 2023. Despite this background, the Guardian Council disqualified him from running in the 2012 Majles election, almost certainly because of his ties to pragmatic clerical leaders and his perceived reformist leanings.[99]

Following his inauguration as president, Hassan Rouhani, a centrist cleric intent on securing the regime through selective domestic policy reforms and improved foreign relations, nominated an apparently like-minded Alavi to be intelligence minister. The Rouhani-led pragmatist faction took a technocratic approach to reforms. It emphasized economic planning and some accommodations to the West to foster greater integration into the global economy. But the faction remained committed to maintaining the nezam and using autocratic means, as necessary, to protect the regime. During his Majles confirmation hearing in August 2013, Alavi suggested that his term as minister would focus on reforming MOIS operations and administration. He proposed corrections to what he saw as ministry activities that were outside the law, violated citizens' rights, and lacked accountability.[100] The nominee also promised reforms to change an internal security environment that he believed weakened confidence in the ministry and the government. Alavi told the legislators that he intended to build public trust by strengthening the MOIS public relations department while being accountable to relevant authorities, watchdog agencies, and public institutions.[101]

Iran's other intelligence services did not follow Alavi's lead. The IRGC Intelligence Organization (IRGC-IO), created in the aftermath of the 2009 election protests, greatly expanded its operations against political activists following Rouhani's election.[102] By late 2016 competition with the Revolutionary Guard appeared to push the MOIS to intensify its arrests of regime critics. Human rights organizations reported increased MOIS targeting of civil and women's rights advocates, journalists, and ethnic and religious minorities. They also charged that the ministry had become more involved in the soft war campaign against Internet activists and social media administrators, possibly to assuage hard-liners who accused the Rouhani administration of inadequately controlling online political discourse.[103]

The expansion of intelligence activities from 2013 to 2017 probably reflected regime perceptions of increased security threats. During this period, the UN Security Council imposed damaging sanctions that for the first time restricted European and Asian purchases of Iranian oil and gas, shaking an important foundation of the regime. Other dangers included alleged US efforts to promote sedition, Israeli threats to attack Iran's nuclear facilities, and the rise of the virulently anti-Shia Sunni terrorist group Islamic State of Iraq and al-Sham (ISIS).[104] Founded as al-Qaeda's regional affiliate in the Levant before becoming an independent entity, ISIS considered Shia apostates. From its inception, the group had actively tried to recruit, build an offshoot, and conduct terrorist attacks in Iran.[105] In late 2014 Alavi announced plans to expand internal and external intelligence activities, with a focus on the ministry's essential security missions.[106] Despite significant MOIS successes in disrupting terrorist cells, ISIS was able to launch major terrorist attacks in Tehran on June 7, 2017. The MOIS quickly recovered from the attacks by locating the terrorists and killing the group's leader.[107]

Alavi ended his tenure as minister while several controversies raised questions about MOIS counterintelligence effectiveness and undermined his reputation as a pragmatic official. In early 2018 Mossad stole approximately one hundred thousand secret documents about Iran's nuclear program from a warehouse in Tehran and moved them out of the country. Several years earlier, from 2013 to 2015, the Rouhani administration had negotiated with the United States and other major powers to place additional constraints on Iran's nuclear power program in return for the end of international and select US sanctions.[108] The resulting Joint Comprehensive Plan of Action (JCPOA) placed significant curbs on Iran's nuclear capabilities in exchange for substantial sanctions relief.[109] Although international monitors judged that the Iranians were abiding by their commitments,[110] President Donald J. Trump, who had strongly opposed the JCPOA, cited the Israelis' stolen information when he withdrew the United States from the agreement in May 2018.[111]

Iran suffered multiple instances of sabotage and cyberattacks on its nuclear facilities in 2020 and 2021 that humiliated the MOIS and Iran's other security services. In addition, assassins directed by Mossad killed Mohsen Fakhrizadeh, the architect of Iran's nuclear program, in November 2020. In response to conservative calls for a purge of Iran's intelligence and counterintelligence community, Alavi blamed the IRGC-IO for the failures and accused it of being compromised by Mossad.[112] In February 2021 the minister angered regime leaders when he suggested that Khamenei's purported fatwa forbidding nuclear weapons might be abandoned if US economic sanctions continued.[113]

A final embarrassment for Alavi occurred in July 2021 when a New York federal court indicted Iranian assets, including one linked to the MOIS, for conspiring to kidnap Brooklyn-based Iranian human rights activist Masih Alinejad. The failed endeavor was only one of a series of Iranian attempts in 2019 and 2021 to lure or forcibly return to Iran regime critics residing in Canada, Europe, and the United Arab Emirates.[114] The abduction bids undercut Alavi's professed desire to have his ministry respect citizens' rights and improve its reputation.[115]

Esmail Khatib (August 2021–)

Following his 2021 election, President Ebrahim Raisi nominated his longtime colleague Esmail Khatib to become intelligence minister.[116] Born in 1961, Khatib, an established member of Iran's conservative elite, reportedly studied Islamic jurisprudence under Khamenei and other influential regime clerics. He joined the IRGC intelligence branch in 1980 and around 1991 moved to the MOIS. The ministry assigned him to its regional office in Qom, where his counterintelligence and security duties extended to working with the Office of the Supreme Leader and keeping watch on the city's seminaries. From 2012 to 2019 Khatib headed the Judiciary Protection and Intelligence Center, where he worked with Raisi, then serving as the deputy judiciary chief. After Raisi became chair in 2014 of one of Iran's largest and most influential charitable endowments, the Astan Qods Razavi, he put Khatib in charge of the organization's security.[117]

Khatib serves a presidential administration intent on taking a stronger approach to security affairs as it completes a reorganization of Iran's military and security structures that began in 2019 under the banner of "The Second Step of the Islamic Revolution."[118] The plan was prepared by Khamenei to ensure his ideology dominated Iran for decades to come regardless of the regime's shrinking base of political support and increasing domestic unpopularity. Meanwhile, Khatib, in one of his initial public statements, announced a transformation program that would focus on providing improved surveillance to protect national security along with greater emphasis on the production of intelligence information. He held to the regime's line that Iran's primary threat was Western cultural influence that aimed to create popular dissatisfaction and destabilize the country.[119] His major challenges, however, appeared to be the sabotage and cyberattacks on Iran's nuclear, defense, and other critical infrastructure and sporadic and often widespread antigovernment protests that reignited in September 2022 and lasted for several months.

In 2023 Khatib led the MOIS in a series of claimed successful operations that disrupted networks allegedly directed by the MEK, ISIS, and Israel along with the activities of Iranian separatist groups.[120] The intelligence minister also seemed to have a higher profile in Iran's foreign policy, taking a leading role in repeatedly charging the United States,

Israel, various European countries, and some nongovernmental organizations with trying to destabilize Iran by promoting antigovernment protests.[121] He also used remarks praising President Raisi's efforts to improve relations with neighboring Arab states to warn them against normalizing relations with Israel.[122] After the October 7 attack on Israel by the Iranian-supported Palestinian militant group Hamas, Khatib confidently declared the initial aggression a strategic victory for Iran's interests and regional allies.[123] When Tehran quickly claimed to have been surprised by the Hamas attack, however, the intelligence minister had nothing to say about his service's apparent failure to discover and warn Iran's leaders about the Palestinian militants' plans.[124]

All eight intelligence ministers demonstrated a strong commitment to the MOIS and its role in defending Iran and the nezam. Their similarities generally have overshadowed their political differences when it came to supporting policies and activities approved by the supreme leader and coordinated among the regime's most senior security officials. While the Chain Murder investigations forced the regime to discard extrajudicial killings, the last five intelligence ministers simply worked more closely with the judiciary to arrest, isolate, and punish regime opponents with the clear goal of deterring others from challenging the ruling establishment. Similarly, Iran stopped its political murders of exiled dissidents from 1996 to 2015. But as concern about foreign-instigated sedition and soft war continued to grow in Tehran, the MOIS ministers competed with the IRGC-IO to conduct assassinations and abductions abroad to silence regime opponents directly or through intimidation. Finally, as discussed in chapter 5, all eight sought to strengthen coordination among the numerous members of Iran's intelligence community, but the steady operational expansion of Iran's parallel intelligence organizations demonstrated the limits of the ministry's ostensible leading role.

Notes

1. Mehrzad Boroujerdi and Kourosh Rahimkhani, *Postrevolutionary Iran: A Political Handbook* (Syracuse, NY: Syracuse University Press, 2018), 697; Buchta, *Who Rules Iran?*, 19.
2. Boroujerdi and Rahimkhani, *Postrevolutionary Iran*, 343.
3. Hoseyni, "Unsaid Words of Shariatmadari."
4. Library of Congress, *Iran's Ministry of Intelligence and Security*, 18.

5. "Iran: Former Justice Minister Elaborates on 1990s Serial Murders," BBC Monitoring Middle East [Sharq Daily in Persian], July 13, 2019, ProQuest.

6. Axworthy, *Revolutionary Iran*, 343; Buchta, *Who Rules Iran?*, 97.

7. In the United States the leak led to the Iran-Contra Affair, in which congressional investigations revealed that President Ronald Reagan's administration had illegally used money obtained from the arms sales to Iran for a Cold War covert action to fund the Contras, Nicaraguan insurgents fighting a guerrilla war to overthrow the country's communist Sandinista government.

8. This discussion of Hashemi was derived from Buchta, *Who Rules Iran?*, 92–94.

9. This paragraph is derived from a more detailed account of Hashemi's arrest and trial that can be found in Abrahamian, *Tortured Confessions*, 162–66.

10. Abrahamian, 162–66.

11. Ward, *Immortal*, 296.

12. For details on the fatwa and the victims, see "Deadly Fatwa: Iran's 1988 Prison Massacre," Iran Human Rights Documentation Center, February 5, 2011, https://iranhrdc.org/deadly-fatwa-irans-1988-prison-massacre/.

13. Amnesty International, *Iran: Blood-Soaked Secrets: Why Iran's 1988 Prison Massacres Are Ongoing Crimes against Humanity*, index no. MDE 13/9421/2018, December 4, 2018, https://www.amnesty.org/en/documents/mde13/9421/2018/en/; Nasser Mohajer and Kaveh Yazdani, "Iran's New President Has Blood on His Hands," Atlantic Council, September 8, 2021, https://www.atlanticcouncil.org/blogs/iransource/irans-new-president-has-blood-on-his-hands/; Boroujerdi and Rahimkhani, *Postrevolutionary Iran*, 666.

14. Andrew Hanna, "Raisi: Role in 1988 Massacre," United States Institute of Peace (USIP) Iran Primer, July 21, 2021, https://iranprimer.usip.org/ blog/2021/jul/21/raisi-role-1988-massacre.

15. Buchta, *Who Rules Iran?*, 97–98.

16. The Expediency Council's formal title is "Expediency Discernment Council of the System." In addition to its mediating duties between the Majles and the Guardian Council described in box 1.1, one of its main roles is to determine whether the regime can circumvent Islamic laws and Iran's constitution to serve government interests and protect the revolution. Expediency is a recognized concept in Islamic jurisprudence that allows flexibility to act as needed to preserve the religion, ruling system, and people. Boroujerdi and Rahimkhani, *Postrevolutionary Iran*, 697; Axworthy, *Revolutionary Iran*, 343; Buchta, *Who Rules Iran?*, 19.

17. Boroujerdi and Rahimkhani, *Postrevolutionary Iran*, 456.

18. The USIP Iran Primer keeps an updated chronology of Iranian assassinations at https://iranprimer.usip.org/blog/2020/sep/16/timeline-iran-assassinations-and-plot.

19. Dan Geist, "'A Darker Horizon': The Assassination of Shapour Bakhtiar," PBS, August 6, 2011, https://www.pbs.org/wgbh/pages/frontline/tehranbureau/2011/08/a-darker-horizon-the-assassination-of-shapour-bakhtiar.html.

20. Geist.

21. US Department of State, Office of the Coordinator for Counterterrorism, *Patterns of Global Terrorism, 1993*, April 1993, https://www.hsdl.org/?abstract&did=481510.

22. Buchta, *Who Rules Iran?*, 128.
23. See Israel Ministry of Foreign Affairs, "Terror Attack on the Israeli Embassy in Buenos Aires," n.d., https://mfa.gov.il/MFA/ ForeignPolicy/Terrorism/Hizbullah /Pages/Terror-attack-Israeli-Embassy-Buenos-Aires-17-Mar-1992.aspx. For a thorough discussion of this attack and the subsequent AMIA bombing, see Matthew Levitt, *Hezbollah: The Global Footprint of Lebanon's Party of God* (Washington, DC: Georgetown University Press, 2013), 75–102.
24. Ronen Bergman, "Mossad Sheds New Light on Argentina Terrorist Attacks in 1990s," *New York Times*, July 22, 2022, https://www.nytimes.com/2022/07/22 /world/middleeast/argentina-mossad-hezbollah-bombings.html. Israeli media also reported on this study. See, e.g., "Hezbollah Acted Alone in 90s Attacks on Jews in Argentina, Mossad Report Finds," *Haaretz*, July 22, 2022, https://www.haaretz .com/world-news/americas/2022-07-22/ty-article/.premium/mossad-hezbollah-ac ted-alone-in-argentina-attacks-on-jews-in-90s/00000182-2711-dfa9-a5c7-27dd84 230000.
25. Boroujerdi and Rahimkhani, *Postrevolutionary Iran*, 456.
26. Scott Peterson, *Let the Swords Encircle Me: Iran—A Journey behind the Headlines* (New York: Simon & Schuster, 2010), 232.
27. Boroujerdi and Rahimkhani, *Postrevolutionary Iran*, 441.
28. Buchta, *Who Rules Iran?*, 41, 147n47.
29. A. William Samii, "Factionalism in Iran's Domestic Security Forces," *Middle East Intelligence Bulletin* 4, no. 2 (February 2002), https://www.meforum.org/meib/ar ticles/0202_me2.htm.
30. "Covert Terror: Iran's Parallel Intelligence Apparatus," Iran Human Rights Documentation Center, February 3, 2011, https://iranhrdc.org/covert-terror-irans-paral lel-intelligence-apparatus/.
31. This discussion of the murders and subsequent events is drawn primarily from Buchta, *Who Rules Iran?*, 156–68.
32. Sarah Fowler, "Iran's Chain Murders: A Wave of Killings That Shook a Nation," BBC News, December 2, 2018, https://www.bbc.com/news/world-middle-east-46 356725.
33. Buchta, *Who Rules Iran?*, 158.
34. Buchta, 167.
35. Buchta, 167.
36. The Office of the Supreme Leader is the executive arm and administrative office that assists the leader in performing his duties and supervising the regime. It also employs advisers for military, economic, cultural, and other fields. For more detail, see Mehrzad Boroujerdi and Kourosh Rahimkhani, "Office of the Supreme Leader: Epicenter of a Theocracy," Iran Data Portal, https://irandataportal.syr.edu /data-by-individual-researchers/the-office-of-supreme-leader.
37. Buchta, *Who Rules Iran?*, 167–68.
38. Buchta, 168.
39. Peterson, *Let the Swords Encircle Me*, 231; Shirin Ebadi with Azadeh Moaveni, *Iran Awakening: One Woman's Journey to Reclaim Her Life and Country* (New York: Random House, 2006), 131–32.
40. Buchta, *Who Rules Iran?*, 162.

41. "Iran: Information Minister's Letter of Resignation," BBC Monitoring Middle East [Vision of the Islamic Republic of Iran Network 1 in Persian], February 9, 1999, ProQuest.
42. Bill Samii, *RFE/RL Iran Report*, vol. 2, no. 32, August 9, 1999, Global Security, https://www.globalsecurity.org/wmd/library/news/iran/1999/32-090899.html; Buchta, *Who Rules Iran?*, 163.
43. "New Iranian Information Minister: 'Reforms Will Definitely Be Made,'" BBC Monitoring Middle East [Islamic Republic News Agency (IRNA) in English], February 24, 1999, ProQuest.
44. Buchta, *Who Rules Iran?*, 160; Samii, "Factionalism in Iran's Domestic Security Forces"; Samii, *RFE/RL Iran Report*.
45. "Iran: Supreme Court Condemns Two Main 'Serial Murderers' to Life in Prison," BBC Monitoring Middle East [IRNA in English], January 28, 2003, ProQuest.
46. "The Outcome of Karroubi's Remarks Will Be Announced in a Three-Member Committee," Mehr News, September 5, 2009, https://www.mehrnews.com/news/941953; "The Result of the Investigations of the Three Member Board of the Judiciary," Islamic Republic News Agency, September 12, 2009, https://www.irna.ir/news/4362095; Boroujerdi and Rahimkhani, *Postrevolutionary Iran*, 441.
47. Buchta, *Who Rules Iran?*, 163.
48. Boroujerdi and Rahimkhani, *Postrevolutionary Iran*, 784–85; Samii, "Factionalism in Iran's Domestic Security Forces."
49. "Iran President's Senior Advisor Says Intelligence Minister Not in Full Control," BBC Monitoring Middle East [Fars News Agency in Persian], October 6, 2014, ProQuest.
50. Boroujerdi and Rahimkhani, *Postrevolutionary Iran*, 784–85.
51. "New Iranian Information Minister: 'Reforms Will Definitely Be Made'"; Buchta, *Who Rules Iran?*, 163–64.
52. "Iran President's Senior Advisor Says Intelligence Minister Not in Full Control."
53. Buchta, *Who Rules Iran?*, 163.
54. "Iran: New Minister Promises 'To Safeguard Power' of Information Ministry," BBC Monitoring Middle East [IRNA in English], February 24, 1999, ProQuest; "Covert Terror."
55. Maziar Bahari, "We Know Where You Live," *New Statesman*, November 12, 2007, 30–31, 33, ProQuest; "Iran: Minister-Designate Outlines His Strategies for Information Ministry," BBC Monitoring Middle East [IRNA in English], February 18, 1999, ProQuest; "Minister of Information: We Do Not Give Information According to Anyone's Wishes, We Act According to National Interests," Iranian Students News Agency, July 16, 2005, https://www.isna.ir/news/8404-10272.
56. Library of Congress, *Iran's Ministry of Intelligence and Security*, 19.
57. "IRGC Commanders Letter to Khatami," translation, Iran Data Portal, https://irandataportal.syr.edu/irgc-commanders-letter-to-khatami; *RFE/RL Iran Report*, vol. 2, no. 30, July 26, 1999, https://www.rferl.org/a/1342938.html.
58. On MEK attacks, see US Department of State, Office of the Coordinator for Counterterrorism, "Chapter 6: Foreign Terrorist Organizations," *Country Reports on Terrorism 2010*, August 18, 2011, https://2009-2017.state.gov/j/ct/rls/crt/2010/170264.htm. A very detailed listing of MEK actions against Iran that appears to be generally accurate despite being prepared by the anti-MEK Nejat Society can be

found in Xavier Rauf, "Mujahedin Khalq Organization as a Terrorist Group," *Atlas of Radical Islam*, June 19, 2008, https://www.nejatngo.org/en/posts/1863.

59. Steven R. Ward, "The Continuing Evolution of Iran's Military Doctrine," *Middle East Journal* 59, no. 4 (Autumn 2005): 564–65.

60. "Iran: Blogger Sentenced to 14 Years in Prison: Government Broadens Its Crackdown on Freedom of Expression," Human Rights Watch, February 23, 2005, https://www.hrw.org/news/2005/02/23/iran-blogger-sentenced-14-years-prison; "Iran: Web Writers Purge Underway," Human Rights Watch, November 7, 2004, https://www.hrw.org/ news/2004/11/07/iran-web-writers-purge-underway.

61. For brief summaries of Iranian activities, see Lionel Beehner and Greg Bruno, "Iran's Involvement in Iraq," Council of Foreign Relations, March 3, 2008, https://www.cfr.org/backgrounder/irans-involvement-iraq; and Sajjan M. Gohel, "Iran's Ambiguous Role in Afghanistan," *CTC Sentinel* 3, no. 3 (March 2010): 13–16, https://ctc.usma.edu/irans-ambiguous-role-in-afghanistan/.

62. Philip Bump, "Why the Administration Claims That Soleimani Killed Hundreds of Americans," *Washington Post*, January 8, 2020, https://www.washingtonpost.com/politics/2020/01/08/why-administration-claims-that-soleimani-killed-hundreds-americans/; Kyle Rempfer, "Iran Killed More US Troops in Iraq Than Previously Known, Pentagon Says," *Military Times*, April 4, 2019, https://www.militarytimes.com/news/your-military/2019/04/04/iran-killed-more-us-troops-in-iraq-than-previously-known-pentagon-says/.

63. For a brief synopsis and timeline of European-led nuclear negotiations with Iran, see "Official Proposals on the Iranian Nuclear Issue, 2003–2013," Arms Control Association, January 2022, https://www.armscontrol.org/factsheets/Iran_Nuclear_Proposals.

64. Zimmt, "Intelligence Organization of the IRGC," 9.

65. Boroujerdi and Rahimkhani, *Postrevolutionary Iran*, 784–85.

66. Boroujerdi and Rahimkhani, 604; "Who Iran's New Judiciary Chief Is," *Iran News*, July 3, 2021, ProQuest; "Biography of New Iranian Intelligence Minister Mohseni-Ezhe'i," BBC Monitoring Middle East, August 31, 2005, ProQuest; "Background on Proposed Intelligence Minister," BBC Monitoring Middle East, August 14, 2005, ProQuest; "Iran Cabinet: Biography of Proposed Intelligence Minister," BBC Monitoring Middle East [IRNA in English], August 14, 2005, ProQuest.

67. Roghayeh Rezaei, "Chief Justice Mohseni Ejei Signals an Even Bleaker Future for Iran Human Rights," IranWire, July 2, 2021, https://iranwire.com/en/features/69856/; September 2012 Hajjarian interview.

68. "Biography of New Intelligence Minister."

69. "Judicial System to Be Used to Further Suppress Dissent," Iran Human Rights Documentation Center, July 6, 2021, https://iranhumanrights.org/2021/07/ejeis-appointment-as-irans-judiciary-chief-poses-grave-threat-to-rights-activists/; "Biography of New Intelligence Minister."

70. "Judicial System to Be Used."

71. Peterson, *Let the Swords Encircle Me*, 404.

72. Several other dual nationals were arrested during this period, but Saberi and Esfandiari are perhaps the best known because of the published accounts of their experiences. See Roxana Saberi, *Between Two Worlds: My Life and Captivity in*

Iran (New York: Harper, 2010); and Haleh Esfandiair, *My Prison, My Home: One Woman's Story of Captivity in Iran* (New York: Ecco, 2009).

73. Saeid Golkar, "Iran's Intelligence Organizations and Transnational Suppression," Washington Institute for Near East Policy, PolicyWatch, no. 3,517, August 5, 2021, https://www.washingtoninstitute.org/policy-analysis/irans-intelligence-organizations-and-transnational-suppression.

74. "Paper Outlines Iran Ex-Vice-President's 'News-Making' Instances," BBC Monitoring Middle East [Hamshahri in Persian], August 10, 2009, ProQuest; Library of Congress, *Iran's Ministry of Intelligence and Security*, 19.

75. Borzou Daragahi, "Iran Intelligence Ministry Purged," *Los Angeles Times*, August 10, 2009; "Iranian Media Urged Not to Name Intelligence Officials," BBC Monitoring Middle East [Iranian Students News Agency (ISNA) in Persian], August 10, 2009, ProQuest; "Iran MPs Question Dismissal of Key Intelligence Ministry Officials," BBC Monitoring Middle East [Etemad in Persian], August 4, 2009, ProQuest.

76. "Judicial System to Be Used."

77. Boroujerdi and Rahimkhani, *Postrevolutionary Iran*, 604; "Judicial System to Be Used"; "Who Iran's New Judiciary Chief Is."

78. Boroujerdi and Rahimkhani, *Postrevolutionary Iran*, 616–17.

79. Ali Akbar Ebrahimpour, "Iran's International Propaganda Machine: The Imam Khomeini Educational Institute," IranWire, December 14, 2020, https://iranwire.com/en/features/8315.

80. "A Brief Biography of Iran's New Ministers," Payvand (originally from Rooz Online), September 7, 2009, http://www.payvand.com/news/09/sep/1068.html.

81. This discussion of Moslehi and the IRGC was derived from "Minister of Intelligence, Reckless Criticism and Support of Representatives: From the Worries of Kavakebian to the Assurances of Hoseynian," Tabnak, August 31, 2009, https://www.tabnak.ir/fa/news/62019, and "Brief Biography of Iran's New Ministers."

82. On the charitable organizations or *bonyads*, see David E. Thaler et al., *Mullahs, Guards, and* Bonyads*: An Exploration of Iranian Leadership Dynamics* (Santa Monica, CA: RAND National Defense Research Institute, 2010).

83. Boroujerdi and Rahimkhani, *Postrevolutionary Iran*, 616–17; "Brief Biography of Iran's New Ministers"; "Minister of Intelligence, Reckless Criticism."

84. "The Minister of Intelligence: Repeating the Statements of the Sedition Leaders by Hashemi Is Shocking," Islamic Republic News Agency, December 10, 2009, https://www.irna.ir/news/ 4422484.

85. Borzou Daragahi, "Hard-Liners Push Ally of Ahmadinejad to Step Down," *Los Angeles Times*, June 22, 2011.

86. "The Unspoken Words of Moslehi from the Time of His Ministry in Ahmadi-Nejad's Government," Tabnak, May 29, 2021, https://www.tabnak.ir/fa/news/105 4855.

87. Eric Randolph, "Iranian IRGC Consolidates Primacy in Intelligence Operations," *Jane's Intelligence Review*, August 19, 2020, https://www.janes.com/defence-news/news-detail/iranian-irgc-consolidates-primacy-in-intelligence-operations.

88. Zimmt, "Intelligence Organization of the IRGC," 9; Library of Congress, *Iran's Ministry of Intelligence and Security*, 10. See also Udit Banerjea, "Revolutionary Intelligence: The Expanding Intelligence Role of the Iranian Revolutionary Guard

Corps," *Journal of Strategic Security* 8, no. 3 (2015): 98, https://scholarcommons .usf.edu/jss/vol8/iss3/6.

89. Catherine A. Theohary, "Iranian Offensive Cyber Attack Capabilities," *Congressional Research Service in Focus*, IF11406, January 13, 2020, 1, https://crsreports .congress.gov.

90. Library of Congress, *Iran's Ministry of Intelligence and Security*, 36; "Commander: IRGC Assigned to Protect Iranian VIPs," Fars News Agency, December 25, 2013, ProQuest.

91. Jay Solomon, *The Iran Wars: Spy Games, Bank Battles, and the Secret Deals That Reshaped the Middle East* (New York: Random House, 2016), 139.

92. "Iran Says US, UK Coordinated Rigi's Attacks on Iran," BBC Monitoring Middle East [Islamic Republic of Iran News Network in Persian], February 23, 2010, ProQuest.

93. US Department of State, Office of the Coordinator for Counterterrorism, Country Reports on Terrorism 2011, chap. 6: "Foreign Terrorist Organizations," July 31, 2012, https://2009-2017.state.gov/j/ct/rls/crt/2011/195553.htm#jundallah. The United States designated Jundallah a terrorist organization later that year. US Department of State, "Designation of Jundallah . . . as a Foreign Terrorist Organization Pursuant to Section 219 of the Immigration and Nationality Act, as Amended," public notice 7222, *Federal Register* 75, no. 213 (November 4, 2010), 68017, ProQuest.

94. Scott Peterson, "Iran Arrests Top Sunni Militant Abdolmalek Rigi," *Christian Science Monitor*, February 23, 2010; "Leader of Iran's Sunni Rebel Group Is Hanged," *Wall Street Journal* (online), June 20, 2010, ProQuest.

95. US Department of the Treasury, "Treasury Designates Iranian Ministry of Intelligence and Security for Human Rights Abuses and Support for Terrorism," February 16, 2012, https://www.treasury.gov/press-center/press-releases/Pages/tg1424 .aspx.

96. Boroujerdi and Rahimkhani, *Postrevolutionary Iran*, 617.

97. Boroujerdi and Rahimkhani, 375.

98. MODAFL was created in 1989 by the merger of the former Ministry of Defense and the short-lived Ministry of Revolutionary Guards (1982–89). It is responsible for supporting and equipping Iran's armed forces but is not in the chain of command or involved in developing defense policy and military plans.

99. Boroujerdi and Rahimkhani, *Postrevolutionary Iran*, 375; Ali Reza Eshraghi, "Iran's Proposed Cabinet: The Old Guard Is Back in Charge," CNN, August 7, 2013, https://edition.cnn. com/2013/08/07/opinion/iran-eshraghi-cabinet.

100. "Rouhani's Intelligence Ministry and Khamenei's IRGC Widen Crackdown Ahead of Election," Center for Human Rights in Iran, March 16, 2017, https://www.iran humanrights.org/ 2017/03/increase-arrest-by-ministry-of-intelligence; "Iranian Intelligence Minister Presents Programs—Paper," BBC Monitoring Middle East [Defa'e-Moqaddas News Agency in Persian], August 19, 2013, ProQuest.

101. "Iranian Intelligence Minister Presents Programs."

102. "Supreme Leader Revives Feared Intelligence Unit of Iran's IRGC," Radio Free Europe / Radio Liberty, September 23, 2015, http://www.rferl.org/a/iran -irgc-intelligence-unit-revived/27265226.html; Nima Gerami, "Iran's Widening Crackdown Pressures Rouhani," Washington Institute for Near East Policy,

November 25, 2015, http://www.washingtoninstitute.org/policy-analysis/view
/irans-widening-crackdown- pressures-rouhani.

103. "Rouhani's Intelligence Ministry and Khamenei's IRGC."

104. In 2014, after ISIS leaders declared the creation of a global caliphate, the core
element renamed itself the Islamic State as it established affiliates in other places,
such as Yemen, Libya, and later Afghanistan, to complement ISIS efforts in the
Levant (al-Sham) and Iraq.

105. Ariane Tabatabai and Dina Esfandiary, "Cooperating with Iran to Combat ISIS in
Iraq," *Washington Quarterly* 40, no. 3 (Fall 2017): 131.

106. "People Caught Unawares by the Ministry of Intelligence," Young Journalists
Club, December 4, 2014, https://www.yjc.news/fa/news/ 5063636.

107. "Iran Minister Says Mastermind behind Tehran Attacks Killed," BBC Monitoring
Middle East [Vision of the Islamic Republic of Iran Network 2 in Persian], June
10, 2017, ProQuest.

108. See the national intelligence estimate *Iran: Nuclear Intentions and Capabilities*,
ODNI, November 2007, https://www.dni.gov/files/documents/Newsroom/Repo
rts%20and%20Pubs/20071203_release.pdf; Peter Baker and Robin Wright, "A
Blow to Bush's Tehran Policy," *Washington Post*, December 4, 2007; William J.
Broad and David E. Sanger, "U.N. Nuclear Agency Says Iran Worked on Weapons
Design until 2009," *New York Times*, December 3, 2015; and Director General to
IAEA Board of Governors, *Final Assessment on Past and Present Outstanding
Issues Regarding Iran's Nuclear Programme*, GOV/2015/68, International Atomic
Energy Agency, December 2, 2015, https://www.iaea.org/sites/default/files/gov
-2015-68.pdf.

109. For a brief discussion of the JCPOA and the results of the subsequent US with-
drawal, see "The Joint Comprehensive Plan of Action (JCPOA) at a Glance,"
Arms Control Association, January 2022, https://www.armscontrol.org/ factsheets
/JCPOA-at-a-glance.

110. Iran's nuclear ambitions and capabilities had been the subject of intense international debate and multinational negotiations since the early 1990s. In 2007 a
controversial US national intelligence estimate judged that Tehran had abandoned
a nuclear weapons program in 2003 but continued to acquire technology and expertise useful for building a nuclear bomb. Subsequently, Iran, as a signatory of
the Nonproliferation Treaty, alternately complied with and reneged on monitoring
agreements with the International Atomic Energy Agency based on changes in
the status of negotiations and sanctions. A year after the US withdrawal from the
JCPOA, the regime began a steady increase of its enriched uranium stockpile, a
first step in creating weapons-grade fissile material. It also resumed testing with
high explosives, and both actions supported a capacity to build a weapon if the
regime chose to do so.

111. Julian E. Barnes, Ronen Bergman, and Adam Goldman, "Israel's Spy Agency
Snubbed the U.S.: Can Trust Be Restored?" *New York Times*, August 26, 2021,
https://www.nytimes.com/2021/08/26/world/middleeast/us-israel-bennett-cia
-mossad.html.

112. Ardavan Khoshnood, "Iran Might Purge Its Intelligence and Counterintelligence
Community," BESA Center Perspectives Paper no. 2,025, May 13, 2021, https://
besacenter.org/iran-intelligence-purge; Erfan Fard, "Iran's Intelligence Minister

Sends a Clear Signal to the Biden Administration," BESA Center Perspectives Paper no. 1,929, February 12, 2021, https://besacenter.org/iran-intelligence-minister/.

113. Maysam Behravesh, "Iran Is Starting to Want the Bomb," *Foreign Policy*, March 10, 2021, https://foreignpolicy.com/2021/03/10/iran-is-starting-to-want-the-bomb.

114. Benjamin Weiser, "Iranian Operatives Charged in Plot to Kidnap a Brooklyn Author," *New York Times*, July 13, 2021, www.nytimes.com/2021/07/13/nyregion/iran-masih-alinejad-kidnapping.html; US Department of Justice, "Iranian Intelligence Services Allegedly Plotted to Kidnap a U.S. Journalist and Human Rights Activist from New York City for Rendition to Iran," July 13, 2021, https://www.justice.gov/opa/pr/iranian-intelligence-officials-indicted-kidnapping-conspiracy-charges; "Iran: Alleged Plot to Kidnap Prominent Dissident in US," Human Rights Watch, July 14, 2021, https://www.hrw.org/news/2021/07/14/iran-alleged-plot-kidnap-prominent-dissident-us.

115. Robin Wright, "Iran's Hollywood Plot Exposes Its Paranoia," *New Yorker*, July 19, 2021, https://www.newyorker.com/news/daily-comment/irans-hollywood-plot-exposes-its-paranoia.

116. Muhammad Sahimi, "The Who's Who of Iranian Players behind the New President," Responsible Statecraft, June 24, 2021, https://responsiblestatecraft.org/2021/06/24/the-whos-who-of-iranian-players-behind-the-new-president/.

117. "Iran's Raisi Forms Cabinet Including Terror and Corruption Suspects," Iran International, August 11, 2021, https://iranintl.com/en/iran/irans-raisi-forms-cabinet-including-terror-and-corruption-suspects; Raz Zimmt, "Look Right: Iranian President Raisi Appoints a Government," Institute for National Security Studies, August 19, 2021, http://www.inss.org.il; "Who Is the Proposed Minister of Information of the 13th Government?" Etemad Online, August 13, 2021, https://www.etemadonline.com/fa/tiny/news-509996.

118. Saeid Golkar and Kasra Aarabi, "Why Iran's Ali Khamenei Removed Hossein Taeb from the IRGC," *Foreign Policy*, July 8, 2022, https://foreignpolicy.com/2022/07/08/iran-irgc-khamenei-hossein-taeb-removal-power/.

119. "Promises of the Minister of Information for Transformation in Ministry," Khabar Online, August 29, 2021, https://www.khabaronline.ir/news/1549535.

120. For example, see "Intelligence Ministry Detains MKO-Linked Network in Iran," Mehr News Agency, January 2, 2023, ProQuest; "Iran Captures Israeli Mercenaries behind Military Workshop Attack," Fars News Agency, February 11, 2023, ProQuest; "Iran Captures Mossad Agents in Another Blow to Israel," Fars News Agency, May 21, 2023, ProQuest; "Iran Neutralized 400 Bombs Recently: Intel. Min," Mehr News, September 10, 2023, ProQuest; "Iran Arrests Last Terrorist Involved in Shah Cheragh Attack," Mehr News, August 19, 2023, ProQuest.

121. "Intelligence Forces Should Be Ready for Schools Incidents," Mehr News, March 7, 2023, ProQuest; "Intelligence Minister: Iran Captures Several European Spies," Fars News Agency, August 20, 2023, ProQuest; "Iran Intelligence Forces Dismantle Network Planning Riots," Mehr News, September 7, 2023, ProQuest; "Intelligence Minister: 200 Terrorists Captured by Iran during Past Months," Fars News Agency, September 12, 2023, ProQuest.

122. "Intelligence Minister: Arab Nations Unable to Buy Security through Normalization with Israel," Fars News Agency, February 26, 2023, ProQuest.

123. "Iran's Intel. Min Hails Palestinians' Al-Aqsa Storm Operation," Mehr News, October 11, 2023, ProQuest; "Iran's Intelligence Minister Vows Harsh Revenge Awaiting Israel over Gaza Carnage," Fars News Agency, October 2023, ProQuest; Sina Toossi, "How Iran Really Sees the Israel-Hamas War," *Foreign Policy*, November 2, 2023, https://foreignpolicy.com/2023/11/02/how-iran-really-sees-the-israel-hamas-war.

124. Adam Entous, Julian E. Barnes, and Jonathan Swan, "Early Intelligence Shows Hamas Attack Surprised Iranian Leaders, US Says," *New York Times*, October 11, 2023, https://www.nytimes.com/2023/10/11/us/politics/iran-israel-gaza-hamas-us-intelligence.html.

3

Organization and Organizational Culture

Since its formal establishment in 1984, Iran's Ministry of Intelligence has been shaped by a variety of influences, including its primary intelligence missions and perceptions of persistent threats to the Islamic Republic. Over the years Khamenei repeatedly told ministry personnel to be prepared to counter an intelligence war directed against Iran.[1] Meanwhile, the ministry developed a religiously inspired organizational culture and recruited "pious believers" in the nezam's ideals to protect its "soft inner core of values."[2] These influences and legislated MOIS responsibilities, occasional public official statements, and purported leaks of sensitive information provide a general outline of the service's composition and operational ethos.

Organization

The ministry's organization and the exact responsibilities of its various directorates and subordinate offices are unpublicized. A 1995 MOIS employment law indicates that the ministry is obliged to prepare its organizational chart for approval by the president "while avoiding its uncontrolled publication."[3] The same law dictates that all MOIS documents, locations, and information are classified and, except within the limits of administrative duties, prohibits their disclosure. In addition, the number and role of Iran's multiple parallel intelligence bodies obscure some of the structure and functions of the Iranian intelligence community from outside observers, shielding the MOIS with an additional "cloak of anonymity."[4] Still, the ministry's structure probably mirrors that of other countries' intelligence organizations, with major offices for core functions such as human and technical intelligence collection, analysis, counterintelligence, covert action, and security. Said Hajjarian claimed that he and others in the prime minister's intelligence bureau developed the ministry's initial organization based on the study of other intelligence services, including SAVAK, Mossad, and Turkish intelligence.[5]

Over the years, various speculative claims have been made about the ministry's configuration that, while plausible, have not been verified. Many of these uncorroborated claims came from expatriate opposition organizations and Iranian social media. For example, exiled former Iranian officials in 1980 claimed that the regime's alleged intelligence service was a carbon copy of SAVAK and had nine directorates.[6] A French research center specializing in intelligence organizations determined in 2010 that the MOIS consisted of five primary directorates with more than a dozen secondary ones.[7] According to a 2012 Library of Congress report, the ministry had at least fifteen directorates, but this assessment relied on information from a website belonging to former Iranian president Abdolhassan Banisadr and a blog described as having questionable reliability.[8]

In determining the likely organizational components of the ministry, the 1983 establishment law is an essential starting point. As noted in chapter 1, the law's first article tasks the MOIS with obtaining and processing foreign intelligence information, protecting intelligence information, and conducting counterintelligence operations to prevent domestic and foreign conspiracies against Iran.[9] For conducting these missions, Ali Yunesi suggested during the 1999 Chain Murder investigations that the MOIS structure went from the minister to an unstated number of deputy ministers leading directorates and then to a tier of directors general managing subcomponents of the main directorates.[10] Khamenei in 2016 publicly suggested the need for greater ministry focus on missions to counter infiltration and information theft, influence operations targeting Iranian decision-makers and the public, and foreign attempts to create "economic, financial and security turmoil," which likely entailed a shifting of resources and possibly a reorganization of subcomponents.[11]

A review of the available unclassified evidence suggests that the ministry probably has at least eight principal directorates, centers, and organizations. These include offices for internal security, counterterrorism, foreign intelligence operations, counterintelligence, analysis, protection (security), technical collection, and economic/anticorruption operations. In addition, the MOIS almost certainly has a mix of other necessary directorates and components for personnel, training, finance, administration, and similar responsibilities. The ministry also has regional centers across Iran to monitor and combat regime opponents.[12]

Internal Security

In protecting the Islamic Republic of Iran, the ministry seems to prioritize internal security duties. The MOIS has a significant component devoted to its duty to prevent "domestic conspiracies" against the Islamic Revolution.[13] Based on investigations into Iranian assassination plots against exiled oppositionists, the European Union in 2019 described the office as the Directorate for Internal Security when sanctioning its purported head, Deputy Minister Said Hashemi Moghadam.[14] These charges suggest that the directorate's mission to counter internal threats can lead to operations beyond Iran's borders.

From the start, the conservative establishment has used the MOIS to counter political opponents and enhance clerical control at home. MOIS officers, working closely with the judiciary, actively suppress dissent and help prosecute regime critics under vaguely defined national security laws.[15] A 2010 law gave the MOIS the additional task of combating "soft security threats," a reference to perceived Western cultural interference through information and psychological operations as well as the general appeal of popular Western media.[16] As Mohammad Reyshahri complained, the 1983 establishment law lacked needed authorities for the ministry to conduct its assigned internal security tasks. The Majles corrected this by using other laws to assign MOIS personnel the status of "special judicial officers."[17] With this status, MOIS officers can investigate suspected crimes, gather evidence, detain the accused, deliver summons, and implement judicial orders.[18] Because the 1983 and later laws do not specify the scope of MOIS judicial powers, "the general missions effectively grant . . . intelligence officials a blanket authorization to act as judicial officers in a wide range of offences."[19]

Counterterrorism

A known related office, which has been mentioned in Iranian media, is the Directorate for Counterterrorism. Its officers concentrate on violent terrorist and separatist groups that conduct attacks on government facilities, military and police bases, and Iranian personnel.[20] Over the past decade, MOIS and IRGC counterterrorism officers have developed a deep understanding of militant Sunni terrorist networks in Afghanistan and Pakistan and established extensive arrangements to counter terrorists in Iraq and Syria.[21] After 2014 and the rise of ISIS, Mahmud Alavi regularly touted his ministry's success in disrupting terrorist operations, capturing terrorists and arms, and preventing Iranians from joining the "takfiris" (those who consider other Muslims apostates and thus nonbelievers subject to death).[22] The counterterrorism directorate's responsibilities apparently extend to activities outside Iran's immediate neighbors. In October 2020 MOIS officers lured Habib Chaab, the leader of the separatist group Arab Struggle Movement for the Liberation of Ahwaz (ASMLA), from exile in Sweden to Turkey, where they abducted him and returned him to Iran.[23] Following the capture of the Swedish Iranian, the MOIS released documents purportedly showing a direct connection between ASMLA and Saudi intelligence and broadcast Chaab's confession to supporting a September 2018 terrorist attack on a military parade in Ahvaz.[24]

Foreign Intelligence

Another publicized directorate runs foreign intelligence operations. Since its creation, the Islamic Republic of Iran has used intelligence officers deployed overseas to monitor and target expatriate dissidents and defectors, abduct regime opponents, conduct espionage against foreign governments and commercial interests, and liaise with foreign intelligence services. This component, sometimes referred to as the Foreign Intelligence and Movements Directorate, almost certainly handles these duties and works with Iranian-supported terrorist groups and sympathetic foreign political movements. In December 2015 the directorate for the first time since the late 1990s resumed sporadic lethal operations abroad when its officers in the Netherlands directed the murder of an MEK member suspected of involvement in the 1981 bombing of the Islamic Republican Party's headquarters. A few months later, an MOIS official publicly suggested that intelligence collectors operated in other countries to enable the ministry to prevent threats and conspiracies from reaching Iran.[25]

In February 2017 Tehran expanded the directorate's powers and responsibilities by elevating it to an "organization."[26] In an echo of the early 1980s debate over creating an executive branch intelligence ministry or an independent intelligence organization, its new designation as the Foreign Intelligence Organization implied greater autonomy, a budget separate from the rest of the ministry, and potentially less oversight of its activities, although it apparently remains subordinate to the ministry. According to a Harvard Kennedy School cyber study, the MOIS foreign intelligence arm almost certainly is involved in Iranian cyberespionage against foreign government and commercial targets.[27] The study also found that MOIS cyber operations to spread supportive proregime narratives and suppress political opposition abroad possibly are conducted within this organization's purview.

Counterintelligence

The MOIS has acknowledged publicly the existence and work of its Directorate of Counterintelligence (or Counterespionage), which protects Iran against foreign intelligence activities.[28] In addition to searching for foreign espionage networks, the directorate supervises, along with other regime intelligence bodies, the appointment of government officials to "important posts," probably in the security and nuclear fields.[29] The directorate also defends against sabotage and similar covert actions, as suggested by the MOIS claim in 2019 that its counterintelligence operations had uncovered an American effort to supply defective parts "to a sensitive industry," presumably the nuclear or missile program.[30] That same year, after purportedly disrupting an American spy network, Alavi announced that the MOIS had "changed its defensive counter intelligence approach to an offensive counter intelligence approach, and . . . seriously damaged the foreign intelligence services."[31] The counter- intelligence directorate also shares responsibilities in the cyber realm, as shown by its claiming credit for the management of operations to identify and destroy an extensive cyberespionage network in 2019.[32]

Analysis

A major MOIS mission is the production of assessments and other intel- ligence analysis. The ministry calls its primary office for these duties the National Security Strategic Research Center, which was established in 1989. According to Jamal Shafii, the deputy minister leading the center in the mid-2010s, its duties include combining information from vari- ous outside open sources, "expert information" from statistics and re- search centers, and intelligence received from various bodies to provide a product with "a predictive characteristic."[33] At a 2016 National Con- ference on Intelligence Analysis Methods in Tehran, Alavi suggested that the MOIS tried to manage intelligence analyses "scientifically" and intended its assessments to be solution-based and realistic.[34] Shafii in- dicated that the MOIS uses Iranian universities, research centers, and think tanks to study and make plans for various contingencies and then submits the results to the leader and the president.[35] In addition, the ministry sponsors polling on issues of interest to the government as part of its analytic function.[36]

Protection

The MOIS Directorate of Protection appears to cover the range of se- curity fields involving safeguarding ministry personnel, facilities, in- formation, and operations as well as intelligence sources and methods. During the 2009 purge of MOIS officials, press reports indicated that one of the deputy ministers dismissed by President Ahmadinejad headed the directorate and had been in that post since 2001.[37] The directorate coordinates the activities of Iran's military and other protection organi- zations.[38] In 2019 Alavi praised these organizations' "unparalleled coop- eration" on activities that probably included background investigations for personnel, physical and technical security measures for facilities, executive protection, and possibly some elements of cyber defense.[39] Given its experience in background investigations and comments by Hajjarian about the directorate's focus on opposition politicians, it probably is involved in the ministry's role in vetting candidates for elective office.[40]

Technical Collection

As revealed during the 1999 Chain Murders investigations, the ministry has an office responsible for signals intelligence and other electronic surveillance using various eavesdropping and monitoring systems. During the 2009 purge, an Iranian news site reported that the head of the ministry's technology department, a twenty-five-year MOIS veteran, had been forced to leave.[41] The office almost certainly supports the activities of the internal security, foreign intelligence, and other directorates. For example, leaked MOIS cables concerning operations in Iraq in 2014 and 2015 revealed that ministry officers used telephone bugs and other listening devices to keep tabs on Iraqi informants.[42] This directorate also likely participated in a 2019 operation that used a volunteer asset with access to hack the mobile phone of Benny Gantz, a former chief of the Israeli armed forces and a candidate that year to become Israel's prime minister.[43] In 2016 the Majles required the MOIS to make "quantitative and qualitative improvements" to its technical and scientific activities.[44]

Economic/Anticorruption Operations

An Iranian official involved in the creation of the MOIS has stated that the ministry was not involved initially in economic or, more accurately, anticorruption issues.[45] The official asserted that the misuse of assets confiscated from the shah's government eventually drew the ministry into these operations. Over the years, statements by Iranian officials about ministry anticorruption responsibilities and operations suggest that a directorate-level economic office exists.

In the early 1990s, the head of the judiciary informed judicial authorities that MOIS officers could legally pursue all cases of financial corruption in government organizations and act with the same authority as judicial officers.[46] By 1999, however, the ministry's own businesses, whose income supplemented its budget, numbered more than one hundred and provided opportunities for MOIS corruption and interference with other economic enterprises. When Yunesi became minister that year, Khamenei insisted on the closure of the MOIS-affiliated companies.[47] Yunesi agreed with the decision, noting in a 2012 interview that his experience in the judiciary familiarized him with violations by the ministry's economic activities.[48] Yunesi explained that he wanted to use the reform to demonstrate that the MOIS was not acting to benefit its own business interests as it pursued corruption cases. The Khatami administration assisted with this reform by compensating the ministry with additional funds to close the budget deficit caused by the suspension of MOIS economic activities.[49]

In 2002 Khamenei initiated an anticorruption campaign that expanded MOIS personnel's role as judicial officers for the investigation of economic corruption and cultural heritage thefts.[50] Other anticorruption and anti-money-laundering laws since the mid-2000s extended MOIS authorities to investigate suspicious transactions, large foreign deals and contracts, smuggling, and other cases of large-scale financial corruption.[51] In 2020 an unidentified deputy intelligence minister, who presumably had the economic portfolio, noted that the MOIS had signed an agreement with Iran's judiciary to coordinate a campaign against corruption.[52]

Beyond these more traditional intelligence missions, the MOIS has other directorates to perform evolving missions and manage the ministry.[53] In mid-2022 Iranian media indicated the existence of a political, cultural, and social affairs directorate under an unnamed deputy minister. Yunesi apparently referenced this directorate in 2018 when he stated that a "cultural section" separate from the counterintelligence directorate was involved in establishing the criteria for initiating espionage cases.[54] Based on these press reports, it probably injects political-ideological considerations into the definitions of infiltration and spying, conducts political indoctrination at the ministry, and supports the vetting of candidates for elective office. Other major MOIS offices mentioned in Iranian media include the Public Relations and Information Center,[55] a parliamentary liaison (legislative affairs) directorate,[56] and likely an office focused on supporting law enforcement counternarcotic operations.[57] In the latter case, a 2021 Iranian press report noted that a 2010 amendment to counternarcotic legislation required the MOIS to collect intelligence on regional and international drug-trafficking networks.[58]

Staff Size, Employment, and Training

The ministry's size has remained secret, and estimating its personnel strength is complicated by Iran's multiple intelligence organizations and their overlapping roles. In 2010 the French Center for Research on Intelligence estimated that the MOIS had roughly fifteen thousand employees, with several thousand deployed outside the country covertly or under official cover.[59] The 2012 Library of Congress study offered an estimate of thirty thousand personnel that was disputed at the time but was repeated in an unclassified 2019 US Defense Intelligence Agency publication.[60] Given the ministry's focus on internal security, its provincial offices spread throughout a country of more than eighty million people, and its foreign intelligence responsibilities, it seems likely that it employs a range of up to thirty thousand employees.

Employment at the ministry starts with recruitment and vetting to determine the qualification of candidates. The 1995 Employment Law of the Ministry of Intelligence, which appears to remain in effect,[61] divides employees into permanent, temporary, and contractor categories. According to the law, formal employment occurs through identification, introduction, and vetting based on merit, efficiency, and competence. A Central Vetting Board, set out by the law, examines all applicants and determines the hiring policies, codifies the required regulations, and establishes vetting subboards.[62]

The law's conditions for entering MOIS service are belief in Islamic principles, the Islamic Revolution, and the nezam and a commitment to the leader's absolute authority. The regime expects applicants to express a willingness to sacrifice to achieve Iran's security goals. If hired, employees must adhere to Iran's laws and Islamic ethical standards. Other conditions in the law include Iranian citizenship (not naturalized or acquired) and no affiliation with political parties, groups, and organizations or affiliation with or support for non-Islamic, atheistic, or illegal groups. Candidates cannot have a drug addiction, a criminal record, or a foreign spouse or one with acquired Iranian citizenship.[63]

Other criteria for employment in the law are a minimum and maximum age of eighteen and forty years and required educational and professional qualifications. An applicant needs the intelligence, talent, health, and physical and mental abilities commensurate with the position sought. A potential hire also must have a good reputation, suitable temperament, and a background of "commitment and honesty, trustworthiness, confidentiality, [and] compassion."[64] In addition, candidates must accept a minimum service commitment of ten years. Under the law, the ministry gives priority of employment to veterans and their immediate family members. Moreover, the ministry is allowed to hire individuals subject to Iran's mandatory military service, who, at the end of the commitment period, are then exempted from conscription.[65]

The law requires new hires to serve a probationary period that lasts a minimum of six months and a maximum of two years. Employees during the probationary period have the same salary and benefits as permanent employees. After the end of employees' probationary service, they will be permanently hired if the central vetting board approves their ideological, moral, and political competence. If an employee fails the probationary period, his or her service will be terminated.[66]

The 1995 legislation dictates that the ministry provide housing or housing allowances to its employees as well as transportation services and transportation reimbursements. The law also provides for overtime pay and relocation allowances to employees along with hardship post differentials, hazard pay, and other extraordinary expenses. The MOIS can pay its employees annual and performance bonuses and even a marriage gift (once) to newly wedded staff equal to two months' salary and benefits. According to the law, the ministry pays tuition fees and other educational expenses for employees who study in required fields at its request. Deductions from pay are taken to fund retirement accounts and pay health insurance premiums.[67]

The ministry conducts annual employee evaluations to determine eligibility for new job appointments, promotion, annual pay increases, and bonuses.[68] An unacceptable evaluation requires the ministry to move the employee into another job or arrange for suitable training to improve the employee's performance. Employees are offered ongoing professional development opportunities because the 1995 law obliges the ministry to organize training courses in ideological, political, and professional fields to "cultivate and create a spirit of initiative and creativity and promote the insight and scientific and practical abilities of employees."[69] MOIS employees are expected to retire after reaching thirty years of acceptable service or at sixty years of age. Employees also can retire with the ministry's consent after age fifty with twenty-five years of service if male and at any age with at least twenty years of service if female. The law prohibits any foreign contacts by its officers, except in accordance with administrative requirements and with the notification of relevant authorities. In addition, all current, former, and retired MOIS employees must obtain the ministry's permission to travel outside the country.[70]

Although employees can be recruited directly into the MOIS, many male officers enter through the ministry's University of Intelligence and National Security (UINS), also known as Imam Baqer University. Originally created as the Faculty of Intelligence in 1986, the university offers bachelor's, master's, and doctoral degrees, which allows MOIS officers to continue their education throughout their careers. Entry into UINS begins with Iran's national exam, which all candidates for admission to Iranian universities must take. Prospective students select the UINS code, and then the university contacts approved applicants for interviews.[71]

According to the university, student applicants must be male, Muslim, Iranian citizens who are no more than twenty-three years old after serving their compulsory military service, which applicants can complete by serving with the MOIS. They must be qualified under MOIS ideological and loyalty requirements and hiring regulations and meet minimum grade-point averages in the humanities and math and sciences. The selection process then occurs in several stages over the course of a year and includes IQ and personality tests; physical and mental health medical examinations; face-to-face interviews to address personal issues and cultural, ideological, political, social, and economic views; and background investigations into the applicant and his family. All admitted students are offered scholarships and accommodations, plus an employment guarantee if they earn their degree. Because each receives a paid allowance, all students are expected to be present for classes, and students who withdraw must repay their education and recruitment costs.[72]

For the school year 2021–22, the university listed the availability of undergraduate courses in intelligence, economic, international, and "soft" security.[73] Other courses covered security research, intelligence protection, counterterrorism, and security technical science. Finally, students could study courses on information and communication technology along with intelligence and communication management. After students fulfill their commitments, the graduates receive a certificate approved by the Ministry of Science, Research, and Technology. Students

دانشگاه اطلاعات و امنیت ملی

U.I.N.S

Figure 3.1. University of Intelligence and National
Security seal

also must learn at least one foreign language and attend extracurricu-
lar programs. In 2016 the university announced that its new cohort of
postgraduate student applicants under the age of twenty-seven could
take programs in intelligence management, intelligence protection, Iranian security studies, criminology sciences, security telecommunication
engineering, and information technology and security engineering.[74] It
also offered the subtopics of coding, cybersecurity, bioterrorism, and
crisis management.

Organizational Culture: "The Unknown Soldiers of the Hidden Imam"

When the MOIS was established, Iran's leaders emphasized Islam as a
guiding principle in security policies. The requirement for the minister
to be a mujtahid helped to contrast the MOIS with SAVAK, which was
seen as an un-Islamic organization that operated outside the bounds of
Islamic law. Among the Shia clergy, a mujtahid is a cleric with the training and scholarship to perform *ijtihad*, or independent reasoning, which

enables him to make legal decisions based on Islamic sources, such as the Quran, Islam's holy book, and the Hadith, the sayings of the Prophet Muhammad. Khomeini and his followers sought to have the ministry run by fair and pious men who would follow the leader's religious, political, and ideological guidance.

Understanding some of the other key influences shaping MOIS organizational culture requires some brief background on the Shia sect of Islam. Most Iranians today are Twelver Shia, the mainstream Shia denomination that follows the line of twelve imams regarded as the divinely appointed, sinless, and infallible successors of the Prophet. These imams are descended from Ali, Muhammad's son-in-law and cousin, whose followers became known in Arabic as *shiat Ali*, the partisans of Ali. This partisanship grew out of the first split in Islam over the faith's leadership. The Shia believed Muhammad wanted his successors to come from his household's bloodline, while the Sunni, the majority sect, held that it was up to the community of believers to select their caliph (leader) based on his integrity, honesty, and righteousness.

Shia traditions feature a history of martyrdom and persistent threats that appear to form part of the narrative the regime uses to shape its security services' beliefs. In 680 Hussein, Ali's surviving son and the Prophet's closest remaining male relative, led a small band of followers to confront a much larger Sunni army at the Battle of Karbala. Surrounded in the desert, the Shia eventually succumbed, and Hussein, the third Shia imam, was martyred, a key event in Shia history commemorated every year during Ashura. The fourth through eleventh imams of Ali's line encountered continued Sunni repression and, according to Shia beliefs, were murdered.

When the eleventh imam died, his purported son, Muhammad, went into occultation, or supernatural hiding, to avoid being killed by the Sunni caliph. The Shia believe this twelfth or "hidden" imam, also known as the *imam zaman*, or "imam of time," will return one day as the *mahdi* (messiah) to lead and win the final battle between good and evil.[75] With the hidden imam's disappearance in the ninth century, the Shia began relying on learned men to serve as interpreters of the Quran and as leaders of their community. In some cases, these pious and knowledgeable men garnered substantial political influence. This foundation partially accounts for Khomeini's ability to use his popular appeal to gain political power. Khomeini later underscored the ministry's linkage to this history by calling Iran's MOIS officers the "Unknown Soldiers of the Hidden Imam." (The Persian word for "unknown" also is translated as "anonymous" and "nameless," which appear in some sources.)[76]

Many of the elements of MOIS organizational culture expressed in statements by the ministry are aspirational. Over the decades, those elements directed outward toward the Iranian people have been observed only sporadically depending on the ministers' goals. At the start, Khomeini and his lieutenants, steeped in their experience with SAVAK, were sensitive about the power inherent in a clandestine intelligence service. According to an MOIS founder, regime leaders sought to reduce the potential threat by instilling a sense of responsibility, self-sacrifice, and dedication among the personnel of the new ministry under its clerical head.[77] In 2014 the MOIS presented its desired personnel traits in a publication issued to mark the ministry's thirtieth anniversary. Asserting that the qualities were based on the Quran and sayings of the Prophet and Ali, it listed complete obedience to the leader, moral behavior, courage, sincerity, honesty, and devotion.[78] Calling the ministry the "discerning and vigilant eye of the Islamic Establishment," Khamenei told MOIS staff they had to maintain the "orientations of the Islamic Revolution," which were based on Khomeini's writings and speeches.[79] During his tenure, Alavi claimed that the ministry's work was based on Islamic law, "the Prophet's ethics," and the guidance of Khomeini and Khamenei.[80]

Nonpolitical Service

An important element of Khomeini's guidance, codified in Article 12 of the 1983 establishment law, was the development of a culture of political neutrality in the ministry. Although the law prohibited MOIS personnel from being members of political parties and groups, Hajjarian thought the ministry's establishment suffered from a range of political tendencies among its new staff members that hindered cooperation and fanned suspicions within the service.[81] The former SAVAK officers, transferred IRGC personnel, leftists, and future reformists who staffed the new ministry, in Hajjarian's view, had political inclinations even if they were not party members. Still, the limit on participation in political parties was important because the MOIS worked with the judiciary and Ministry of the Interior in conducting background investigations of candidates for president and parliament for the Guardian Council, whose vetting powers allowed it to prohibit some from running for office.[82]

By the late 1990s, greater differences emerged within the ministry and the broader Iranian intelligence and security communities as officials aligned with hard-line conservative factions and those favoring President Khatami's reformist policies became more polarized. Starting as early as 1996 and expanding dramatically in the years following Khatami's reelection in 2001, the IRGC and Basij became active in elections.[83] They began to undermine reformist candidates with propaganda and arrests of their supporters and, in some cases, offered Basij support to favored candidates' political rallies. In 2008, during Ahmadinejad's presidency, Mohseni-Ejei saw an apparent need to remind the heads of the intelligence community's protection organizations publicly to avoid allowing factional tendencies to affect their work and interpretation of the law.[84] Later, in the months before the 2009 presidential election, he warned some of the political factions about their conduct ahead of the campaign and election.[85]

Other signs of politicization included Iranian lawmakers' accusations in the aftermath of the initial Green Movement protests that Ahmadinejad worked with the IRGC to remove senior MOIS officers for unspecified disloyalty to the president.[86] Years later, in mid-2016, Alavi warned against analysts' "self-censorship" inhibiting the decision-making process at higher levels.[87] He added that analyses to justify an officer's thoughts and opinions would hinder decision-makers facing new situations. In 2017, as the MOIS joined the IRGC and Basij in cracking down on political and social activists, the reformist deputy parliament speaker threatened to impeach Alavi for political interference, a consequence the IRGC and Basij commanders, answerable only to the supreme leader, did not face.[88]

Popular Intelligence

During the Khatami administration and continuing to varying degrees subsequently, the MOIS has tried to foster a culture that elicited the participation of the Iranian people in intelligence activities to support the country. In September 1998 Khatami visited the ministry and urged its employees to abandon their intimidating self-image as *mosht-e nezam* (fist of the regime).[89] In 2008 Mohseni-Ejei espoused the observance of Islamic values based on kindness, compassion, and sympathy to deter espionage.[90] The Rouhani administration and Alavi, however, made a more significant effort to advance the idea of popular intelligence to enhance the country's security.[91]

During his confirmation hearing, Alavi stated that MOIS policies included observing the legal, religious, and moral rights of society and protecting the rights of the citizens and their constitutional freedoms.[92] He stated that his goal was to create public trust and enhance the social status of the MOIS. Within the limits allowed by Khamenei, Alavi joined Rouhani in trying to promote a political vision that emphasized democratic governance, a free press, vibrant civil society, fair elections, and détente and dialogue abroad.[93] This contrasted with the conservative hard-liners' efforts to preserve Iran's revolutionary character, the primacy of velayat-e faqih, and the nezam's interests. As a result, the ministry's reputation temporarily improved, and, at least among the reform-minded parts of Iranian society, it was seen as a relatively "good cop" in contrast to the "bad cop," the IRGC-IO.[94]

An example of popular intelligence at work can be seen in the MOIS public hotline. Since at least late 2006, the MOIS has broadcast announcements urging Iranians to call the ministry to report suspicious activities. It set up a special hotline, with the number 1-1-3, to allow easier contact. Early ministry messages warned about the distribution of illegal opposition leaflets and suspicious phone calls by people who introduced themselves as government officials in order to extract information.[95] A 2008 MOIS video mixing film and computer animation featured a supposed White House meeting involving the late US senator John McCain, a vocal opponent of Iran and candidate that year for the US presidency; billionaire investor and philanthropist George Soros; and notional CIA officials planning a campaign against Iran.[96] In the video, an Iranian caller to the hotline helps to foil the plot to influence Iranian "hearts and minds." In 2018, as the ministry battled ISIS terrorists, it reminded Iranians to report any observed terrorist activity and suspicious individuals.[97] Interestingly, MOIS public messages in 2022 appealed to Iranian nationalism and patriotism as they emphasized protection of the "homeland" rather than the Islamic Revolution and Islamic Republic.

Figure 3.2. 2022 MOIS website screenshots. *Top*: "We take care of our homeland. . . . Unknown Soldiers of Imam Zaman (may God hasten his fate)." In this graphic, the first digit of 113 uses the Iranian flag to form a 3, which symbolically refers to the 313 companions prophesized to accompany the Hidden Imam on his return to battle evil. *Bottom*: "I take care of my homeland. . . . Share your security reports with the Ministry of Intelligence's 113 press office."

In May 2017 Alavi claimed that kind and tactful encounters had raised the popular appeal of the intelligence services among the Iranian people. He added that "hostile treatment towards the enemy is good, but we do not always need it in relation to the country's academic and economic activists, producers, and artists."[98] He argued that the ministry's ethical operations provided "psychological security" with an impact on society "no less than a physical security."[99] He later indicated that MOIS goals were to "protect the people's lives, assets, and reputations."[100] The ministry's tolerance, however, was not open-ended. In 2016 National Security Strategic Research Center head Shafii publicly suggested that political activists needed to act as part of the "family of the revolution."[11] This meant, per Khomeini's guidance, activists had to be loyal to the leader and the revolution's Islamic values. The MOIS director of research and analysis also hinted that the ministry's goal was to boost conformity and national unity rather than allow diversity of political thought.[102]

As part of his popular intelligence approach, Alavi said that the Ministry of Intelligence's attitude toward political and social activists was based on "protection" and "guidance."[103] At the height of the ISIS threat in 2016, Alavi claimed that the MOIS had prevented more than fifteen hundred Iranians from joining the group or its affiliates. A senior MOIS official claimed that the ministry knew how ISIS recruited people and, following the guidance approach, would send officers to talk to and discourage the young Iranians suspected of being interested in the group.[104] Later, after uncovering purported CIA intelligence networks, Alavi suggested the ministry's approach involved education rather than intimidation as he warned Iranians to be extra vigilant against falling into the "elusive traps of the enemy's spy networks."[105]

By early 2022 even the relatively hard-line Khatib credited public collaboration with the security forces for helping to "neutralize enemy conspiracies."[106] However, the MOIS culture of popular intelligence and its aspirational avoidance of harsh police state tactics had already started to weaken during the final years of the Rouhani administration. The IRGC-IO increased its repressive activities concurrent with the US imposition of "maximum pressure" after Washington's 2018 withdrawal from the JCPOA agreement. In an apparent response to the subsequent impact of renewed sanctions and sabotage operations targeting nuclear and missile sites, the MOIS stepped up its internal security operations.[107]

Rouhani administration reforms sought important policy adjustments to normalize foreign relations, advance trade, and improve Iran's domestic economy rather than a significant change in the nature of the regime. This approach suggested that the tolerance implied by popular intelligence was always limited. Alavi may have initiated more arrests because of rising unrest in the late 2010s and early 2020s, genuine concerns about feared US infiltration activities, and a desire to retain the leader's trust and support.[108] He also may have been seeking to prevent the IRGC-IO from becoming more powerful and to influence the ultimate disposition of the arrested activists.[109] In some instances, for example, the ministry pushed back against IRGC-IO targeting of dual nationals, lawyers, environmentalists, and women's rights and labor activists. In either case, MOIS organizational culture emphasized its adherence to the nezam's principals and priorities. Ultimately, the ministry reserved its supposed values of kindness, compassion, and sympathy for Iranians it deemed to be within the family of the revolution.

Notes

1. Peterson, "Why Europe Is Again a Battlefield"; "Iran's Supreme Leader Warns"; "Official Says USA Formed 'Intelligence NATO' against Iran," BBC Monitoring Middle East [ISNA in Persian], August 18, 2016, ProQuest.
2. "Intelligence Min. Provides System with 'Hard Outer Shell,'" Mehr News Agency, August 9, 2016, ProQuest.
3. Islamic Consultative Assembly, "Employment Law of the Ministry of Intelligence," July 16, 1995, https://rc.majlis.ir/fa/law/show/90455 (hereafter cited as 1995 Employment Law); "Iranian Media Urged."
4. Carl Anthony Wege, "Iran's Intelligence Establishment," *Intelligencer: Journal of U.S. Intelligence Studies* 21, no. 2 (Summer 2015): 67.
5. September 2012 Hajjarian interview.
6. Getler, "Khomeini Is Reported."
7. Rodier, "Iranian Intelligence Services."
8. Library of Congress, *Iran's Ministry of Intelligence and Security*, 17–18.
9. 1995 Employment Law.
10. "New Iranian Information Minister."
11. "Iran's Supreme Leader Warns"; "Official Says USA Formed 'Intelligence NATO.'"
12. Wege, "Iran's Intelligence Establishment," 64–65.
13. 1983 Ministry of Intelligence Establishment Law.
14. "EU Agrees Fresh Sanctions on Iran over Alleged Assassination Plots," BBC,

January 8, 2019, https://www.bbc.com/news/world-europe-46800868; "EU Names Two Iranian Officials Blacklisted for Suspected Roles in Assassination Plots," Radio Free Europe / Radio Liberty, January 9, 2019, https://www.rferl.org /a/eu-names-two-iranian-officials-blacklisted-for-suspected-roles-in-assassination -plots/29699600.html.

15. Hadi Ghaemi, "The Islamic Judiciary," USIP Iran Primer, August 1, 2015, https:// iranprimer.usip.org/resource/islamic-judiciary; "Covert Terror."

16. "Flawed Reforms: Iran's New Code of Criminal Procedure," Amnesty Inter-national, February 11, 2016, 28, https://www.amnestyusa.org/reports/flawed -reforms-irans-new-code-of-criminal-procedure/.

17. "Flawed Reforms," 28; "Legal Duties of the Ministry of Information in the Ca-pacity of Bailiff," ISNA, March 16, 2021, https://www.isna.ir/news/14001225204 ‎وظایف-قانونی-وزارت-اطلاعات-در-مقام-ضابط-دادگستری‎/95‎.

18. "Flawed Reforms," 27–28.

19. "Flawed Reforms," 28.

20. "Iran: Article Details Petrol Unrest in Khuzestan, Sistan-Baluchestan Provinces," BBC Monitoring Middle East [Mardom-Salari in Persian], December 6, 2019, ProQuest.

21. Wege, "Iran's Intelligence Establishment," 67.

22. "Iran Security Official Claims Stopping US Affiliated Intelligence Operatives," BBC Monitoring Middle East [Entekhab in Persian], May 3, 2019, ProQuest; "Iran News Round Up," AEI Critical Threats Project, June 20, 2016, https:// www.criticalthreats.org/briefs/iran-news-round-up/iran-news-round-up-june -20-2016; "Iran News Round Up," AEI Critical Threats Project, May 20, 2016, https://www.criticalthreats.org/briefs/iran-news-round-up/iran-news-round-up-may-20-2016-1.

23. Scott Peterson, "Kidnapping Dissidents Abroad, Iran Is Sending a Message at Home," *Christian Science Monitor*, December 18, 2020, www.csmonitor.com/Wo rld/Middle-East/2020/1218/Kidnapping-dissidents-abroad-Iran-is-sending-a-mes sage-at-home.

24. "Intel Min. Releases Docs on SA, Terror Group Relation," Mehr News, November 18, 2020, ProQuest; Peterson, "Kidnapping Dissidents Abroad."

25. "Official Says USA Formed 'Intelligence NATO.'"

26. Golkar, "Iran's Intelligence Organizations and Transnational Suppression"; "Iran's Foreign Intelligence Bureau Given Higher Status," BBC Monitoring Middle East [Tasnim in Persian], February 8, 2017, ProQuest.

27. James Shires and Michael McGetrick, *Rational Not Reactive: Re-evaluating Ira-nian Cyber Strategy* (Cambridge, MA: Belfer Center for Science and International Affairs, 2021), 18, 42.

28. "Iran MPs Question Dismissal"; Daragahi, "Iran Intelligence Ministry Purged."

29. "Iran Intelligence Ministry Criticises Weekly for Report on 'Failure' in Duties," BBC Monitoring Middle East [IRNA in Persian], June 14, 2016, ProQuest.

30. "Iran Security Official Claims."

31. "Iran Security Official Claims."

32. "Hardline Daily Says Iran Intelligence Ministry Infiltrates into America's Secure Systems," BBC Monitoring Middle East [Siyasat-e Ruz in Persian], June 22, 2019, ProQuest.

33. "Official Says USA Formed 'Intelligence NATO.'"
34. "The Minister of Intelligence: Censorship and Self-Censorship Are Serious Harms to Intelligence Analysis," Iran Student Correspondents Association, June 5, 2016, https://www.iscanews.ir/news/650384.
35. "Iran Prepared for Every Eventuality in Nuclear Talks—Official," BBC Monitoring Middle East [Fars News Agency in Persian], October 16, 2014, ProQuest.
36. "Polls Show 84 Per Cent of Iranians Assured of Armed Forces' Vigilance—Commander," BBC Monitoring Middle East [Fars News Agency in Persian], February 23, 2015, ProQuest.
37. "Iran MPs Question Dismissal"; Daragahi, "Iran Intelligence Ministry Purged."
38. "Agency Outlines Iran's Intelligence Units, Duties," BBC Monitoring Middle East [Fars News Agency in Persian], October 15, 2014, ProQuest.
39. "Iran Security Official Claims." For more on protection organizations, see Carl Anthony Wege, "Iranian Counterintelligence," *International Journal of Intelligence and CounterIntelligence* 32, no. 2 (2019): 292n62.
40. September 2012 Hajjarian interview.
41. Daragahi, "Iran Intelligence Ministry Purged."
42. James Risen, "Spying on the US," *Intercept*, February 7, 2021, https://theintercept.com/2021/02/07/iran-iraq-spies-mois/.
43. "Israel Suspects Iran of Hacking Election Frontrunner Gantz's Phone: TV," Reuters, March 14, 2019, https://www.reuters.com/article/us-israel-election-iran/israel-suspects-iran-of-hacking-election-frontrunner-gantzs-phone-tv-idUSKCN1QV2RR; "House Cleaner for Israel's Gantz Charged over Iranian Spying Attempt," *Al-Monitor*, November 18, 2021, https://www.al-monitor.com/originals/2021/11/house-cleaner-israels-gantz-charged-over-iranian-spying-attempt#ixzz7L10jTV6c.
44. "Duties of the Ministry of Intelligence to Promote the Interests and National Security of the Country Specified," Tasnim, May 2, 2016, www.tasnimnews.com/fa/news/1395/02/13/1064484.
45. Hoseyni, "Unsaid Words of Shariatmadari."
46. "Legal Duties of Ministry of Information."
47. "Why Was Economic Activity Closed?"
48. "Why Was Economic Activity Closed?"
49. "Why Was Economic Activity Closed?"
50. "Legal Duties of Ministry of Information"; "Iran: Leader Khamenei Reiterates Need for 'All-Out' Anti-Corruption Campaign," BBC Monitoring Middle East [Voice of the Islamic Republic of Iran in Persian], January 9, 2002, ProQuest.
51. "Intelligence Minister Says Iran's Problems Have Domestic Roots," BBC Monitoring Middle East [Fars News Agency in Persian], July 17, 2018, ProQuest; "Iran Security Official Claims"; "Legal Duties of Ministry of Information."
52. "Iran: Judiciary, Intelligence Ministry Sign Anti-corruption Agreement," BBC Monitoring Middle East [ISNA in Persian], August 4, 2020, ProQuest.
53. "Senior Iranian Intelligence Official Urges Elite Unity," BBC Monitoring Middle East [ILNA in Persian], July 14, 2022, ProQuest.
54. "Iran: Official Says Spy Cases Must Be Handled Only by Intelligence Ministry," BBC Monitoring Middle East [IRNA in Persian], March 5, 2018, ProQuest.
55. "Intel Min. Releases Docs."

56. Daragahi, "Iran Intelligence Ministry Purged."

57. "Iran President Underlines More Counter-narcotics Measures," BBC Monitoring Middle East [president.ir website in Persian], July 31, 2019, ProQuest.

58. "Legal Duties of Ministry of Information."

59. Rodier, "Iranian Intelligence Services"; Wege, "Iran's Intelligence Establishment," 65.

60. Library of Congress, *Iran's Ministry of Intelligence and Security*, 24; Defense Intelligence Agency, *Iran Military Power*. On disputed figure, see Elliot, "How a Government Report Spread"; and Elliot, "Widely Cited Government Study."

61. The regime apparently allows private employment agencies to help candidates with the recruitment and selection process. In 2022 one company's Iran-based website, which declared the MOIS to be one of the most popular government agencies for job seekers, summarized a 2022 employment manual that repeated the information contained in the 1995 law. "Comprehensive Manual of Employment for Ministry of Intelligence 1402," Iran Tahsil, April 4, 2022, https://irantahsil.org/استخدام-وزارت-اطلاعات/.

62. 1995 Employment Law.

63. 1995 Employment Law.

64. 1995 Employment Law.

65. 1995 Employment Law.

66. 1995 Employment Law.

67. 1995 Employment Law.

68. 1995 Employment Law.

69. 1995 Employment Law.

70. 1995 Employment Law.

71. For complete details, see *The Booklet of the National [Entrance] Exam Registration of 1400 [2021–22]*, Education Assessment Organization of the Ministry of Science, Research and Technology, February 2021, https://dl.heyvagroup.com/admin/Files/upload/943672488daftarche_sabte_nam_konkoor_sarsari_1400.pdf; and "Interview Questions from the University of Intelligence and National Security," Seda-ye Moshaveran, n.d., https://sedayemoshaveran.com/سوالات-مصاحبه-دانشگاه-اطلاعات-و-امنیت-ملی/.

72. "Iran Intelligence University Calls for Applicants," BBC Monitoring Middle East [ILNA in Persian], June 18, 2016, ProQuest; *Booklet of National Exam Registration*.

73. *Booklet of National Exam Registration*.

74. "Iran Intelligence University Calls for Applicants."

75. Kamran Taremi, "Iranian Strategic Culture: The Impact of Ayatollah Khomeini's Interpretation of Shiite Islam," *Contemporary Security Policy* 35, no. 1 (2014): 7.

76. Library of Congress, *Iran's Ministry of Intelligence and Security*, 2.

77. "Iran: Former Justice Minister Elaborates on 1990s Serial Murders," BBC Monitoring Middle East [Sharq in Persian], July 13, 2019, ProQuest.

78. Golnaz Esfandiari, "Desired Traits of a Nameless Soldier of the Hidden Imam," Radio Free Europe, October 20, 2014, ProQuest.

79. "Daily Questions Performance of Iran's Intelligence Ministry," BBC Monitoring Middle East [Keyhan in Persian], August 24, 2016, ProQuest.

80. "Iran Security Official Claims."
81. Sariati, "Said Hajjarian on Formation."
82. "Access Denied: Iran's Exclusionary Elections," Human Rights Watch, n.d. (ca. 2005), https://www.hrw.org/legacy/backgrounder/mena/ iran0605/2.htm.
83. See Ali Alfoneh, "The Revolutionary Guards' Role in Iranian Politics," *Middle East Quarterly* (Fall 2008): 3–14, http://www.meforum.org/1979/the-revolutiona ry-guards-role-in-iranian-politics.
84. "Iran Minister Asks Security Forces to Observe Law," BBC Monitoring Middle East [Jomhuri-ye Eslami in Persian], February 24, 2008, ProQuest.
85. "Iranian Press Menu on 08 Oct 08," BBC Monitoring Middle East [Etemad in Persian], October 8, 2008, ProQuest.
86. Daragahi, "Iran Intelligence Ministry Purged."
87. "Minister of Intelligence: Censorship and Self-Censorship."
88. Ahmad Majidyar, "Latest Crackdown in Iran Points to I.R.G.C.'s Meddling in Elections," Middle East Institute, March 20, 2017, https://www.mei.edu/pub lications/latest-crackdown-iran-points-irgcs-meddling-elections.
89. Buchta, *Who Rules Iran?*, 123–24.
90. "Iran Minister Asks."
91. "Iran's Intelligence Agency Enjoys Vast Popular Appeal," Mehr News, May 9, 2017, ProQuest.
92. "Iranian Intelligence Minister Presents Programs."
93. Maysam Behravesh, "Iran's Spies Are at War with Each Other," *Foreign Policy*, August 9, 2019, https://foreignpolicy.com/2019/08/09/irans-spies-are-at-war-with -each-other/.
94. Behravesh.
95. "Iranian Intelligence Ministry Urges Officials to Report Suspicious Calls," BBC Monitoring Middle East [Khuzestan Provincial TV in Persian], November 1, 2006, ProQuest; "Iranian Ardabil TV Airs Intelligence Ministry Clip," BBC Monitoring Middle East [Ardabil Provincial TV in Persian], April 3, 2007, ProQuest.
96. "Iran: Intelligence Ministry Video Clip Urges People to Inform 'Suspicious Moves,'" BBC Monitoring Middle East [Vision of the Islamic Republic of Iran West Azarbayjan Provincial TV in Persian], February 1, 2008, ProQuest.
97. "Iran Asks Citizens to Report on 'Terrorist' Activity," BBC Monitoring Middle East [IRIB's News Agency in Persian], June 4, 2018, ProQuest.
98. "Iran's Intelligence Agency Enjoys."
99. "Iran's Intelligence Agency Enjoys."
100. "Iran Security Official Claims."
101. "Official Says USA Formed 'Intelligence NATO.'"
102. "Official Says USA Formed 'Intelligence NATO.'"
103. "Iran's Intelligence Agency Enjoys."
104. "Minister Says over 1,500 Iranian Youths Prevented from Joining Islamic State," BBC Monitoring Middle East [Tasnim in Persian], August 26, 2016, ProQuest; "Official Says USA Formed 'Intelligence NATO.'"
105. "Mole Hunt: Story of Busting CIA's 'House of Cards,'" Press TV, July 22, 2019, ProQuest; "Hardline Daily Says."
106. "Iran Intelligence Minister Says 'Enemies' Exploit Protests," BBC Monitoring Middle East [IRNA, ISNA in Persian], December 15, 2021, ProQuest.

107. Scott Peterson, "In Iran, a Hardline Hunt for 'Infiltrators' Has Political Target, Too," *Christian Science Monitor*, February 6, 2019, ProQuest.
108. "Intelligence Ministry and IRGC Widen Crackdown."
109. "Intelligence Ministry and IRGC Widen Crackdown."

4

Operations and Tradecraft

The success of an intelligence service's operations and its tradecraft effectiveness generally are gauged by its achievements in gathering and exploiting secret information. The opacity of Ministry of Intelligence activities and its emphasis on internal security operations, the bulk of which occur beyond scrutiny, generally deny outside observers the information needed for detailed performance assessments. The announcement or exposure of successful and failed intelligence operations, however, reveal some insights into MOIS missions, activities, and tradecraft. At a minimum, such operations provide a closer look into the means, leadership guidance, personnel capabilities, and culture behind their conduct.

The ministry's history allows broad generalizations about its tradecraft and other practices. Its SAVAK inheritance, for example, suggests that some commonality with Western intelligence processes within the MOIS is possible, if not likely. MOIS human intelligence (HUMINT) operations appear to follow standard practices involving spotting, recruiting, vetting, tasking, and running agents. Although evidence is lacking, ministry counterintelligence officers and analysts could be expected to assist in assessing the reporting from the Foreign Intelligence Organization. Similarly, details are unavailable on the ministry's collection, processing, decrypting, and analyzing of signals intelligence (SIGINT). But the MOIS likely follows procedures gained from Iran's shah-era SIGINT cooperation with the United States even as it has undoubtedly acquired techniques from its cooperation in this century with countries such as Russia and China, as discussed in the next chapter.

Beyond such inferences, however, clarity is lacking on how the MOIS manages its version of the intelligence cycle and the elements of planning and direction; collection, processing, and exploitation; analysis and production; dissemination; and evaluation.[1] Alavi, however, indicated in 2017 that MOIS employees develop an organizational strategy for the supreme leader that provides a road map for ministry planning and actions, which suggests standard procedures exist.[2] Another unknown is the ministry's practices for organizing, supporting, and using the open-source, geospatial, measurement and signature, and other intelligence disciplines. Finally, while Iranian intelligence community elements are supposed to share information, available legislation and official statements do not explain the process of warning and intergovernmental notifications.

The following examination of MOIS activities uses publicized Iranian intelligence successes and failures. The most noteworthy failures, many of which involved Iran's other security services, have been in the protection and counterintelligence fields. These range from the assassinations of key figures in Iran's nuclear program through sabotage inflicted on Iran's nuclear and missile programs to the theft of Iranian nuclear archives. Successes include the capture of Abdulmalik Rigi, arrests of alleged conspirators in the scientist assassinations, destruction of foreign intelligence networks, and penetrations of foreign governments. Another important source of information is the "Iran Cables,"[3] an archive of hundreds of secret intelligence cables and reports written in 2014 and 2015 by MOIS officers serving in Iraq that were obtained, verified, summarized, and published by two American news organizations in 2019.[4]

This chapter also benefits from a 2022 study prepared by Matthew Levitt, a former US Treasury Department intelligence official and scholar specializing in terrorism, that examined an unclassified and open-source dataset of ninety-eight cases of Iranian external operations from 1979 to 2021.[5] Drawn from publicly available court documents, government reports, press releases, and news articles, the Levitt study helps to categorize and understand Iranian external operations. The study, however, relies exclusively on Western sources and in instances of disputed Iranian involvement does not appear to have taken Iranian denials and counterclaims into consideration. Reports by Western cybersecurity analysts, meanwhile, provide insights into the ministry's cyber activities and tools.

Overall, MOIS performance in some areas is more than adequate for the regime's internal security and foreign intelligence needs. With no responsibility to the Iranian public to protect civil liberties, the ministry, working with the judiciary and other security forces, has stifled ethnic political violence and terrorist threats along with peaceful dissent. In other areas, such as operational security, performance is woefully inadequate, judging from repeated blown operations and an apparent lack of correction. In recent disrupted Iranian operations in Europe, for example, the European services were able to identify the operatives and track their communications back to a specific ministry office.[6] The MOIS and IRGC-IO bureaucratic conflict, meanwhile, seems a weak point that potentially denies or limits the interoperability and avoidance of duplicative missions needed to confront effectively the challenges from foreign intelligence services, violent domestic separatists, and Sunni terrorist organizations.

MOIS Officer Characteristics and Tradecraft

In Iran the ministry tries to maintain a reputation for professionalism. Accounts of MOIS officers' work as judiciary agents and their detention of suspects have shown them to be alternately abusive toward suspects and detainees and careful about acting within Iranian laws. These laws, however, generally are permissive for security service actions and restrictive on individual liberties. In stressing that the MOIS acts within the law, Yunesi in 2018 referenced the case of Zahra Kazemi, an Iranian Canadian freelance photographer who died in custody in 2003. He described ministry counterintelligence officers carefully interviewing Kazemi and "technically and scientifically" determining she was not a spy.[7] He lamented that the MOIS assessment was rejected by the judiciary's prosecutor and that Kazemi subsequently died after being beaten. Yunesi added that the judiciary's obstinacy and politicization of the case imposed heavy political costs on Iran. In the aftermath of Kazemi's death, however, a Majles investigatory committee criticized the MOIS for being uncooperative and suggested that some MOIS officers had been involved in her killing.[8]

When MOIS officers have acted outside the law, the ministry has tried, at least under Yunesi and Alavi, to hold its personnel accountable. The ministry in 2019 admitted that when Heydar Moslehi was minister it had mistakenly arrested fifty-three suspects in the nuclear scientists' assassinations case despite disagreements among MOIS counterintelligence officers over the alleged perpetrators' involvement. After the suspects were acquitted, the ministry dealt with the offending officers through "training, inspection, and correctional supervision" while the government paid nearly a million dollars in compensation to the victims.[9] This incident severely damaged the ministry's reputation as the relatively rational and responsible good cop.[10]

Human rights advocates have long charged that MOIS personnel behave with impunity in civil and human rights cases when acting as judicial officers. The advocates charge that the detention of suspects for political reasons with scant evidence and the obstruction of Iran's limited due process protections to achieve predetermined results are standard MOIS procedures.[11] Since 2010 the United States has designated the MOIS and the last four ministers for complicity in the commission of serious human rights abuses against the Iranian people.[12] For example, in late 2018 the MOIS arrested a group of labor activists, two of whom went public after their release with charges that the ministry had tortured them and harassed their families.[13] The MOIS then rearrested the two in reprisal, which led to their eventual prosecution and imprisonment.[14] In late 2021 two Iranian defense lawyers and a civil rights activist charged the MOIS with torture and violations of due process laws after they were held in solitary confinement and harshly interrogated.[15]

MOIS officers are very active in HUMINT collection and related foreign intelligence operations, especially in countries neighboring Iran.[16] The leaked MOIS reports from Iraq during the period when ISIS violence was at its peak portray MOIS officers as patient, professional, and pragmatic.[17] Described as some of the ministry's best by Iranian sources familiar with MOIS operations, these officers appeared to be focused intently on their mission to keep Iraq from falling apart and threatening Iranian territorial integrity and regional stability.[18] This focus included prioritized surveillance of American activity in Iraq through the development of Iraqi informants who could gain access to US personnel and facilities.[19] The officers also demonstrated some practical foresight along with a thorough understanding of Tehran's policy goals by cultivating Sunni and Kurdish partners to help Iraq recover from the conflict with ISIS.[20] At the same time, MOIS officers exposed their susceptibility to bureaucratic backbiting by keeping watch on and regularly criticizing IRGC operations in Iraq.[21]

MOIS officers overseas operate out of Iranian diplomatic facilities and other fronts. Officers assigned to an Iranian embassy typically serve three- to five-year tours, which allows them to acquire significant local expertise and time to recruit and develop assets.[22] A 2018 European investigation revealed that in one instance an MOIS officer worked out of Iran's Vienna embassy for more than a decade.[23] The Levitt study determined that Iranian diplomats or operatives with diplomatic cover were involved in at least thirteen external operations involving the surveillance and targeting of dissidents from 2011 to 2021.[24] In 2013 and 2015, purported Iranian diplomats in Bosnia-Herzegovina and Uruguay were expelled after being accused of being MOIS officers involved in threatening activities.[25]

Various investigations into Iranian activities have revealed that over the decades the ministry has used multiple forms of nonofficial cover. In some cases, the MOIS has set up intelligence bases in cultural and charitable organizations and even mosques.[26] In addition, MOIS officers are believed to have operated as journalists, students, and medical personnel as well as employees of private businesses, the foreign branches of Iranian banks, and Iran Air, the state-owned airline.[27] MOIS officers also have proven adept at identifying and exploiting lax border security and active trade routes in regions such as Latin America to acquire technology and materials that Iran could not otherwise get because of trade restrictions by the United States and other nations.[28]

The Iran Cables show that the MOIS recruitment process involves spotting and meeting with potential recruits followed by offers of a salary, gold coins, and other gifts.[29] MOIS officers also use informants and recruited assets to help develop others. In one report from Iraq, for example, an MOIS handler claimed to have used an asset to prepare a friend who would be working for the United States at Al-Asad Airbase for recruitment and direction.[30] In another example of successful recruitment, MOIS officers were able to enlist and direct Iraqi assets to penetrate and gather detailed information on ISIS.[31] Other recruitment methods involve the use of the Internet and the development of elaborate cover stories. An Israeli investigation that resulted in the arrest of five Jewish immigrants from Iran in early 2022 revealed that Iranian intelligence officers used financial incentives to recruit the assets, who were initially contacted and then directed over the Internet. The Israelis reported that the Iranian officers, whose affiliation was not provided, used the assets' family members in Iran to transport funds to them in Israel.[32]

MOIS officers historically have infiltrated expatriate communities to recruit assets to penetrate exiled opposition groups and spy on other Iranians overseas.[33] Iranian intelligence officers, almost certainly including MOIS personnel, also have assumed identities as political intellectuals or human rights defenders to travel abroad and participate in dissident gatherings and activities, according to claims in a 2010 reformist news site report on the experience of Iranian dissident groups outside of Iran.[34] In working with its own officers, recruited former dissident group members, and other cooperative Iranians, the ministry develops backstories for its undercover officers and assets with temporary prison stays to develop their reputation among the other prisoners as antiregime activists.[35] The regime then allows each asset to be released or "escape" to go abroad and connect with regime opponents. In addition to collecting information about expatriate opposition organizations, especially those suspected of receiving US funding, these officers and assets try to sow mistrust and spread disinformation to influence the oppositionists' actions.[36] According to the dissidents, even after returning to Iran, the suspected intelligence officers maintain contact and try to remain active with the exiled groups.[37]

Breaking Foreign Espionage Networks

Among its most notable claimed successes, the Ministry of Intelligence has repeatedly declared that it infiltrated and broke CIA espionage networks directed against Iran. The MOIS uses these counterintelligence accomplishments to boast of its effective operational and analytic capabilities, sow doubt about the veracity of information gathered by foreign intelligence networks, and denigrate foreign intelligence services' capabilities. As discussed below, while disparaging CIA operations, the ministry touts its knowledge of alleged CIA methods along with the implied omnipresence of its surveillance to deter Iranians from accepting recruitment pitches from foreign intelligence services. Despite the claims of past successes, continued announcements of the discovery of new networks suggest MOIS efforts to deter Iranians from cooperating with foreign services are not fully effective.

In 2019 the MOIS announced that it had broken up an American spy network by arresting seventeen Iranian nationals who allegedly had been recruited and trained by the CIA.[38] MOIS officials claimed that, working with other foreign intelligence services, 290 purported CIA assets in various countries had been identified over the preceding year.[39] They also acknowledged that some CIA assets had managed to infiltrate "critical centers" inside Iran.[40] But the officials added that some of the arrested suspects cooperated as double agents against the United States, suggesting they were used to feed false information, undermine the previously reported information, and gather more details on CIA operations.[41]

The MOIS director general of counterintelligence used the episode to denigrate the CIA by suggesting without evidence that it failed to fulfill promises of visas, jobs, money, medical assistance, and citizenship to its assets. He also implied that the alleged assets' CIA training in complex, supposedly secure communication methods was insufficient to avoid MOIS detection. The director general claimed that documents provided by the CIA to its assets were poorly forged and that MOIS officers, after penetrating the communication system, fooled CIA handlers into communicating with them.[42] Perhaps hinting at the double agents' actions or the loss of the network's information, MOIS chief Alavi suggested that perceived US policy miscalculations during this period were the result of MOIS efforts to create "a lack of access to reliable intelligence."[43]

Alavi credited the claimed 2019 success to ministry efforts that extended back to an earlier disruption of another CIA network.[44] Iran reportedly started hunting for a mole in 2009 after Washington announced the discovery of a secret Iranian uranium enrichment facility.[45] Because Iran had long been a denied area to Americans, MOIS counterintelligence officers apparently began to focus on tracing Iranians who traveled out-side the country and who might have been approached by the CIA. US officials later assessed that Iran probably unwound the CIA's asset net-work analytically and, aided by turned assets, the MOIS identified the covert communication system used by the network. MOIS officers then scoured the Internet for websites with similar digital signifiers and com-ponents. They eventually located other secret CIA websites and began to unravel the wider espionage program.[46] The MOIS announced in May 2011 that it had dismantled a CIA spy network and claimed that after sharing information with its intelligence partners forty-two CIA-linked spies had been identified in other countries.[47]

Over the years, the MOIS has claimed the disruption of various Mos-sad networks, although these actions usually came after damaging Is-raeli operations had already occurred. In 2012 the MOIS announced the discovery of an alleged Israeli network targeting Iran's nuclear activities as well as the arrests of the operatives involved in the assassinations of Iranian nuclear scientists.[48] One of the conspirators, Majid Jamali-Fashi, confessed on television to receiving training and a payment of $120,000 from Mossad.[49] However, the claimed counterintelligence successes suffered from credibility problems stemming from the ministry's harsh interrogation tactics. As discussed in more detail in chapter 6, the MOIS in 2019 reluctantly acknowledged that some of the other conspirators' confessions had been obtained under torture. More recently, in late July 2021, the ministry claimed that it had arrested alleged members of an Israeli intelligence network on Iran's western border, seized arms in-tended to support riots in Iranian cities, and disrupted a plan to conduct "acts of sabotage" during Iran's presidential election that June.[50] A few weeks earlier, Iranian press reported that rockets, presumably fired by Iraqi militias aligned with Iran, had struck a Mossad base in Erbil, Iraq.[51]

In early 2023 Iran revealed another significant, if somewhat mixed and delayed, MOIS counterintelligence success. Four years earlier in 2019, according to press reports, the MOIS had arrested Alireza Akbari, a dual British citizen, former deputy defense minister, and associate of former defense minister and then SNSC secretary Ali Shamkhani, for allegedly spying for London.[52] British intelligence purportedly had re-cruited Akbari in 2004 while he was still serving in Iran's government.[53] The MOIS detained Akbari for four months in 2008 on suspicion of espionage, but the case was closed after powerful supporters intervened on his behalf. Akbari then retired from government and was allowed to travel freely, which enabled him to build businesses outside of Iran and eventually gain British citizenship. The former deputy minister also continued to consult with Shamkhani and the foreign ministry.

Before and after his 2008 arrest, according to the same press reports, Akbari allegedly provided intelligence on Iranian nuclear and missile programs, nuclear negotiations, and economic issues related to sanctions, including the names of Iranian nuclear scientists and the existence of a clandestine Iranian nuclear program site at Fordo.[54] In 2019 the retired former minister returned to Iran for consultations at Shamkhani's request. The MOIS then arrested Akbari and held him in secret for three years. MOIS officials later told state media that during this time they had Akbari regularly use a British-provided computer to communicate with his handlers to mislead them.[55] In January 2023 the Raisi administration revealed Akbari's detention, conviction, and death sentence.[56]

Counterterrorism Operations

The ministry regularly touted its success against various terrorist groups, especially against ISIS from 2014 to 2017. In mid-2016 Alavi disclosed details on the disruption of one of the "largest takfiri-Wahhabi [Saudi] terrorist plots" in Iran, in which MOIS officers arrested ten terrorists in Tehran and three other provinces and confiscated one hundred kilograms of explosives. Alavi stated that the terrorists intended to target crowded public areas with suicide attacks and vehicle-born improvised explosive devices.[57] These and other public comments in 2016 and 2017 revealed little about MOIS counterterrorism operations, but the ministry apparently intended to bolster its reputation for identifying and disrupting terrorist plots. It also wanted to deter Iranians from joining terrorist and opposition groups.[58]

Despite these successes, on June 7, 2017, ISIS launched nearly simultaneous daylight attacks on the Majles and Khomeini's mausoleum in Tehran. An hours-long battle with security personnel that resulted in the deaths of seventeen people and injuries to at least fifty stunned the regime and the Iranian public. Iranian security forces killed four terrorists in the fighting, while the MOIS quickly tracked down the remaining terrorists, killed the reputed mastermind, and arrested other ISIS members.[59] Alavi later claimed that his ministry provided the location where ISIS leaders were assembled in Syria to IRGC missile units that targeted the camp in a retaliatory strike.[60]

After the start of the Trump administration's "maximum pressure" campaign and the imposition of more restrictive sanctions on Iran in May 2018, regime officials judged that the economic warfare was accompanied by renewed clandestine operations by the United States, Israel, and Saudi Arabia. In particular, Iran suspected its foes of backing the MEK and ethnic-minority Arab, Kurd, and Baluch separatist groups that had been stepping up antiregime actions.[61] The MOIS responded with additional efforts against the armed opposition and terrorist groups, stepping up surveillance and interdiction operations. Alavi claimed in May 2019 that during the preceding year the MOIS had dealt with 114 ISIS-related cells, 116 groups of *monafeqin* (hypocrites, a term usually reserved for the MEK), and 44 antirevolutionary organizations, disrupting 188 operations in the process.[62] Nonetheless, during that same time frame, Iran suffered three significant terrorist attacks in Arab and Baluch regions of southwestern and southeastern Iran.[63]

Continued attacks through early 2024 showed Iran's vulnerability to infiltration by extremist groups despite the efforts of the MOIS and Iran's other intelligence services and police. In late October 2022, for the first time since 2018, ISIS terrorists conducted an attack in Iran, assaulting a Shia shrine in Shiraz and reportedly killing fifteen people and injuring at least forty. Nearly a year later in August 2023, the MOIS arrested the perpetrators of another ISIS shooting spree days earlier at the same Shiraz shrine.[64] On January 3, 2024, ISIS claimed responsibility for a "dual martyrdom operation" in Kerman, boasting how two militants approached a memorial procession and killed eighty-four people by detonating explosive belts strapped to their bodies.[65] An MOIS investigation reported days later that the attack was carried out by a team of Tajik operatives based in Afghanistan—where ISIS-Khorasan is based.[66] In response, on January 16 Iran launched missiles at purported ISIS camps in Syria and at a suspected Mossad base in Iraqi Kurdistan for Israel's alleged support of ISIS and an earlier Israeli airstrike in Syria that killed eleven IRGC personnel. On the same day, Iran fired missiles against camps in Pakistan supposedly belonging to the Baluch separatist group Jaish al-Adl (Army of Justice, previously called Jundallah) in retaliation for its mid-December attack on a police station in Rask that killed at least eleven officers.[67]

Protection Failures: Assassinations and Sabotage in Iran

Domestic breakdowns in counterintelligence and protection missions reveal that the MOIS and Iran remain vulnerable to foreign intelligence operations against the regime and its interests. Most of these incidents involved generally sophisticated and carefully run Israeli operations where details on MOIS protective actions are lacking. The consequences of the Israeli successes suggest some shortcomings in MOIS capabilities and performance as well as the ministry's ability to coordinate operations among Iran's intelligence community members. This assessment, however, must be balanced against the potential foreign intelligence operations that were disrupted, assuming that at least some of the ministry's claims of success against spy networks are true. In addition, MOIS "police work" after an attack has often resulted in successful investigations leading to the arrest of foreign intelligence service assets.

Regime leaders in late 2020 credited the MOIS with nearly preventing one of a string of high-profile assassinations of Iranian nuclear scientists stretching back more than a decade and attributed to Israel and Mossad-recruited operatives. The regime believes the assassinations may have started in 2007 when a nuclear scientist at a uranium plant in Esfahan died in a mysterious gas leak. In subsequent years, six other scientists and military officials alleged to be critical to Iran's nuclear efforts have been assassinated, while a seventh was wounded (see box 4.1).[68] Mohsen Fakhrizadeh—the reputed "father" of Iran's nuclear program—was killed in November 2020 in an ambush of his four-car convoy on a rural road forty miles east of Tehran. The Mossad hit team, comprising more than twenty Israelis and Iranians, carried out the high-tech assassination following months of painstaking surveillance. The ambush reportedly used a one-ton remote-controlled machine gun smuggled piece-by-piece into Iran, a car bomb, and two snipers.[69]

Government spokesperson and former MOIS deputy minister Ali Rabii said that the Ministry of Intelligence had identified the people who brought the "devices and technologies" used for the killing.[70] He added

Box 4.1. Attacks on Iranian Nuclear, Missile, Cyber, and Other Officials

Although the IRGC has primary responsibility for protecting Iranian officials, the MOIS shares the mission to identify and disrupt plots by foreign intelligence services inside Iran. Iranian nuclear scientists, other technical experts, and military commanders targeted inside Iran since 2010 include:

- Masoud Ali Mohammadi, killed on January 12, 2010, in Tehran when a booby-trapped motorcycle parked next to his vehicle exploded
- Majid Shahriari, killed on November 29, 2010, while driving in Tehran, by a magnetic bomb attached to his car by a team of assassins on a motorcycle
- Fereydoun Abbasi Davani, the former head of Iran's Atomic Energy Organization, wounded by a magnetic bomb attached to his car by a man on a motorcycle on November 29, 2010, while driving in Tehran
- Daryoush Rezaei Nejad, killed on July 23, 2011, by a team of motorcycle-riding gunmen who shot him five times near his house in Tehran and wounded his wife and daughter
- IRGC major general Hassan Tehrani Moghaddam, a pioneer in Iran's missile development, killed in an explosion at an IRGC missile base near Tehran on November 12, 2011
- Mostafa Ahmadi Roshan, killed along with his driver in Tehran on January 11, 2012, by a team of motorcycle-riding assailants who planted a bomb on his car
- Mojtaba Ahmadi, head of Iran's Cyber War Headquarters, found dead after allegedly being shot by two people on a motorcycle near Karaj on or around September 29, 2013
- Mohsen Fakhrizadeh, the former head of Iran's nuclear program and reputed mastermind of Iran's nuclear weapons effort, killed on November 27, 2020, in an ambush while traveling outside Tehran
- IRGC colonel Sayyad Khodai, an alleged IRGC-QF deputy commander, killed by two gunmen on motorcycles outside his home in Tehran on May 22, 2022

that the MOIS, after warning about the danger for several years, had "noticed movements in advance and was almost in control of the area."[71] SNSC secretary Shamkhani, a former senior IRGC officer, repeated that Iran's intelligence services had information about the plot—including the location—but blamed the breakdown in protection on a complacent failure to observe precautions after years of frequent warnings.[72] Alavi later claimed in an interview that the Fakhrizadeh assassination was organized by a member of the Iranian armed forces, but no evidence or subsequent confirmation were offered. If true, Iran's security and intelligence apparatus suffers significant operational weaknesses and potentially is compromised by foreign service penetrations. Consumed by soft war dangers, security officials seem to have been caught repeatedly looking in the wrong places for threats.[73]

Other recent protection failures in the period surrounding Fakhrizadeh's death included the August 2020 assassination of al-Qaeda's second-in-command, Abu Muhammad al-Masri, who had been held in loose custody in Tehran from 2003 to 2015 before settling there, and the July 2020 and April 2021 explosions at a nuclear facility in Natanz.[74] The 2020 blast at Natanz was traced to explosives sealed inside a heavy desk that had been placed in the facility months earlier.[75] The 2021 Natanz attack sparked official criticism of the intelligence and security community over "the Israel within," a reference to perceived Mossad penetrations of Iranian facilities and organizations.[76] A few years earlier, in 2018, Israeli operatives conducted a daring nighttime raid to steal a half ton of secret nuclear program archives—more than one hundred thousand documents, images, and videos related to Iranian nuclear plans—from a warehouse in Tehran.[77] These operations revealed an MOIS inability to prevent Israeli intelligence from establishing effective networks of collaborators inside Iran and repeatedly gaining access to sensitive sites.[78]

The MOIS claimed additional successes against Israeli and other militant efforts in 2023, starting in late January when Khatib announced that more than twelve terrorist teams allegedly affiliated with Israel had been dismantled.[79] A few weeks later, the MOIS announced the arrest of alleged Israeli saboteurs but only after a military production facility in Esfahan had been attacked by drones launched from inside Iran.[80] In

September Khatib announced that since March the MOIS had discovered and defused four hundred bombs and claimed the Israelis, Americans, and British were supporting the terrorist and saboteur groups.[81] He also claimed that more than two hundred terrorists from ISIS and other groups allegedly created by foreign states (probably a reference to Kurdish and Baluch separatists) had been arrested, preventing the serial assassinations of judges, Sunni clerics, and IRGC personnel in eastern Iran intended to aggravate ethnic and religious differences.[82] The Kerman bombing at the start of 2024 undercut MOIS claims of sustained improvement in the protection field, especially after the United States claimed that following a long-standing "duty to warn" policy, it had secretly alerted Iran about ISIS attack preparations,[83] which, despite Iranian denials, raised questions about how the ministry and the regime handle such information.

Fighting Intelligence and Soft Wars Overseas

Iran's external operations have focused on regime opponents but do not ignore espionage against foreign political, security, and economic interests. In 2012, for example, the MOIS recruited Gonen Segev, a former Israeli cabinet minister living in Africa who had been jailed in the 1990s on narcotics charges. Captured by Mossad, Segev was sentenced to prison for giving Iran information related to Israeli political and security officials and the country's security sites and energy sector. The court case revealed that MOIS handlers had twice brought Segev to Iran for meetings and had given him a communication system for encrypted messages.[84] More recently, in 2019, the MOIS turned to the Internet and cyber operations to hack the cell phone of former Israeli armed forces chief Benny Gantz, who was Israel's defense minister from 2020 to 2022.[85] Gantz claimed no classified information was compromised, but political opponents questioned whether his lost personal information made him vulnerable to blackmail. Supplying Iran with materials subject to embargo, especially weapons, military spare parts, and nuclear-related materials, is another long-standing MOIS external mission.[86]

From 2012 to 2022, the MOIS joined the IRGC in stepping up operations overseas to remove the threat from the external Iranian opposition.

These moves to enhance regime security occurred during a period when Tehran perceived itself as facing constant threats from Western- and Saudi-supported opposition groups, US-led economic warfare and cultural invasion, Israeli assassinations and sabotage, and heightened Sunni-Shia tensions stemming from its rivalry with Saudi Arabia over the civil war in Yemen and other disputes. The surge in attacks on Iranian oppositionists in Europe in the late 2010s seemed to reflect an MOIS attempt, perhaps goaded by domestic political rivalries over the Rouhani administration's reform-oriented policies, to compete with the IRGC-IO in protecting the nezam.[87] US and Israeli officials alleged to reporters that the MOIS also operated in Africa, citing the Ethiopian intelligence agency's announcement that it had uncovered an Iranian cell of fifteen locals casing the embassy of the United Arab Emirates.[88] Iran denied any involvement and noted that the Ethiopians had not publicly blamed Tehran.[89] The US and Israeli authorities stated that this operation was part of an MOIS effort to identify soft targets to avenge the assassinations of Mohsen Fakhrizadeh and IRGC-QF commander Qassem Soleimani, who was killed by an armed US drone strike at Baghdad International Airport on January 3, 2020.[90]

In examining Iranian external operations over the past four decades, the Levitt study categorized them as targeted assassinations, abductions, indiscriminate attacks (i.e., bombings), and surveillance operations in support of these plots, all of which have involved the MOIS.[91] An example of the latter category occurred in 2018 when the FBI arrested two Iranian American dual citizens affiliated with the MOIS and charged them with acting as agents of Iran.[92] The pair had been secretly monitoring Jewish centers and MEK members in the United States. In early December 2023 the United States designated alleged MOIS officers Majid Dastjani Farahani and Mohammad Mahdi Khanpour Ardestani for recruiting individuals for various surveillance and lethal operations in the United States, including targeting current and former US government officials to avenge the death of Soleimani.[93] Overall, these external activities were part of a campaign of transnational repression to deter opposition to the regime that, according to one scholar, the Islamic Republic has waged for decades on the psyches of Iranian-born people living overseas.[94]

Targeted Assassinations

The Levitt dataset includes eighteen assassination plots from 2011 to 2021, not all of which were successful.[95] Across the world, in an effort to carry out attacks with relative deniability, the MOIS and IRGC have deployed non-Iranian and dual-national operatives, who travel on their non-Iranian or false passports, including forged Israeli ones.[96] Iran also has outsourced some operational activities to criminal organizations, such as the 2015 contract killing of Mohammad Reza Kolahi Samadi. Iran believed that this former MEK member living under an assumed name in the Netherlands was responsible for the 1981 IRP headquarters bombing.[97] Iran also used Dutch criminals for the late 2017 murder of Ahmad Mola Nissi, an ASMLA founder, outside his home in The Hague.[98] Similarly, an employee of a Turkish crime boss was the prime suspect in MOIS lethal operations in Istanbul in the late 2010s against regime critics Massoud Molavi Vardanjani and Said Karimian, the latter accused of spreading Western culture and anti-Islamic values by broadcasting foreign programs dubbed into Persian on his Gem TV network.[99]

In the former case, Molavi had been a high-ranking director of the Armed Forces General Staff's Cyber Defense Command before moving to Turkey in 2018. He claimed to have worked as a technical adviser to the MOIS protection office, including a component in charge of "video control and protection" of the Supreme Leader's Office. He reportedly had been jailed three times in 2009 and 2010 on the charge of "acting against national security."[100] In Turkey Molavi ran a Telegram channel and several other accounts on various social networks called "the Black Box."[101] The Black Box Telegram channel published articles critical of Iranian leaders and government institutions, including the MOIS, the IRGC, the Supreme Leader's Office, and the judiciary. His articles also provided details about the security organs' tracking methods and their techniques for kidnapping, assassination, and theft outside Iran, particularly in Turkey.[102] Two Iranian security sources claimed Molavi had been warned and threatened numerous times during his stay in Turkey.[103] The Black Box Telegram channel published an audio file in early 2019 in which an Iranian security official appeared to threaten the channel's administrators.[104]

Turkish officials charged two probable MOIS officers at Iran's consulate in Istanbul, nine other Iranians, and six Turkish citizens with Molavi's murder.[105] The Turks alleged that Ali Esfanjani, one of the likely MOIS officers under diplomatic cover, was the leader of the assassination plot. Over several months Esfanjani had worked to become Molavi's friend while passing information about the dissident to Iranian intelligence. He allegedly met with the Turkish gunman to discuss the murder before accompanying Molavi to the location where the killing occurred, a scene captured on closed-circuit television. Esfanjani was spirited across the border into Iran three days later by an Iranian smuggler reportedly connected to the MOIS, using false documents allegedly provided by the Iranian consulate.[106]

Another high-profile MOIS assassination plot that occurred in Europe in 2018 demonstrated other elements of ministry tradecraft. According to media accounts quoting European security officials, Asadollah Assadi, an MOIS officer operating under diplomatic cover as the third secretary of Iran's embassy in Vienna, ran an operation to bomb the annual convention of the People's Mojahedin Organization of Iran, another name used by the MEK. Investigators said the bomb was intended to assassinate Maryam Rajavi, the leader of the National Council of Resistance of Iran, an umbrella opposition group dominated by the MEK. The indiscriminate explosive, however, could have killed many others, including President Trump's personal lawyer, Rudy Giuliani, who was scheduled to speak at the rally near Paris.[107]

The media accounts reported that Assadi had recruited an Iranian Belgian couple, Amir Saadouni and Nasimeh Naami, to plant the bomb.[108] Saadouni reportedly was an MEK member, possibly having joined the group to aid his earlier application for asylum in the West. Assadi, under the alias Daniel, had first approached Saadouni around 2008, identifying himself as an Iranian intelligence officer seeking information about the MEK. Assadi alternatively offered to pay thousands of euros for the intelligence and threatened to make life difficult for Saadouni's family in Iran if he refused. Saadouni, joined by Naami, worked for the ministry for the next ten years. The two traveled several times to Tehran starting in 2010 for meetings and training.[109]

Although it is unclear when intelligence-gathering operations switched to preparations for the attack, European officials charged that Assadi arranged to meet the couple in Luxembourg at the end of June 2018 to transfer the bomb.[110] Some MOIS operational security shortcoming had allowed Israeli intelligence to detect the plot, and acting on its tip Belgian intelligence officers observed the transfer and then intercepted the couple.[111] German officials arrested Assadi and extradited him to Belgium, where, in February 2021, a court convicted him for his role in the attempted bombing.[112] French authorities traced responsibility for the attack to the head of the MOIS Internal Security Directorate, Said Hashemi Moghadam, who, along with Assadi and the ministry, was sanctioned by the European Union.[113]

In January 2024 the US Department of Justice charged Naji Sharifi Zindashti, an alleged criminal living in Iran, and two Canadians affiliated with the Hells Angels motorcycle group with conspiracy to use interstate commerce for a murder-for-hire plot against two Iranian expatriates in Maryland in December 2020 and January 2021. Concurrent with the indictment, the US Department of the Treasury took joint action with the British government to sanction Zindashti's narco-trafficking criminal network, alleging that it was directed by the MOIS to target Iranian dissidents and opposition activists for kidnapping and assassination.[114] The Treasury announcement identified Reza Hamidiravari as the MOIS officer overseeing Zindashti's MOIS-directed operations and alleged that Zindashti had previously cooperated with the MOIS in abducting regime opponents.[115]

Abductions

A key element of Iran's transnational repression campaign has been its abduction operations against dissidents. The Levitt study identified ten Iranian abduction plots over the past four decades, all of which involved Iranian operatives, with three that included local, non-Iranian assets.[116] Four of the ten plots occurred in 2020 and 2021, with one, the failed attempt to kidnap Masih Alinejad in New York, possibly including plans to abduct journalists in Canada and the United Kingdom.[117] In one example of the ministry's use of non-Iranians and criminals, the US Department of Justice in January 2023 charged three MOIS-linked members of an Eastern European criminal organization from Iran, the Czech Republic, and Azerbaijan with plotting against Alinejad.[118] Another scheme involved an effort to kidnap a former Iranian military officer in Turkey in September 2021 that was foiled by the Turkish National Intelligence Organization.[119] The MOIS and the IRGC-IO have had the most abduction successes in neighboring countries, where Iran presumably has more access, assets, and other resources.[120]

MOIS spycraft and coercive techniques have contributed to some of the ministry's successes. The kidnapping of Habib Chaab, the former ASMLA leader, is a noteworthy example of MOIS abduction methods and use of dual national and other assets. In late September 2019, five gunmen opened fire on a military parade in the southwestern Iranian city of Ahvaz, killing twenty-five soldiers and civilians and injuring more than sixty. An ASMLA splinter group claimed responsibility for this terrorist attack.[121] A few days later, Danish police observed a Norwegian citizen of Iranian descent conducting reconnaissance near the residence of an ASMLA leader in Denmark. The Iranian, Mohammad Davoudzadeh Lolei, was later arrested and convicted for being part of an MOIS assassination plot.[122]

Just over a year later, the MOIS successfully conducted an alleged "honey trap"—the use of an operative to create a sexual or romantic relationship—to lure Chaab to Istanbul.[123] Footage from closed-circuit cameras showed the female Iranian operative getting off a flight from Tehran in Istanbul, having her fake Iranian passport stamped, and communicating with her Iranian handler. In the complex operation, aided by the Zindashti criminal network, the MOIS drugged Chaab, transported him in a van across Turkey, and then smuggled him into Iran. Turkey later announced that it had detained eleven people for participating in the abduction.[124]

The MOIS forced Chaab to confess to terrorism-related crimes on Iranian state television.[125] The ministry claimed that ASMLA had been planning new terrorist operations and released documents alleging a direct connection between ASMLA and Saudi intelligence. According to the indictment, Chaab admitted to receiving an encrypted computer from Saudi intelligence to upload information on an IRGC barracks near Ahvaz and other military installations across Iran.[126] Chaab reportedly confessed to participation in an attempt to move arms and bomb-making equipment from Iraq to Iran, which Iranian security forces purportedly intercepted. A Danish police investigation into ASMLA reported in 2020 that Riyadh had paid the group roughly $3 million to provide intelligence on Iran and that ASMLA had been fundraising for antiregime operations by separatist Arab, Baluch, and Kurdish groups in Iran.[127] For the MOIS, the operation apparently was intended to demonstrate its ability to capture an alleged terrorist outside Iran and restore the ministry's damaged reputation following the major intelligence failures from 2018 to 2020.[128]

The ministry managed to seize Jamshid Sharmahd, a spokesman and leader for the promonarchy, California-based opposition group Kingdom Assembly of Iran, in the United Arab Emirates in July 2020. Iran alleged that Sharmahd was behind the 2008 bombing of the Hosseynieh Seyed al-Shohada Mosque in Shiraz that killed at least fourteen people and wounded 215. The regime also charged him and the group's militant wing, Tondar (Thunder), with planning other attacks inside Iran. In what MOIS officials described as a complex operation, ministry officers kidnapped Sharmahd in Dubai as he attempted to get a connecting flight to India after his initial flight schedule was disrupted by coronavirus pandemic restrictions.[129] Although details are unavailable, the MOIS apparently was able to detect Sharmahd's arrival in Dubai, track the dissident's movement, and quickly arrange for its officers and operatives to grab and move him to Iran.

In its efforts to abduct dissidents, the MOIS regularly uses coercion against family members and loved ones to exert pressure on a target. During the Alinejad plot, Iran tried to denigrate the activist and embarrass her family by broadcasting propaganda accusing her of spying for Western governments and being a drug addict. Her parents and siblings in Iran were repeatedly harassed, threatened with job loss, and pressured to lure Alinejad to Turkey. In 2018 the MOIS forced a sister to go on television to say that the family had disowned Alinejad over her disgraceful behavior. A year later, the ministry arrested Alinejad's brother and sentenced him to eight years in prison for acting against Iran's security, insulting the leader, and spreading "propaganda against the regime."[130] Similarly, during the ministry's failed September 2021 plot to kidnap a former military officer in Turkey, the MOIS reportedly offered the intended victim's wife $10,000 to aid the abduction and threatened to harm her family in Iran if she refused.[131]

The Islamic Republic of Iran has a long history of arresting dual and foreign nationals for use as hostages for prisoner swaps and for diplomatic and security purposes. For example, in May 2010 France released Vakil Rad, one of Shahpour Bakhtiar's murderers, after he became eligible for parole. While French officials denied any quid pro quo, Rad's release came just two days after Iran freed a French academic who had been detained for ten months on espionage charges. In 2016 the United States arranged the release of *Washington Post* reporter Jason Rezaian and several others being held in Iran in exchange for commuting the sentences or pardoning several Iranians held in US prisons for nonviolent crimes.[132] In all of these cases, the IRGC-IO played the leading role in the arrests.[133] The regime, however, turned to the Ministry of Intelligence for the prisoner swap, asking it to lead the negotiations, possibly because it viewed the ministry as more pragmatic and likely to be successful.[134]

In December 2020 the Trump administration imposed sanctions on two senior MOIS officers, Mohammad Baseri and Ahmad Khazai, for their alleged involvement in the probable death of retired FBI special agent Robert A. Levinson. The White House stated that senior Iranian officials were responsible for Levinson's disappearance from Iran's Kish Island in March 2007 and had used an extensive disinformation campaign to obscure their involvement.[135] Working as a private investigator, Levinson had flown to the Iranian resort island to meet Dawud Salahuddin, the expatriate American who had killed a former Iranian diplomat and regime opponent in Maryland in 1980.[136] Baseri and Khazai have backgrounds in counterintelligence and protection activities, and their duties may have involved them with Levinson. US officials, however, provided no evidence for their claims of the two MOIS officers' culpability.[137]

More recently, in September 2023, the United States sanctioned the MOIS and former Iranian president Mahmud Ahmadinejad for enabling the wrongful detention of US citizens by the service.[138] The announcement occurred on the same day that Tehran and Washington exchanged five American detainees for five Iranian prisoners. In the deal, the Joe Biden administration also gave Tehran access to $6 billion of its money—then frozen by sanctions—through a controlled account in Qatar that limited spending to humanitarian purposes.[139] After the

Israel-Hamas War began, the United States again blocked Iran's access to the $6 billion with Qatar's tacit agreement.[140]

Other MOIS Tradecraft Techniques

Exposed operations have revealed other elements of general MOIS activities and tradecraft. According to the Iran Cables, MOIS officers were involved in the planning of influence operations to counter Iraqi resentment of Iranian activities—especially heavy-handed IRGC operations—and diminish strife between Iraqi Shia and Iraqi Arab and Kurdish Sunnis.[141] The Levitt dataset shows a wide variety of MOIS financial activities, including money laundering for assets and operations. In some cases, MOIS officers carried a few thousand dollars in cash on their person to pay local assets. In other instances, Iranian intelligence officers have offered significant amounts (up to $1 million) to dual citizens and other assets for surveillance missions and assistance in plots to abduct or attack targeted dissidents.[142]

The Iran Cables show that MOIS officers, like other intelligence professionals, use surveillance detection routes to meet assets.[143] As one reported, "I left the base by foot an hour before holding the meeting and after twenty minutes walking on foot and carrying out the necessary checks, took two taxis through the neighboring streets to the site of the meeting."[144] The leaked cables also revealed that MOIS officers used electronic surveillance of their Iraqi informants to vet the accuracy of the reports they provided.[145] Moreover, like in any spy organization, some MOIS reports from Iraq contained questionable raw intelligence, while others appeared to represent the views of intelligence officers and sources with their own agendas.[146]

Iranian operations occasionally demonstrate poor tradecraft, as in Iraq, where the activities of some Iranian officers and assets showed "bumbling and comical ineptitude."[147] In a 2009 example, Iranian officers recruited a naturalized US citizen of Iranian descent with no relevant experience to surveil Jamshid Sharmahd. The asset was easily spotted and arrested before quickly pleading guilty.[148] The MOIS operatives involved in the 2021 Alinejad kidnap plot explored renting a speedboat for an escape of roughly twenty-two hundred nautical miles to Venezuela, a trip that was beyond the capabilities of the craft under discussion.[149]

Technical and Cyber Operations

Since its founding, the Ministry of Intelligence has conducted technical operations, although little information is available about these activities. The MOIS appears to remain responsible for Iran's nonmilitary SIGINT and related collection efforts targeting electronic communications.[150] The ministry inherited this mission and equipment from SAVAK and the prime minister's intelligence bureau, which used the capabilities to run a monitoring station in the Iranian embassy in Kuwait to intercept Iraqi communications.[151] The leaked Iran Cables show that MOIS officers sometimes depended on electronic technology to conduct their espionage operations in Iraq in 2014 and 2015.[152] In 2017 Alavi revealed that the MOIS sent collection equipment to Syria to gather intelligence on and monitor terrorist movements.[153]

Over time, the ministry has added cyber activities to its operational tool kit, deploying cyber capabilities to spy on dissidents, surveil enemies, and engage in disinformation campaigns.[154] Iran's use of cyberspace has evolved from an internal means of information control and repression to retaliatory and offensive cyber operations against foreign targets. Cyberespionage was initially based in the Ministry of Intelligence, but other Iranian intelligence services are involved, which complicates attribution of domestic and external cyber operations.[155] Similarly, the ministry or contractors working for it have joined the IRGC in conducting offensive cyber operations to suppress the political opposition and retaliate for adversary cyber operations and other threats against the Islamic Republic.[156] A February 2019 US Department of Justice indictment of various Iranian cyber operatives suggests that Iranian security services share resources and that operatives are likely to provide their skills to more than one organization.[157]

Defense against cyberattacks and Western soft war influence and psychological operations seem to drive MOIS intelligence activities in cyberspace. Since at least the early 2000s, the MOIS and other governmental entities have sought to control Iranians' access to the Internet.[158]

As part of Iran's long-term soft war strategy, the regime censors the Internet and tries to eliminate its ability to offer Iranians an unfettered avenue for free expression. As early as 2001, the regime established a Committee in Charge of Determining Unauthorized Sites composed of representatives from the Ministry of Intelligence, the Ministry of Communications, and the Ministry of Islamic Guidance to develop criteria for blocking websites. In 2006 the Majles voted into law regulations governing censorship and punishment for Web content violations. The MOIS appears to play an investigative role in collaboration with other security services and judiciary prosecutors to enforce Iran's cybercrime laws.[159]

The ministry uses offensive cyber operations to target oppositionists and critics inside Iran, such as a 2007 deployment of malware to help trace and disrupt dissident activities.[160] In the past decade, the MOIS reportedly has gained unauthorized access to legitimate websites to spy on Iranian citizens. For example, after compromising Iran's National Library computer network to obtain personal information, the ministry allegedly sent phishing emails with malicious attachments from the library's official email account.[161] Since 2015 Iran's Supreme Council of Cyberspace has coordinated cyberspace policy. It uses the National Cyberspace Center to coordinate offensive and defensive cyber operations among the various ministries and related institutions and develops internal Internet security controls to counter "cultural war" from Iran's enemies.[162]

The MOIS, at least under Alavi, presented itself as sensitive to perceptions that it was a threat to Iranian Internet users as it fulfilled its duties to police security crimes in cyberspace.[163] Iran's Computer Crimes Law allows judicial officers the discretion to arrest and charge political activists caught disseminating antiregime material or participating in online protests.[164] Following government detention of Internet activists in March 2017, Alavi stated that the ministry had not conducted the apprehensions but acknowledged that the MOIS supervised and, as needed, removed immoral and "anti-value" social media and Internet content.[165] In the same statement, the minister claimed that the MOIS preferred not to arrest people but to prevent security problems by talking to the Internet activists. In September 2022 the Department of the Treasury designated the MOIS and Khatib for engaging in cyberespionage and ransomware attacks against the United States and its allies in support of Iran's political goals.[166]

Cyber Proxies

For some cyber operations, the MOIS employs proxies, who range from individual hackers to private sector contractors and quasi-governmental organizations. The use of proxies probably provides needed capacity and capabilities but also allows the regime to maintain plausible deniability for aggressive cyber operations, potentially avoiding bilateral escalation.[167] According to leaked documents from early 2019, the MOIS hired the Rana Institute as a contractor to conduct social engineering and develop malware and similar tools.[168] The ministry also used a company, Ravand Cybertech, to host domains for an MOIS disinformation campaign to discredit the MEK.[169] In October 2022 the US State Department and Department of the Treasury designated the MOIS-related Ravin Academy, an institute that specialized in cybersecurity and hacker training, for sanctions.[170] Founded by two MOIS officers, the Ravin Academy trained the hackers who disrupted protestor communications during antigovernment demonstrations in late 2022, according to the US designation.

The US government refers to Iranian groups that conduct cyber operations as "advanced persistent threats" (APTs), some of which are better known by the names US cybersecurity companies use to track Iranian cyber activity. Iranian government-associated groups likely connected to the MOIS include APT33 (aka Refined Kitten), APT35 (aka Charming Kitten), and APT39 (aka Remix Kitten).[171] APT33 has carried out cyberespionage operations against aviation, military, and energy targets in the United States, Saudi Arabia, and South Korea. APT35 attempted to breach the email accounts of President Trump's reelection campaign in 2019 and has targeted accounts of US government officials, journalists, and Iranians living outside Iran. According to the Treasury Department, Charming Kitten was linked to an Iranian company, Net Peygard Samavat, that provided services to the MOIS and various IRGC organizations for social engineering and malware targeting of US defense personnel and was involved in Iranian cyber operations against Israeli infrastructure.[172] In September 2020 Treasury sanctioned APT39 for conducting a yearslong malware campaign with a front company owned or controlled by MOIS, Rana Intelligence Computing Company, that targeted Iranian dissidents, journalists, and international companies in the travel sector.[173]

According to one US cybersecurity company, operations by APT33, APT35, and other Iranian hackers have since 2014 become relatively methodical and more focused on data exfiltration from strategic intelligence targets.[174] In 2021 Facebook announced that it had taken down some two hundred accounts run by a group of Iranian hackers who were targeting US military personnel and employees at major defense agencies. The hackers created sophisticated fictitious profiles—often across multiple platforms—and pretended to be recruiters in American defense, aerospace, medical, travel, and journalism companies to collect information, install malware, and trick targets into providing personal information.[175] During the late 2022 unrest in Iran, Charming Kitten hackers targeted high-profile activists, journalists, researchers, academics, diplomats, and politicians working on Middle East issues in an ongoing social engineering and credential-phishing campaign.[176]

Cyberwar

In early 2022 the US director of national intelligence testified to Congress that Iran's growing expertise and willingness to conduct aggressive cyber operations made it a major threat to the security of US and allied networks and data. The director added that Iranian cyberattacks on Israeli and US targets over the preceding two years showed that Iran was more willing to target countries with stronger cyber capabilities.[177] For more than a decade, Iran and the MOIS have responded to cyberattacks by investing resources in developing cyber forces. When the regime is under pressure, it often takes "a good offense is the best defense" approach to protecting its national security. Unsurprisingly, Iran has regularly responded to perceived cyber provocations by conducting offensive cyber campaigns, usually by relying on proxies and front organizations such as those linked to MOIS cyberespionage.[178]

From Iran's perspective, the United States and its allies have waged a cyberwar against Iranian government computer systems since at least the late 2000s. In addition, the regime views cyberattacks as part of the intelligence war with the United States that involves US cyber operations being combined with psychological warfare, public diplomacy, military provocations, and other intimidation tactics.[179] One of Iran's first known cyber responses occurred in mid-2009 when a group of hackers called the Iranian Cyber Army—probably connected to the IRGC—defaced Twitter's homepage in response to perceived US involvement in the Green Movement protests. A primary motivation for the expansion of the regime's cyber organizations was the 2010 Stuxnet virus attack that damaged nearly one thousand centrifuges and infected thirty thousand computers at Iran's Natanz uranium enrichment facility and was followed by other computer viruses that targeted the country's oil infrastructure.[180]

US and allied interests soon experienced an increase in the severity and duration of cyberattacks originating in Iran.[181] Notable attacks include the 2012–13 Operation Ababil campaign against US financial institutions and the 2012 Shamoon attack against Saudi Aramco. At the time, the Shamoon operation was one of the most damaging cyberattacks ever reported, destroying more than thirty thousand computers, wiping out large portions of the Saudi oil producer's information technology infrastructure, and crippling the company's business operations.[182] In May 2018 the cybersecurity firm CrowdStrike warned its clients about a "notable" increase in Iranian phishing activity a day after President Trump's withdrawal from the JCPOA nuclear deal.[183]

The cyber domain became a battlefield in the shadow war between Iran and Israel. Probable MOIS-related actors conducted multiple successful disruptive cyberattacks from April to July 2020 against Israeli water facilities in retaliation for Israeli cyberattacks that targeted Iranian fuel infrastructure.[184] Starting in February 2022, an MOIS-backed group of Lebanese hackers targeted Israeli organizations in critical manufacturing, information technology, and defense industries. That spring APT35 Charming Kitten conducted a spear-phishing campaign aimed at Israeli military, diplomatic, and think tank officials.[185] Soon thereafter, Israel's cyber director called Iran a top rival in cyberspace and, along with Hezbollah and Hamas, one of the country's chief adversaries in the cyber realm.[186]

MOIS efforts in cyberspace probably will continue to expand offensively and defensively. In 2018 former MOIS minister Yunesi claimed that during his tenure in the early 2000s the ministry had concluded that because of the Internet its approaches to collecting and protecting information had to change.[187] He added that "the question is: should we control the cat [information gatherers] or the meat [information]?"[188] Yunesi believed that, given the expansion of cyberspace, the cat was uncontrollable, which meant that intelligence organizations needed to focus on protecting the meat. Subsequently, Iran has done more to control information inside Iran. Khamenei, meanwhile, has expressed the desire to grow Iran into a global cyber power, and the MOIS probably will follow his guidance.[189] The ministry will remain a key player in cyber operations, devoting significant attention to cyber-related counterintelligence, protection, domestic surveillance, and social media censorship along with information collection to support its and other Iranian offensive cyber operations.

Notes

1. For a brief introduction to the intelligence cycle, see Director of National Intelligence, *U.S. National Intelligence: An Overview* (Washington, DC: ODNI, 2011), 10–12, https://www.dni.gov /files/documents/IC_Consumers_Guide_ 2011.pdf.
2. "Narration of the Proposed Minister of Intelligence from Two Anti-Espionage Programs: We Have Good Cooperation with IRGC Intelligence," *Donya-e-Eqtesad*, August 16, 2017, https://www.donya-e-eqtesad.com/fa/tiny/news-3247340.
3. An anonymous source leaked the roughly seven hundred pages of MOIS reports to the news organization The Intercept, which translated them from Persian to English and shared them with the *New York Times*. While verified as genuine by the news organizations, the published material appears to be based on raw, uncorroborated reporting from MOIS officers in the field.
4. Tim Arango, James Risen, Farnaz Fassihi, Ronen Bergman, and Murtaza Hussain, "The Iran Cables: Secret Documents Show How Tehran Wields Power in Iraq," *New York Times*, November 19, 2019, https://www.nytimes.com/interactive/2019 /11/18/world/middleeast/iran-iraq-spy-cables.html.
5. Matthew Levitt, "Trends in Iranian External Assassination, Surveillance, and Abduction Plots," *CTC Sentinel* 15, no. 2 (February 2022): 2, https://ctc.usma.edu /trends-in-iranian-external-assassination-surveillance-and-abduction-plots/.
6. Peterson, "Why Europe Is Again a Battlefield."
7. "Iran: Official Says Spy Cases."
8. "Iran: Intelligence Ministry Criticized for Failure in Death of Journalist Case," BBC Monitoring Middle East [ILNA in Persian], November 17, 2003, ProQuest.
9. "Iran Report on Intelligence Ministry Lawsuit against MP over Nuclear Killings," BBC Monitoring Middle East [Etemad in Persian], December 20, 2019, ProQuest.
10. Behravesh, "Iran's Spies Are at War."

11. Saeid Dehghan, "Walking in a Minefield without a Map: The Life of an Iranian Human Rights Lawyer," Center for Human Rights in Iran, April 15, 2021, https:// iranhumanrights.org/2021/04/the-life-of-an-iranian-human-rights-lawyer/.

12. Daphne Psaledakis and Humeyra Pamuk, "U.S. Imposes Sweeping Sanctions on Iran, Targets Khamenei-Linked Foundation," *U.S. News & World Report*, November 18, 2020, https://www.usnews.com/news/world/articles/2020-11-18/us-impo ses-fresh-iran-related-sanctions-targets-khamenei-linked-foundation-website; US Department of the Treasury, "Treasury Sanctions Iranian Ministry of Intelligence and Minister for Malign Cyber Activities," September 9, 2022, https://home.trea sury.gov/news/press-releases/jy0941.

13. "Activist Challenges Intelligence Minister to TV Debate," IranWire, January 24, 2019, https://iranwire.com/en/features/65752.

14. "Iran: Labour Rights Activists at Imminent Risk of Further Torture," Amnesty International, January 22, 2019, https://www.amnesty.org/en/latest/news/2019/01 /iran-labour-rights-activists-at-imminent-risk-of-further-torture/.

15. "Human Rights Lawyers and an Activist Are Scheduled to Be Tried after Being Denied Access to Their Case Files," Center for Human Rights in Iran, October 12, 2021, https:// iranhumanrights.org/2021/10/human-rights-lawyers-activist-to-be-il legally-tried-as-their-legal-team-is-denied-case-files/.

16. Library of Congress, *Iran's Ministry of Intelligence and Security*, 33.

17. Arango et al., "Iran Cables."

18. Arango et al.

19. James Risen, "Spying on the US," The Intercept, February 7, 2021, https://theinter cept.com/ 2021/02/07/iran-iraq-spies-mois/.

20. Murtaza Hussain, "Iran's Shadow War on ISIS," The Intercept, November 18, 2019, https:// theintercept.com/2019/11/18/iran-isis-iraq-kurds/.

21. James Risen, "A Secret Summit," The Intercept, November 18, 2019, https://the intercept.com/ 2019/11/18/iran-muslim-brotherhood-quds-force/.

22. Wege, "Iran's Intelligence Establishment," 65.

23. Matthew Dalton, "Bags of Cash and a Bomb Plot: Inside a Covert Iranian Oper- ation in Europe," *Wall Street Journal*, October 31, 2018, https://www.wsj.com/ar ticles/bags-of-cash-and-a-bomb-plot-inside-a-covert-iranian-operation-in-europe -1540978201; David M. Herszenhorn, "Terror Trial in Antwerp to Test EU-Iran Relations," *Politico*, November 27, 2020, https://www.politico.eu/article/terror-tr ial-in-antwerp-will-test-eu-iran-relations.

24. Levitt, "Trends in Iranian External Assassination," 4.

25. Ardavan Khoshnood, "Iran's Killing Machine: Political Assassinations by the Is- lamic Regime," BESA Center Mideast Security and Policy Studies Paper no. 185, December 2020, 11, 14, https://besacenter.org/iran-political-assassinations/.

26. Mark P. Sullivan and June S. Beittel, *Latin America: Terrorism Issues*, Report for Congress no. RS21049 (Washington, DC: Congressional Research Service, 2013), 24; Rodier, "Iranian Intelligence Services."

27. Library of Congress, *Iran's Ministry of Intelligence and Security*, 29; Rodier, "Ira- nian Intelligence Services."

28. Greg Miller, "Closing a Peephole into Iran," *Los Angeles Times*, March 27, 2005.

29. Arango et al., "Iran Cables."

30. Risen, "Spying on the US."

31. Hussain, "Iran's Shadow War on ISIS."
32. Judah Ari Gross, "Shin Bet Arrests 5 Jewish Israelis Suspected of Spying for Iran," *Times of Israel*, January 13, 2022, https://www.timesofisrael.com/shin-bet-arrests -5-jewish-israelis-suspected-of-spying-for-iran/.
33. Library of Congress, *Iran's Ministry of Intelligence and Security*, 30; Rodier, "Iranian Intelligence Services."
34. "How Do Iran's Intrusive Intelligence Forces Operate Abroad?" Khabar Online, June 9, 2010, https://www.khabaronline.ir/news/67593/ان‌‌یرا‌-اطلا‌عاتی‌-نفوذی‌های‌‌و‌نیر کنند‌-می‌-عمل‌-چگونه‌-کشور‌-از‌-خارج‌-در-.
35. Library of Congress, *Iran's Ministry of Intelligence and Security*, 30; Rodier, "Iranian Intelligence Services"; "How Do Iran's Intrusive Intelligence Forces Operate Abroad?"
36. Library of Congress, *Iran's Ministry of Intelligence and Security*, 30; Rodier, "Iranian Intelligence Services."
37. "How Do Iran's Intrusive Intelligence Forces Operate Abroad?"
38. Scott Peterson, "Behind Iran Spy Drama, a Broader Escalation," *Christian Science Monitor*, July 22, 2019, https://www.csmonitor.com/World/Middle-East/2019/07 22/Behind-Iran-spy-drama-a-broader-escalation.
39. "Iran Security Official Claims."
40. "Iranian Minister of Intelligence: We Have Identified Dozens of Spies in Sensitive Centers," Radio Farda, April 19, 2019, https://www.radiofarda.com/a/iran-intelli gence-minister-says-tens-spies-caught-us-british/29891534.html.
41. Library of Congress, *Iran's Ministry of Intelligence and Security*, 35–36; Peterson, "Behind Iran Spy Drama"; "Iranian Lawmakers Laud Intelligence Ministry for Disbanding CIA-Linked Spy Team," Fars News Agency, July 28, 2019, ProQuest; "The Director-General of the Ministry of Intelligence Counter-Espionage: The Second Major Blow to the US Intelligence Service; Details of the Destruction of a CIA Network in Iran," Al-Alam, July 22, 2019, https://fa.alalam.ir/news/4336576.
42. "Director-General of Ministry of Intelligence Counter-Espionage."
43. Douglas London, "Iran's Lit Fuse Does Not Necessarily Favor the US," Middle East Institute, January 13, 2020, https://www.mei.edu/publications/irans-lit-fuse -does-not-necessarily-favor-us.
44. "Iran Security Official Claims."
45. Zach Dorfman and Jenna McLaughlin, "The CIA's Communications Suffered a Catastrophic Compromise. It Started in Iran," Yahoo News, November 2, 2018, https://finance.yahoo.com news/cias-communications-suffered-catastroph ic-compromise-started-iran-090018710.html; "Mole Hunt"; Peterson, "Behind Iran Spy Drama."
46. Dorfman and McLaughlin, "CIA's Communications Suffered."
47. "Mole Hunt"; Peterson, "Behind Iran Spy Drama."
48. Library of Congress, *Iran's Ministry of Intelligence and Security*, 36; "Commander: IRGC Assigned."
49. Sebastien Roblin, "Israel Tried to 'Eliminate' Iran's Nuclear Program by Killing Scientists," *National Interest*, May 16, 2019, https://nationalinterest.org/blog/buzz /israel-tried-eliminate-irans-nuclear-program-killing-scientists-57932.
50. "Iranian Intelligence Says It Busted Alleged Israeli Spy Network," Al-Monitor,

July 27, 2021, https://www.al-monitor.com/originals/2021/07/iranian-intelligence
-says-it-busted-alleged-israeli-spy-network.

51. "Mossad Base in Erbil Reportedly Targeted amid Lapid UAE Visit," Mehr News, June 29, 2021, ProQuest.

52. Farnaz Fassihi and Ronen Bergman, "The Double Life of Britain's Spy in Iran's Regime," *New York Times*, May 1, 2023; "Alireza Akbari Executed over Spying for British Intelligence Agency," Press TV, January 14, 2023, ProQuest.

53. Fassihi and Bergman, "The Double Life of Britain's Spy in Iran's Regime."

54. "The Double Life of Britain's Spy in Iran's Regime"; "Alireza Akbari Executed over Spying."

55. "The Double Life of Britain's Spy in Iran's Regime."

56. Farnaz Fassihi, "Iran Executes Former Defense Official, a Dual U.K. Citizen, on Spy Charges," *New York Times*, January 14, 2023, ProQuest; "Iran Has Executed an Iranian-British Dual National over Spying Claim," National Public Radio, January 14, 2023, https://www.npr.org/2023/01/14/1149239774/iran-hangs-for mer-defense-ministry-official.

57. "Several Terrorist Attacks Foiled in Tehran, Other Iranian Provinces," Fars News Agency, June 20, 2016, ProQuest.

58. "Minister Says over 1500 Youths Prevented"; "Iran's Intelligence Agency Enjoys"; "Official Says USA Formed 'Intelligence NATO.'"

59. Thomas Erdbrink and Mujib Mashal, "Dual Sieges by Terrorists Shatter Calm in Tehran," *New York Times*, June 8, 2017; "Iran Minister Says Mastermind."

60. "Minister of Intelligence's Untold Story about IRGC's Missile Attack on ISIS Commanders' Location," Eghtesad News, June 21, 2017, https://www.eghtesadne ws.com/fa/tiny/news-172726; "Iran Guards Issue Pointed Statement about Syria Operations," BBC Monitoring Middle East [Tasnim in Persian], June 21, 2017, ProQuest.

61. Peterson, "Why Europe Is Again a Battlefield."

62. "Iran Security Official Claims."

63. Peterson, "Why Europe Is Again a Battlefield."

64. "Iran Arrests Last Terrorist Involved in Shah Cheragh Attack," Mehr News, August 19, 2023, ProQuest.

65. Vivian Yee, Hwaida Saad, and Eric Schmitt, "Islamic State Claims Responsibility for Deadly Bombings in Iran," *New York Times*, January 4, 2024, https://www.nyt imes.com/2024/01/04/world/middleeast/us-isis-iran-general-suleimani.html.

66. Michael R. Gordon, "U.S. Secretly Alerted Iran ahead of Islamic State Terrorist Attack," *Wall Street Journal*, January 25, 2024, https://www.wsj.com/world/midd le-east/u-s-secretly-alerted-iran-ahead-of-islamic-state-terrorist-attack-af77a19a.

67. Mohammad Mazhari, "Iran Hits Irbil and Pakistan to Retaliate for Terrorist Attacks and the Assassination of a Key General," Stimson Center, January 19, 2024, https://www.stimson.org/2024/iran-irbil-pakistan-missile-strikes/.

68. Ben Hubbard, Farnaz Fassihi, and Ronen Bergman, "Iran Rattled as Israel Repeatedly Strikes Key Targets," *New York Times*, April 20, 2021, https://www.nytimes .com/2021/04/20/world/middleeast/iran-israeli-attacks.html.

69. Scott Peterson, "In Iran, Assassination Shock Spurs Calls to Rethink Security," *Christian Science Monitor*, December 3, 2020, https://www.csmonitor.com/layo

ut/set/print/World/Middle-East/2020/1203/In-Iran-assassination-shock-spurs-cal
ls-to-rethink-security; Jake Wallis Simons, "Truth behind Killing of Iran Nuclear
Scientist Mohsen Fakhrizadeh Revealed," *Jewish Chronicle*, February 13, 2021,
https://www.thejc.com/news/world/world-exclusive-truth-behind-killing-of-iran
-nuclear-scientist-mohsen-fakhrizadeh-revealed-1.511653.

70. "Iran Identifies Those Involved in Killing Nuclear Scientist," BBC Monitoring
    Middle East [Vision of the Islamic Republic of Iran Network 2 in Persian], De-
    cember 2, 2020, ProQuest.

71. "Iran Identifies Those Involved."

72. "Iran Identifies Those Involved"; Peterson, "In Iran, Assassination Shock."

73. Peterson, "In Iran, Assassination Shock"; Ardavan Khoshnood, "Russia and Iran
    Sign an Intelligence Pact," BESA Center Perspectives Paper no. 1,948, March 4,
    2021, https://besacenter.org/russia-iran-intelligence-pact.

74. Hubbard, Fassihi, and Bergman, "Iran Rattled."

75. Hubbard, Fassihi, and Bergman.

76. Scott Peterson, "Why Iran Nuclear Talks Are Moving Ahead, De-
    spite Israeli Attack," *Christian Science Monitor*, April 19, 2021, https://
    www.csmonitor.com/layout/set/print/World/Middle-East/2021/0419/Why
    -Iran-nuclear-talks-are-moving-ahead-despite-Israeli-attack#.

77. Hubbard, Fassihi, and Bergman, "Iran Rattled"; Simons, "Truth behind Killing."

78. Hubbard, Fassihi, and Bergman, "Iran Rattled."

79. "Intelligence Minister: Over 12 Israel-Backed Terrorist Teams Dismantled by
    Iran," Fars News Agency, January 25, 2003, ProQuest; "Over 12 Israel-Linked
    Terrorist Teams Arrested in Iran," Mehr News, January 25, 2023, ProQuest.

80. "Iran Captures Israeli Mercenaries behind Military Workshop Attack," Fars News
    Agency, February 11, 2023, ProQuest.

81. "Intelligence Minister: 400 Explosive Devices Neutralized in Iran in Past Few
    Months," Fars News Agency, September 11, 2023, ProQuest; "Intelligence Min-
    ister: 200 Terrorists Captured by Iran during Past Months," Fars News Agency,
    September 12, 2023, ProQuest.

82. "Iran Thwarts Plots against Sunni Clerics, IRGC Officers," Fars News Agency,
    September 29, 2023, ProQuest.

83. Michael R. Gordon, Vivian Salama, and Warren P. Strobel, "US Secretly Alerted
    Iran ahead of Islamic State Terrorist Attack," *Wall Street Journal*, January 26,
    2024.

84. "Gonen Segev: Israel Ex-Minister Admits Spying for Iran," BBC, January 9, 2019,
    https://www.bbc.com/news/world-middle-east-46808797.

85. David M. Halbfinger and Ronen Bergman, "Gantz, Netanyahu's Challenger, Faces
    Lurid Questions after Iran Hacked His Phone," *New York Times*, March 15, 2019,
    https:// www.nytimes.com/2019/03/15/world/middleeast/gantz-netanyahus-chal
    lenger-faces-lurid-questions-after-iran-hacked-his-phone.html.

86. Rodier, "Iranian Intelligence Services."

87. Peterson, "Why Europe Is Again a Battlefield."

88. Declan Walsh, Eric Schmitt, Simon Marks, and Ronen Bergman, "Arrests in
    Ethiopia Thwarted Iran Terror Plot, Officials Say," *New York Times*, February 15,
    2021.

89. "Iran Strongly Rejects Claims about Scheme to Attack UAE Embassy in Ethiopia," Fars News Agency, February 16, 2021, ProQuest.

90. Walsh et al., "Arrests in Ethiopia."

91. Levitt, "Trends in Iranian External Assassination," 4.

92. Golkar, "Iran's Intelligence Organizations"; Spencer S. Hsu, "U.S. Court Detains Calif. Man Charged with Serving as Agent of Iran, Surveilling Americans," *Washington Post*, August 21, 2018, https://www.washingtonpost.com/local/public-safe ty/us-charges-two-men-with-serving-as-agents-of-iran-spying-on-americans-and -jewish-center/2018/08/20/e6d69252-a4bf-11e8-8fac-12e98c13528d_story.html.

93. US Department of the Treasury, "Treasury Designates Perpetrators of Human Rights Abuse and Commemorates the 75th Anniversary of the Universal Declaration of Human Rights," December 8, 2023, https://home.treasury.gov/ne ws/press-releases/jy1972.

94. Sommerville, "Transnational Repression."

95. Levitt, "Trends in Iranian External Assassination," 4.

96. Levitt, 5.

97. Levitt, 4; Peterson, "Why Europe Is Again a Battlefield."

98. Peterson, "Why Europe Is Again a Battlefield."

99. Ebrahim Ramezani, "More Defendants Released on Bail in Masoud Molavi Assassination Case," IranWire, December 13, 2021, https://iranwire.com/en/world /70951; Humeyra Pamuk, "U.S. Believes Iran Was 'Directly Involved' in Killing of Iranian Dissident in Turkey," Reuters, April 1, 2020, https://www.reuters.com/ar ticle/us-turkey-iran-killing-usa/u-s-believes-iran-was-directly-involved-in-killing -of-iranian-dissident-in-turkey-idUSKBN21K027; Sommerville, "Transnational Repression."

100. "One Person's Story: Mas'ud Molavi Vardanjani," Abdorrahman Boroumand Center for Human Rights in Iran, n.d., https://www.iranrights.org.

101. Telegram, a freeware, cross-platform, cloud-based instant-messaging service, provides channels for broadcasting public messages to large audiences.

102. "One Person's Story."

103. "Exclusive: Iranian Diplomats Instigated Killing of Dissident in Istanbul, Turkish Officials Say," Reuters, March 27, 2020, https://www.reuters.com/article/us-tur key-iran-killing-exclusive/exclusive-iranian-diplomats-instigated-killing-of-dissi dent-in-istanbul-turkish-officials-say-idUSKBN21E3FU.

104. "One Person's Story"; Ramezani, "More Defendants Released."

105. "Exclusive: Iranian Diplomats Instigated Killing"; Ramezani, "More Defendants Released."

106. "Exclusive: Iranian Diplomats Instigated Killing"; "One Person's Story."

107. Herszenhorn, "Terror Trial in Antwerp"; Levitt, "Trends in Iranian External Assassination," 1.

108. Dalton, "Bags of Cash"; Herszenhorn, "Terror Trial in Antwerp."

109. Herszenhorn, "Terror Trial in Antwerp."

110. Dalton, "Bags of Cash."

111. Herszenhorn, "Terror Trial in Antwerp."

112. Levitt, "Trends in Iranian External Assassination," 1.

113. Dalton, "Bags of Cash"; Peterson, "Why Europe Is Again a Battlefield."

114. US Department of Justice Office of Public Affairs, "One Iranian and Two Canadian Nationals Indicted in Murder-for-Hire Scheme," January 29, 2024, https://www.justice.gov/opa/pr/one-iranian-and-two-canadian-nationals-indicted-murder-hire-scheme; US Department of the Treasury, "The United States and United Kingdom Target Iranian Transnational Assassinations Network," January 29, 2024, https://home.treasury.gov/news/press-releases/jy2052.

115. The Treasury Department also has repeatedly acted against IRGC and IRGC-QF intelligence officers, including the June 2023 designation of five IRGC-QF officials and affiliates involved in a series of terrorist plots targeting former US government officials and others. US Department of the Treasury, "Treasury Designates Iranian Regime Operatives Involved in Assassination Plots in the United States and Abroad," June 1, 2023, https://home.treasury.gov/news/press-releases/jy1513; US Department of the Treasury, "The United States and United Kingdom Target Iranian Transnational Assassinations Network."

116. Levitt, "Trends in Iranian External Assassination," 4.

117. Golkar, "Iran's Intelligence Organizations."

118. Benjamin Weiser and Glenn Thrush, "Justice Dept. Announces More Arrests in Plot to Kill Iranian Writer," *New York Times*, January 27, 2023, https://www.nytimes.com/2023/01/27/us/politics/masih-alinejad-doj-assassination-plot.html.

119. Ebrahim Ramezani, "Iranian Intelligence Agents Busted in Turkey Kidnap Attempt," IranWire, October 14, 2021, https://iranwire.com/en/features/10554.

120. Golkar, "Iran's Intelligence Organizations."

121. Peterson, "Why Europe Is Again a Battlefield"; "Intel Min. Releases Docs."

122. Kambiz Ghafouri, "Mohammad Davoudzadeh Loloei, a Terror Plot and Lessons Europe Learned," IranWire, May 18, 2021, https://iranwire.com/en/features/69570.

123. Peterson, "Kidnapping Dissidents Abroad."

124. Peterson.

125. "Intel Min. Releases Docs."

126. "Prosecutor Accuses Iranian Arab 'Terrorists' of Links to Former Israeli PM," BBC Monitoring Middle East [Mizan News Agency in Persian], February 2, 2022, ProQuest.

127. Sune Engel Rasmussen, "Trial Exposes Iran, Saudi Battle in Europe," *Wall Street Journal*, June 26, 2020, https://www.wsj.com/articles/trial-exposes-iran-saudi-battle-in-europe-11593158091.

128. Peterson, "Kidnapping Dissidents Abroad."

129. Hannah Somerville, "One Year after Abduction, Jamshid Sharmahd's Family Vows to Fight On," IranWire, November 19, 2021, https://iranwire.com/en/features/70111; Golnaz Esfandiari, "Mystery Surrounds Iran's Detention of Leader of U.S.-Based Exile Group," Radio Free Europe / Radio Liberty, August 4, 2020, https://www.rferl.org/a/mystery-surrounds-iran-s-detention-of-leader-of-u-s--based-exile-group/30766416.html.

130. Wright, "Iran's Hollywood Plot"; Sommerville, "Transnational Repression."

131. Ramezani, "Iranian Intelligence Agents Busted."

132. Karen DeYoung and Carol Morello, "Freeing a Reporter: Secret Diplomatic Talks and Private Back Channels," *Washington Post*, January 17, 2016, www.washingtonpost.com/world/national-security/freeing-jason-secret-diplomatic

-talks-and-private-back-channels/2016/01/17/. On the seven Iranians, see Nicholas Fandos, "Details of 7 Iranians Granted Clemency in Prisoner Swap," *New York Times*, January 17, 2016, www.nytimes.com/2016/01/18/world/middleeast/a-look-at-the-seven-iranians-released-by-the-us.html.

133. Zimmt, "Intelligence Organization of the IRGC," 30–32.
134. Zimmt.
135. "U.S. Sanctions Iran over Missing U.S. Hostage," USIP Iran Primer, December 14, 2020, https://iranprimer.usip.org/blog/2020/dec/14/us-sanctions-iran-over-missing-us-hostage; Carol Morello, "U.S. Sanctions Two Iranians for Abduction and Probable Death of Former FBI Agent Robert Levinson," *Washington Post*, December 14, 2020, https:// www.washingtonpost.com/national-security/iran-sanctions-robert-levinson-death/2020/12/14/d9b7072c-3e1f-11eb-a402-fba110db3b42_story.html.
136. "Former FBI Agent Held in Iran: Report," Reuters, April 13, 2007, https://www.reuters.com/article/topNews/idUSBLA33261120070413; Matt Apuzzo and Adam Goldman, "American Missing Nearly 7 Years in Iran Was on an Unapproved CIA Mission," Associated Press, December 12, 2013, https://www.businessinsider.com/american-missing-nearly-7-years-in-iran-was-working-for-cia-on-unapproved-mission-2013-12; Adam Goldman, "Ex-F.B.I. Agent Who Vanished on C.I.A. Mission to Iran Is Most Likely Dead, U.S. Concludes," *New York Times*, March 25, 2020, https://www.nytimes.com/2020/03/25/us/politics/robert-levinson-cia-iran.html.
137. "U.S. Sanctions Iran over Missing U.S. Hostage"; Morello, "U.S. Sanctions Two Iranians."
138. US Department of the Treasury, "Treasury Designates Former President of Iran," September 18, 2023, https://home.treasury.gov/news/press-releases/jy1739; "Iran-US Prisoner Swap: New US Sanctions," USIP Iran Primer, September 18, 2023, https://iranprimer.usip.org/blog/2023/sep/18/iran-us-prisoner-swap-new-sanctions.
139. Farnaz Fassihi and Michael D. Shear, "US Reaches Deal with Iran to Free Americans for Jailed Iranians and Funds," *New York Times*, August 10, 2023, https:// www.nytimes.com/2023/08/10/us/politics/iran-us-prisoner-swap.html.
140. Michael Crowley and Alan Rappeport, "US and Qatar Deny Iran Access to $6 Billion from Prisoner Deal," *New York Times*, October 12, 2023, https://www.nytimes.com/2023/10/12/world/middleeast/us-qatar-iran-prisoner-deal.html.
141. Arango et al., "Iran Cables."
142. Levitt, "Trends in Iranian External Assassination," 5–6.
143. Risen, "Spying on the US."
144. Hussain, "Iran's Shadow War on ISIS."
145. Risen, "Spying on the US."
146. Arango et al., "Iran Cables."
147. Levitt, "Trends in Iranian External Assassination," 6.
148. US Congress, House Homeland Security Subcommittee on Counterterrorism and Intelligence and Subcommittee on Oversight, Investigations, and Management, *Iranian Terror Operations on American Soil*, 112th Cong., 1st sess., October 26, 2011 (Matthew Levitt statement).
149. Wright, "Iran's Hollywood Plot."

150. Theohary, "Iranian Offensive Cyber Attack Capabilities," 1.
151. Gregory F. Rose, "The Iranian Islamic Armed Forces: An Assessment," August 15, 1983, 60–61, attachment to Department of the Army, Headquarters, Fort Carson, and Headquarters 4th Infantry Division (Mechanized), *Intelligence Bulletin 01-84*, March 16, 1984, author's personal collection.
152. Risen, "Spying on the US."
153. "Intelligence Minister Says Iran Mounts Intel Devices in Syria to Monitor Terrorists," Fars News Agency, March 14, 2017, ProQuest.
154. Levitt, "Trends in Iranian External Assassination," 2–3.
155. Insikt Group, "Despite Infighting and Volatility, Iran Maintains Aggressive Cyber Operations Structure," Recorded Future, CTA-IR-2020-0409, 2020, 2, www.record edfuture.com.
156. Shires and McGetrick, *Rational Not Reactive*, 39.
157. Inskit Group, "Despite Infighting and Volatility," 4.
158. Library of Congress, *Iran's Ministry of Intelligence and Security*, 31.
159. Hamid Farokhnia, "A Kafkaesque Realm of Cyber Censorship," Tehran Bureau, May 9, 2010, https://www.pbs.org/wgbh/pages/frontline/tehranbureau/2010/05/a-kafkaesque-realm-of-cyber-censorship.html.
160. Inskit Group, "Despite Infighting and Volatility," 26.
161. Phishing uses email or malicious websites to solicit personal information by posing as a trustworthy organization. It is a form of social engineering, which involves the use of deception to manipulate individuals into divulging confidential or personal information over computer networks. Intel 471 Global Research Team, "Iran's Domestic Espionage: Lessons from Recent Data Leaks," Intel 471, July 8, 2020, https://blog.intel471.com.
162. Theohary, "Iranian Offensive Cyber Attack Capabilities," 1.
163. "Narration of Proposed Minister of Intelligence."
164. Inskit Group, "Despite Infighting and Volatility," 7.
165. "Iran Intelligence Minister Says Not Responsible for Social Media Crackdown," BBC Monitoring Middle East [Islamic Consultative Assembly News Agency in Persian], June 6, 2017, ProQuest.
166. US Department of the Treasury, "Treasury Sanctions Iranian Ministry."
167. Theohary, "Iranian Offensive Cyber Attack Capabilities," 1. See also Robert McMillan, "Iranian Hackers Have Hit Hundreds of Companies in Past Two Years," *Wall Street Journal*, March 6, 2019, https://www.wsj.com/articles/iranian-hackers-have-hit-hundreds-of-companies-in-past-two-years-11551906036.
168. Inskit Group, "Despite Infighting and Volatility," 26.
169. Levi Gundert, Sanil Chohan, and Greg Lesnewich, "Iran's Hacker Hierarchy Exposed: How the Islamic Republic of Iran Uses Contractors and Universities to Conduct Cyber Operations," Recorded Future, 2018, www.recordedfuture.com.
170. US State Department, "Designation of Iranian Officials and Entities Connected to Ongoing Protest Repression, Censorship, and Prison Abuses," press release, October 26, 2022, https://www.state.gov/designation-of-iranian-officials-and-enti ties-connected-to-ongoing-protest-repression-censorship-and-prison-abuses/.
171. Gundert, Chohan, and Lesnewich, "Iran's Hacker Hierarchy Exposed." For more on Iranian APTs, see Steph Shample, "Iranian APTs: An Overview," Middle East

Institute, February 10, 2023, https://www.mei.edu/publications/iranian-apts-over
view.

172. Inskit Group, "Despite Infighting and Volatility," 36; Shires and McGetrick, *Rational Not Reactive*, 42.
173. "US Imposes Sanctions on Several Iranian Entities and Individuals," Press TV, September 17, 2020, ProQuest; Shires and McGetrick, *Rational Not Reactive*, 42.
174. Gundert, Chohan, and Lesnewich, "Iran's Hacker Hierarchy Exposed."
175. Wright, "Iran's Hollywood Plot."
176. "Iran: State-Backed Hacking of Activists, Journalists, Politicians; Ongoing Phishing Campaign Imperils Independent Groups," Human Rights Watch, December 5, 2022, https://www.hrw.org/news/2022/12/05/iran-state-backed-hacking-activists
-journalists-politicians.
177. ODNI, *Annual Threat Assessment* (2022), 15.
178. Gundert, Chohan, and Lesnewich, "Iran's Hacker Hierarchy Exposed."
179. "Iran, US Locked in Serious War of Intelligence: IRGC Commander," Iranian Students News Agency, May 19, 2019, https://en.isna.ir/news/98022915101/Iran
-US-locked-in-serious-war-of-intelligence-IRGC-Commander.
180. Andrew Hanna, "The Invisible U.S.-Iran Cyber War," USIP Iran Primer, November 1, 2021, https://iranprimer.usip.org/blog/2019/oct/25/invisible-us-iran-cyber
-war.
181. Theohary, "Iranian Offensive Cyber Attack Capabilities," 1.
182. Micah Loudermilk, "Iran Crisis Moves into Cyberspace," Washington Institute PolicyWatch no. 3,150, July 9, 2019, http://info.washingtoninstitute.org/acton/ct
/19961/; Gundert, Chohan, and Lesnewich, "Iran's Hacker Hierarchy Exposed."
183. Hanna, "Invisible U.S.-Iran Cyber War."
184. ODNI, *Annual Threat Assessment* (2022), 15.
185. A. J. Vicens, "Previously Unreported Lebanon-Based Hacking Group Targeting Israel, Microsoft Says," Cyberscoop, June 2, 2002, https://www.cyberscoop
.com/lebanon-polonium-israel-hacking-cyber; A. J. Vicens, "Iranian Hacking Campaign That Included Former U.S. Ambassador Exposed," Cyberscoop, June 14, 2022, https://www.cyberscoop.com/iranian-hacking-us-ambassador-phospho
rus-espionage/.
186. Yonah Jeremy Bob, "Israel Cyber Chief: Iran Has Become Our Dominant Rival in Cyber," *Jerusalem Post*, June 28, 2022, https://www.jpost.com/middle-east/iran
-news/article-710584.
187. "Iran: Official Says Spy Cases."
188. "Iran: Official Says Spy Cases."
189. "Iran News Round Up," AEI Critical Threats Project, September 8, 2015, https://www.criticalthreats.org/briefs/iran-news-round-up/iran-news-round-up
-september-8-2015-1; Theohary, "Iranian Offensive Cyber Attack Capabilities," 1–2; Wege, "Iran's Intelligence Establishment," 64.

5

Intelligence Community and Foreign Intelligence Partners

The role of the Ministry of Intelligence in the nezam and its nominal position as Iran's paramount intelligence organization needs to be understood in relation to Iran's larger intelligence community. Its ongoing relationships with various foreign services and nonstate actors also are important factors. Both areas, however, are as opaque as the ministry itself. Iran has never publicized the complete structure of its intelligence community. Similarly, the Islamic Republic is discreet about its contacts with foreign services, while the cooperating intelligence services have no apparent desire to publicize the relationship beyond a general acknowledgment of some interactions.

Iran's intelligence community probably has sixteen to twenty-one formal members. In late 2014 Fars News Agency, a hard-line conservative-leaning website affiliated with the IRGC, reported that Iran's intelligence community comprised sixteen separate intelligence bodies.[1] The report, however, named only nine members in addition to the Ministry of Intelligence. Three of the named IRGC members of the community were its Intelligence Organization, Protection Organization, and Center for Investigating Organized Crime, which focuses on the cyber realm and has helped to censor websites and identify Internet activists.[2] Another three members were the Office of the Supreme Leader's Intelligence Bureau, the Artesh Intelligence Directorate (J-2), and the Armed Forces General Staff's Protection Organization. The final

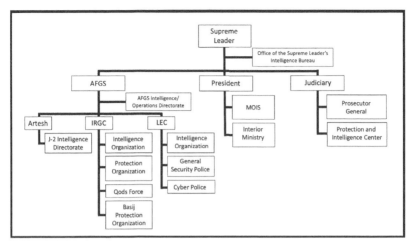

Figure 5.1. Primary Iranian intelligence and related organizations, 2023. Diagram developed by the author.

three members listed in the article were the Law Enforcement Force's Intelligence Unit, its Cyber Police organization, and its protection unit, the General Security and Intelligence Organization. In late 2021 Iran announced that it was dividing the General Security and Intelligence Organization of the renamed Law Enforcement Command (LEC) into two distinct entities, the LEC General Security Police and the LEC Intelligence Organization, which apparently incorporated the LEF Intelligence Unit.[3]

The remaining members of Iran's formal intelligence community probably are the protection units of the Basij, MODAFL, the judiciary, and the MOIS, which would correspond to the other named protection offices on the Fars News list. Given its role in external clandestine operations, the IRGC-QF is a likely member. In addition, the Armed Forces General Staff apparently has an Intelligence and Operations Directorate that,[4] as a counterpart to the Artesh J-2 and IRGC-IO, probably would be considered part of the community.[5] Other members may be existing IRGC, Basij, and Artesh bodies with cyber-related missions similar to those listed by Fars News.

The minister of the interior and the prosecutor general are likely intelligence community members because, as directed by the 1983 MOIS establishment law, they have been part of Iran's Intelligence Coordination

Council since that time.[6] Recall from chapter 1 that the other ICC members are the intelligence minister, who chairs the council, the foreign minister, and the commanders of the IRGC, Artesh, and law enforcement intelligence and protection organizations. According to Article 2 of the establishment law, the ICC brings together select members of the Iranian intelligence community to consult on intelligence issues and operations. The council probably plays a role in implementing the law's Article 14 direction that "all organs of the state must cooperate . . . by placing at the ministry's disposal all necessary means, be they human, technical, or intelligence-related experiences, in order to aid the ministry's work."[7]

ICC collaboration includes the assignment of intelligence operations to the appropriate intelligence units and the exchange of technical intelligence support among members, according to Iranian press reports.[8] Among its duties, the council coordinates joint operations with the SNSC that involve two or more community members, such as the 2010 operation to capture Abdulmalik Rigi. These reports also suggested that the ICC creates intelligence task forces during crises. Other ICC duties include the preparation of community-coordinated intelligence estimates for the regime, the assessment of draft legislation affecting intelligence equities, and the setting of legal guidelines for community activities. Finally, the ICC establishes community standards for "selection" (probably a reference to recruiting and hiring staff) and to enhance training quality.[9]

The Parallel Intelligence Apparatus

Despite the legal construction of intelligence community roles, some of the country's non-MOIS intelligence bodies work as separate and sometimes rival security apparatuses. Since the late 1990s the MOIS has faced persistent competition from the Revolutionary Guard for primacy in intelligence work to safeguard the regime. As a ministry accountable to an elected parliament and directed by an elected president, the MOIS found itself at a disadvantage to the network of intelligence, security, and law enforcement units that operated solely under the leader's control. This system undercut MOIS policies with a harsher approach to intimidating and silencing reformists, political dissidents, and other regime critics.[10]

Going back to the debate over whether to make Iran's main intelligence service a ministry or an organization, the regime has had difficulty finding a balance in centralizing intelligence activities, limiting bureaucratic struggles, and maintaining accountability. According to an expatriate news organization citing former president Rafsanjani's memoirs, when Rafsanjani was Majles speaker in 1987 Reyshahri complained about MOIS-IRGC bureaucratic clashes.[11] Mentioning the difficulty of integrating intelligence operations, the MOIS head unsuccessfully recommended restructuring the ministry to incorporate and direct the judiciary and place the combined organization under the leader's supervision. Rafsanjani also recalled that early in his presidency, MOIS officials called for ministry oversight of and greater restrictions on IRGC intelligence operations.[12]

Tension between the ministry and the hard-line conservatives, including senior IRGC leaders, grew because of the latter's opposition to Yunesi's post-1999 reform efforts. Shortly after Ahmadinejad became president in August 2005, Said Hajjarian and other reformist politicians became concerned that hard-line conservative legislators were laying the groundwork to eliminate Majles supervision and create parallel intelligence bodies.[13] The warnings were a response to the conservatives' proposal to separate the MOIS protection directorate from the ministry.[14] The appointment of Mohseni-Ejei, perceived by conservative parliamentarians as strong and like-minded, possibly made the proposal unnecessary, contributing to its failure to garner enough votes to become law.[15]

Conservative ideologues charged that the MOIS had been compromised by CIA, SIS, and Mossad agents planted inside SAVAK who later embedded themselves in the ministry.[16] Similarly, these hard-liners blamed leftists who supported reformist policies, such as Said Hajjarian, for the bad management that resulted in the Chain Murders. The conservatives also suggested that the reformists inside the ministry had weakened its response to the 2009 election unrest.[17] By then Khamenei appeared committed to creating new intelligence organizations and expanding the roles of existing ones to weaken and silence the reform movement.

From its inception, the Ministry of Intelligence has operated under the supreme leader's guidance, with Reyshahri setting the precedent

Known Intelligence Community (IC) Members
- Ministry of Intelligence
- IRGC Intelligence Organization
- IRGC Protection Organization
- IRGC Center for Investigating Organized Crime
- LEC Intelligence Organization
- LEC General Security Police
- LEC Cyber Police
- Artesh Intelligence Directorate (J-2)
- AFGS Protection Organization
- Office of the Supreme Leader's Intelligence Bureau

Likely Cyber-Related IC Members	Likely Major IC Members	Likely Protection-Related IC Members
o IRGC Electronic Warfare and Cyber Defense Organization	o IRGC–Qods Force	o MOIS Protection Directorate
o Basij Cyber Council	o Ministry of the Interior	o Basij Protection Organization
o Artesh Cyber Defense Command	o Prosecutor General	o MODAFL Protection Organization
	o AFGS Intelligence / Operations Directorate	o Judiciary Protection and Intelligence Center

Figure 5.2. Iran's intelligence community. Chart developed by author.

of deferring to Khomeini when differences arose between the imam and the prime minister.[18] Nonetheless, once Khamenei became leader, he sought to strengthen his control over the government by building strong ties to the security and intelligence services. To facilitate this effort, he expanded the Office of the Supreme Leader and appointed Asghar Mirhejazi, a former MOIS deputy minister and Haqqani Seminary graduate, to supervise the office's intelligence bureau.[19] Mirhejazi, who remained in the post through 2023, provided oversight of Iran's intelligence organizations as well as Basij internal security operations. He ensured Khamenei's views guided the intelligence community's coordinated activities, enhancing the leader's control while privileging the parallel intelligence apparatus over the MOIS.[20]

During the 2009 Green Movement protests, the IRGC led the regime response using Basij paramilitary forces to attack the demonstrators. When Khamenei ordered the expansion of the IRGC intelligence branch to an intelligence organization in the protests' aftermath, he named the Basij commander, Hossein Taeb, as its leader.[21] Born in 1963, Taeb reportedly studied to become a cleric under Khamenei. The young revolutionary fought with the IRGC in the Iran-Iraq War, where he served with Mojtaba Khamenei, the leader's son. Taeb worked for the MOIS from 1984 to the mid-1990s, when he allegedly was dismissed after targeting the son of then President Rafsanjani for investigation.[22] He became a deputy coordinator of intelligence in the Office of the Supreme Leader, where Mojtaba played a leading role for his father.[23] Taeb's background and connections made him a powerful and influential regime official during his nearly thirteen years leading the IRGC-IO from late 2009 to mid-2022.

The MOIS and IRGC-IO generally collaborated on the broader mission of defending the regime and suppressing dissidents, but competition was unavoidable.[24] The expanded Guard unit took on additional security missions, including some, such as capturing regime opponents abroad, that previously had belonged solely to the ministry.[25] Subsequently, the IRGC-IO outmaneuvered the MOIS and ignored the ministry's objections to its activities. For example, in 2017, the IRGC arrested Abdolrasoul Dorri-Esfahani, a dual-national banking expert on Iran's JCPOA negotiating team, and ensured he was sentenced to prison for espionage. Alavi rejected the accusations, but his assertion that the MOIS counterespionage directorate was "the only professional reference for the discernment of espionage activities" was ignored.[26] Similarly, the IRGC overruled the MOIS when it arrested environmental activists in 2018 and managers of the proreformist secure-messaging application Telegram in 2019.[27] In the case of the environmentalists, Yunesi, who had become a frequent defender of ministry equities after his departure, repeated the argument that the MOIS was the proper authority to determine espionage charges. He contrasted the Guard's actions with his assessment that the ministry "dealt with [cases and missions] professionally and expertly."[28] Despite these critiques, the Guard continued to flout MOIS assertions of predominance, which has weakened the executive branch's ability to impede harsh and often counterproductive IRGC actions.[29]

MOIS and IRGC disagreements and competition spread into Iraq, where the IRGC-QF was Iran's primary arm for advancing the regime's policy. According to the leaked Iran Cables, during the rise of ISIS in 2014 and 2015, MOIS officers criticized IRGC-QF activities and reported their assessment of IRGC failings to Tehran.[30] In the cables, MOIS officers regularly warned that Iran's gains in Iraq were being squandered because Iraqis resented the IRGC-QF's sponsorship and direction of Iraqi Shia militias. The greater IRGC focus on keeping political factions loyal to Tehran in power and suppressing Iraqi Sunnis risked, in MOIS officers' assessments, undermining Iranian policy in

Iraq. One report judged that the alienation of Sunnis and rise of ISIS had harmed Iran's interests by allowing US forces to return to Iraq with greater legitimacy. Another report in the leaked cables suggested that Tehran should restrict IRGC-QF actions against innocent Iraqi Sunnis, warning that such violence harmed perceptions of Iran. MOIS officers also accused IRGC-QF commander Qassem Soleimani, whom they saw as a dangerous self-promoter, for using the anti-ISIS campaign as a launching pad for a political career.

Subsequently, the ministry and Revolutionary Guard vied for primacy in combating the terrorist threat to Iran. In June 2017, following a retaliatory Iranian missile strike against ISIS targets in Syria, Alavi claimed that the MOIS had located the target—allegedly a meeting of senior ISIS officials—and provided the information to the IRGC missile unit. Revolutionary Guard officials responded with claims that IRGC-QF ground units had identified the location for the strike.[31] In March 2018 an IRGC supporter in the Majles asserted that, while the MOIS should intervene in crimes pertaining to national security, countering the activities of terrorist groups such as ISIS was the purview of IRGC intelligence.[32] Nonetheless, the ministry has remained active in countering domestic terrorism, including operations against alleged Arab, Baluch, and Kurdish terrorists between 2019 and 2023.[33]

The ministry unsuccessfully confronted an IRGC effort to insert itself into the vetting of candidates for elections and sensitive government jobs. In 2016 the IRGC-IO, which then had no legal role in election investigations, allegedly provided the Guardian Council with information that led to the disqualification from parliamentary elections that February of numerous candidates previously approved by MOIS vetting.[34] Seeking legislation to involve the IRGC-IO in candidate investigations, conservative Majles members charged that the ministry, for political reasons, had avoided answering the Guardian Council's inquiries on as many as 150 reformist and other candidates.[35] The ministry pushed back against conservative criticism, asserting that, while independent, it adhered to the leader's guidance, interacted constructively with Iran's elected administration, and prevented the influence of political factions on its work.[36]

The same legislation added the IRGC-IO to the investigative bodies that cleared the appointment of individuals to sensitive government positions.[37] The list of sensitive positions in the bill focused on executive branch positions, select governmental organizations, and nongovernmental companies and institutions. Notably, the law continued a regime practice of exempting organizations under the leader and the judiciary.[38] More recently, in 2019, the MOIS and IRGC-IO disagreed over their roles in providing security clearances for government jobs in a dispute over which organization should determine the citizenship of children born to Iranian women married to non-Iranian men.[39]

The nezam's worries about infiltration, which these actions sought to counter, and its desire to increase the IRGC role received additional emphasis in April 2021. Then former IRGC commander and Expediency Council secretary Mohsen Rezai responded to the sabotage of nuclear facilities and the Fahkrizadeh assassination by calling for a purge of the intelligence community.[40] His remarks suggested that regime conservatives believed the intelligence community was seriously compromised. Alavi pushed back by criticizing the IRGC-IO's more controversial cases and placed the blame for Fahkrizadeh's assassination on the IRGC, which was responsible for the security of senior officials and other dignitaries.[41] His explicit complaint that the ministry was excluded from some intelligence and security work highlighted the executive branch's diminishing influence on internal security policies.[42] In a June 2021 interview, former MOIS chief Yunesi backed Alavi's complaints while demonstrating that pragmatist officials also were concerned about widespread Mossad infiltration. He blamed the counterintelligence failures on the creation of parallel organizations, competition among the security services, and too much focus on internal dissidents.[43]

In addition to these concerns, increasing popular protests over economic issues from 2019 to late 2021 apparently spurred Khamenei to take additional steps to allow the IRGC to play a greater role in monitoring and preventing domestic unrest. In December 2021 Iran announced it had changed the Law Enforcement Force into a Law Enforcement Command.[44] The new status reportedly placed the organization on par with the IRGC and Artesh. Under this initiative, the LEC, already led by an IRGC major general, was placed under the Armed Forces General Staff, which another IRGC major general commanded. According to the announcement, the interior minister, previously in charge of the LEF, was given the concurrent role of AFGS deputy commander for law enforcement affairs, where his authority apparently is limited to logistics and administrative support. These changes may allow the regime to free MOIS and IRGC-IO resources to focus on counterintelligence, sabotage, and similar threats rather than domestic disturbances. Consistent with other regime actions to strengthen the nezam and IRGC at the expense of Iran's democratic institutions, placing the LEC under Khamenei's military chain of command seems likely to reduce the role of the president, MOIS, and ICC in coordinating intelligence for law enforcement operations.

Overall, the level and quality of ICC-led collaboration amid this competition is difficult to ascertain, but Iranian intelligence leaders regularly suggest that room for improvement exists. In particular, Iranian officials repeatedly offer mixed assessments of the MOIS-IRGC relationship and the effectiveness of ICC-led community collaboration. As early as 2008, before the IRGC-IO was created, Mohseni-Ejei claimed that criticism of Iran's parallel intelligence organizations was unwarranted because of the close collaboration among Iran's intelligence community.[45] At his 2013 confirmation hearing, however, Alavi suggested that one of his policies would be to revive the role of the intelligence community through cooperation and legal interaction to prevent parallel work.[46]

During the final years of the Rouhani administration, Alavi and Taeb tried to maintain good relations by occasionally praising the other organization's successes and emphasizing their cooperation.[47] For example, in May 2019, Alavi used a visit with Maj. Gen. Hossein Salami (the newly installed IRGC commander), Brig. Gen. Mohammad Kazemi (the head of the IRGC Protection Organization), and Taeb to praise the unity and cooperation between his ministry and the Guard.[48] The subsequent period of significant intelligence failures, however, led Yunesi to continue his criticism of the parallel intelligence organizations for ineffectiveness, failing to act within the law, and politicizing security issues in ways that distracted them from identifying and stopping Iran's real enemies.[49] In the early months of President Raisi's administration, efforts to improve cooperation continued as senior MOIS, IRGC-IO, and LEC officials convened the "First Trilateral Convention on Intelligence."[50] The leaders reportedly met to discuss enhancing intelligence cooperation, draft joint guidelines, and implement an earlier MOIS-IRGC memorandum of understanding to improve collaboration.

An opportunity for further improvement in MOIS-IRGC relations occurred in June 2022 when Khamenei had IRGC commander Salami remove Hossein Taeb as head of the IRGC-Intelligence Organization. The Guard announcement gave no indication why Taeb, who had led the IRGC-IO since its establishment in 2009, was being removed.[51] Some Iranian analysts suggested, however, that Taeb lost his position because of repeated failures to prevent and exact revenge for Israeli operations inside Iran in 2022 (see discussion in chapter 7).[52] These alleged failures seem a less likely explanation because his replacement, IRGC Protection Organization chief Kazemi, had as much or more responsibility for countering Israeli sabotage and assassinations.

Despite the change in IRGC-IO leadership and the claimed close collaboration of Iranian protection organizations under MOIS guidance, any opening for better relations and less competition between the two services had not been taken through mid-2023. That summer several senior Iranian officials again called for Iran's intelligence organizations to expand their cooperation.[53] In a written message sent to an intelligence community gathering in June, Khamenei warned about the organizations' lack of mutual understanding.[54] The leader stressed that cooperation must be implemented at all levels, thoughts Khatib and his IRGC-IO counterpart echoed during their remarks.[55]

Foreign Partners

The MOIS has maintained relationships with foreign intelligence services and nonstate organizations since its founding. Characterizing the relationships, however, is difficult because of a lack of information on the scale and scope of the cooperation. Some Iranian relationships appear to be simple, going no further than exchanging intelligence on common security interests. Iran's intelligence relations with stronger powers, meanwhile, are more complex and are a part of larger security relationships involving political, military, economic, and other cooperation. Some involve strategic allies, such as Syria and Hezbollah, and may involve a degree of specialization based on comparative advantage that provides net gains for each party. Iran also has what can be described as adversarial relationships, working with partners in tactical marriages of convenience against a common foe despite opposing strategic interests.[56]

For Iran, foreign intelligence relationships potentially provide information Iranian services are unable to collect. Moreover, in many cases, Iran's partners can act with greater speed and better insight and cultural understanding in intelligence-collection missions. This increased access to others' sources lowers Iran's collection costs and risks. Foreign intelligence relationships also may improve Iran's access to a target through new capabilities provided by the partner service. In addition, these relations potentially establish an infrastructure for future joint operations.[57] Meanwhile, Tehran's knowledge of the region and its access to central authorities, various nonstate groups, and militias can provide value to foreign intelligence partners such as Russia and China.[58] The relationships have costs, especially when conflicting interests limit the amount and quality of shared intelligence. Iran also must counter its partners' attempts to use the cooperation to gain insight into Iranian intentions, intelligence organization, and sources and methods.

In his 2013 confirmation hearing, Alavi emphasized the importance of exchanging information and interacting with other intelligence services, especially those from neighboring countries, to counter international terrorism.[59] Several years later, in 2019, Alavi reported that Iran maintained intelligence sharing and cooperative relationships with "tens of friendly countries."[60] That same year, Iranian intelligence officials claimed to be forming an "international anti-spying network" against the United States as they announced the disruption of a CIA intelligence network.[61] The MOIS director general of counterintelligence praised the intelligence cooperation, saying that information exchanges resulted in some network members being arrested by Iran's partners.[62]

The Iranians avoid offering specifics on liaison partners. Most of the foreign countries, in turn, apparently prefer to hide contacts with Iran for tradecraft reasons and because of Iran's pariah status in the West. The basis of cooperation varies by country, with each party seeking mutual aid for one or more security goals, such as countering militant Sunni terrorists, suppressing ethnic unrest, combating the drug trade, and limiting US influence and power. Countries that have cooperated with the MOIS over the years have ranged across the Persian Gulf region, the larger Middle East, Europe, Asia, and Latin America. The ministry's most important intelligence partners are the services of Russia, China, and Syria along with several nonstate actors.

Russia

While details are scarce, MOIS collaboration with the Sluzhba Vneshnei Razvedki (SVR; Russian Foreign Intelligence Service) extends back to at least the 1990s when the SVR allegedly trained hundreds of Iranian intelligence personnel.[63] Iranian leaders have sought closer ties with Moscow to relieve Iran's diplomatic and economic isolation from the West, support the Syrian government, and reduce US influence in Southwest Asia. During Ahmadinejad's presidency in 2008, Ejei traveled to Moscow to meet SVR chief Alexander Bortnikov and discuss intelligence sharing.[64] While Russia has been a major arms supplier and has welcomed security cooperation against common regional threats, such as Sunni militancy in Central Asia and the Caucasus in the early 2000s, Iranian-Russian relations have fluctuated and seemed to be more of a marriage of convenience rather than a close alliance.

Although the MOIS probably was involved only at the margins, when Moscow entered the fight against ISIS and other opponents of the Assad regime in Syria in 2015, Iran joined with Russia, Syria, and Iraq in an intelligence-sharing agreement. This was followed by the creation of the combined Baghdad Intelligence Center to collect and analyze data to coordinate joint military actions against ISIS.[65] During this period, Iran expressed interest in Russian cooperation on various space programs that had potential intelligence and counterintelligence uses. This included the acquisition of technology for communication and remote-sensing satellites and access to the Russian global positioning and navigation system, GLONASS.[66]

Increasing cooperation remained a subject of discussion when SVR director Sergei Naryshkin visited Tehran in 2019 to meet with the heads of Iran's intelligence organizations on the subjects of combating international terrorism and counteracting common threats, a likely allusion to the United States.[67] That same year, according to press reports, Russian intelligence officials assisted Iranian officers with discovering the alleged British intelligence source Alireza Akbari, who was accused of sharing Iran's nuclear secrets.[68] In January 2021 the two countries formalized a portion of their collaboration when Iran's foreign minister met with his Russian counterpart and signed a cooperation agreement on cybersecurity and information and communication technology.[69] The agreement, coming in the aftermath of Iran's various security failures in 2020, seemed designed to improve the protection function of Iran's intelligence bodies as well as its counterintelligence capabilities. The agreement proposed technology transfers, combined training, coordination in multilateral forums, and cybersecurity cooperation.

According to one technical assessment, the cyber cooperation probably will be more focused on intelligence-sharing and cyber defense improvements than on offensive cyber capabilities.[70] Still, much of the cooperation and intelligence sharing could be focused on US malware and other cyber techniques. Russia also might help Iran to reverse-engineer malware that has been deployed against it, for use by the MOIS, Iran's other intelligence services, and possibly Hezbollah and Iranian-supported Shia militia groups. Some of these nonstate actors, according to the assessment, have already displayed sophisticated hacking capabilities.[71]

The Russian invasion of Ukraine in February 2022 appeared to strengthen Iran-Russia security ties, although both regimes faced Western isolation and have had competing oil and gas production interests. During a meeting in May with his Russian counterpart, SNSC secretary Ali Shamkhani recommended increased cooperation to strengthen security ties as part of a joint strategic plan to overcome Western sanctions and boost economic, trade, and financial relations.[72] When Russian president Vladimir Putin visited Tehran in July, Khamenei vocally supported Russian positions and blamed US policy for the war in Ukraine.[73] Following a mid-November meeting between Raisi and Putin in Tehran that highlighted the deepening security relationship, the United States in December 2022 charged that Iran had become Russia's "top military backer" after it armed Russia with hundreds of drones for Moscow's war with Ukraine.[74]

China

The MOIS may find greater future opportunities in expanding its relationship with its other anti-American partner, China. The extent of Iran-China intelligence collaboration is unknown, but there have been hints of intelligence sharing over the years. Since 2010 the two countries have discussed cooperation on a range of matters, including intelligence sharing, counterterrorism, and technical expertise.[75] More than two dozen American intelligence assets reportedly died in China in 2011 and 2012 after Iran purportedly compromised a CIA communication system.[76] According to a 2018 American press report, around the time Iran announced its uncovering of the CIA network in 2013, senior counterintelligence officials from China's Ministry of State Security visited their counterparts in Tehran.[77] At the same time, Chinese, Iranian, and Russian officials were engaged in senior-level communications on cyber issues that some US intelligence officials viewed as an indicator of enhanced coordination among these countries.[78]

In March 2021 Iran and China signed the Joint Comprehensive Strategic Partnership Agreement on economic and defense collaboration. On the security side, it projected increased military and defense cooperation between Tehran and Beijing and called for intelligence sharing. Should the agreement provide Iran access to the technology, training, and expertise of China's intelligence services, the MOIS likely would be a major beneficiary. In particular, given the wide-ranging types and quality of China's surveillance equipment, the ministry could expect the likely acquisition of Chinese camera, facial-recognition, and similar technology to lead to a larger MOIS role in making Iran a more pervasive digital-surveillance state.[79]

Syria

Going back to its support of Iran during the Iran-Iraq War in the 1980s, Syria has been the regime's most constant ally. Damascus throughout the decades has cooperated with Iranian support to Hezbollah and Palestinian militants and has been central to Iran's creation of a deterrent capability using these and other groups against Israel.[80] In 2016 MOIS National Security Strategic Research Center chief Jamal Shafii highlighted cooperative MOIS-IRGC operations in Syria as being critical to Tehran's forward-defense strategy to confront threats and conspiracies beyond Iran's borders.[81] A few years earlier, in February 2012, the US Department of the Treasury sanctioned the MOIS for providing substantial technical assistance to Syrian intelligence and being complicit in human rights abuses in Syria.[82] Confirming some of these charges, Alavi in early 2017 announced that to combat the militant threat emanating from Syria, MOIS technical teams had installed surveillance equipment in Syria to monitor terrorist bases.[83] Although the IRGC-QF remained the primary Iranian security organization in Syria through the early 2020s, the MOIS probably has sustained its secondary role. As an intersection of Iran's shadow war with Israel, pursuit of residual ISIS terrorists, tensions with Ankara over Turkish military interventions, and opposition to the small US military presence there, Syria seems likely to remain a key area for MOIS and IRGC intelligence operations for years to come.

Neighboring States

Iran's relations with its neighbors have often been hostile, but the regime has been capable of cooperation against mutual threats such as terrorism, narcotics, and smuggling. In 2015 Alavi spoke about the need for enhanced security and economic cooperation among the regional intelligence services. He claimed that Iran then had positive and constructive interactions with most of its regional counterparts.[84] In March 2022 Iran and Uzbekistan signed an agreement to establish a joint security commission that envisioned "intelligence sharing and security collaboration" for combating terrorism, extremism, drug trafficking, and other organized crimes.[85] Such positive interactions, however, almost certainly are constrained when mutual threats are absent.

After 2003 the MOIS played a role with the IRGC-QF in advancing Iran's interests in Iraq. Many of Iraq's leading security officials had worked with Iran as exiles battling the regime of Saddam Hussein during the preceding decades.[86] In dealing with the ISIS threat in 2016, Alavi met with senior Iraqi officials about fighting terrorism and other regional security developments.[87] The following year, when MOIS officers working outside of Iran apprehended the ISIS mastermind behind the Tehran terrorist attack, Alavi credited cooperation with "friendly foreign intelligence services," probably a reference to Iraq.[88]

To Iran's east, the MOIS role over the past two decades has been overshadowed by IRGC-QF operations in support of insurgents in Afghanistan and conventional IRGC campaigns against Baluch militants operating out of Pakistan. The ministry possibly was involved in the background when Iranian law enforcement officials met with counterparts from Afghanistan and Pakistan under United Nations auspices in 2007 to establish a series of trust-building measures and joint operations to combat narcotics smuggling.[89] Similarly, given the MOIS counterterrorism mission, it probably was involved in a 2010 Iran-Pakistan agreement to enhance counterterrorism cooperation and improve intelligence-sharing systems.[90] Following Iran's missile attack on purported Jaish al-Adl camps in Pakistan at the start of 2024, Islamabad retaliated with missile and air strikes on alleged Pakistani Baluch separatist camps in Iran.[91] While such occasional hostile actions are likely to complicate relations between the MOIS and its Pakistani counterparts, their common interests in Baluch separatists and drug trafficking in the border regions between the two countries seem likely to sustain opportunities for MOIS-Pakistani cooperation.

With the departure of the US military from Afghanistan and the restoration of the Sunni Taliban government there in 2021, Iran's intelligence services possibly have fewer reasons to continue past levels of support to the Taliban. The IRGC-QF probably will remain the lead intelligence organization for most cooperation, but Khatib's announcement in September 2023 that Iran and the Taliban were working well together to combat terrorism suggested that the MOIS also has a role.[92] The common threat posed by the ISIS-Khorasan terrorist group, which operates in Afghanistan and Pakistan and conducted the January 2024 suicide bombing in Kerman, seems likely to create additional opportunities for continued collaboration.

Iran's most fraught relationships in the region have been with its Gulf Arab neighbors, particularly Saudi Arabia. In 2011, after the US Justice Department accused the IRGC-QF of plotting to assassinate the Saudi ambassador to Washington, MOIS chief Moslehi still traveled to Riyadh for consultations aimed at removing misunderstandings and discussing security issues.[93] In 2017 Alavi hinted that good relations with the Yemeni and Saudi intelligence services enabled the MOIS operation to free an abducted Iranian diplomat from kidnappers belonging to the terrorist group al-Qaeda in the Arabian Peninsula.[94] Apparently intent on using improving relations with Iran's Gulf Arab neighbors in February 2023 to Iran's advantage, Khatib warned those governments against normalizing relations with Israel, advising that such moves brought no security to the region.[95] He repeated the theme in October after condemning Israel's offensive in Gaza, asserting that because circumstances had changed, normalization attempts would go nowhere.[96]

Nonstate Actors

Iran has relationships with several nonstate actors, some of which are part of an informal coalition called the "Axis of Resistance" or "Resistance Front."[97] Since the 1980s Iran has supported, primarily through the IRGC-QF, multiple armed groups, starting in the fragmented regions of Lebanon and the Palestinian territories, followed by Iraq in the 2000s and Syria and Yemen in the 2010s. Assembled to form a deterrent threat against Iran's enemies, the axis comprised the Lebanese Hezbollah, the Palestinian groups Hamas and Palestinian Islamic Jihad, Iraqi and Syrian Shia militias, and the Ansar Allah or Houthi movement in Yemen. More than terrorist groups, these nonstate actors faced different political and security situations that drove their actions and relationships with Iran. For example, Hezbollah and the Iraqi militias are part of the governments of Lebanon and Iraq, while the Houthis control key areas of Yemen. The Iranian leadership allows each axis member its autonomy while helping with coordination and offering some tactical guidance for unified actions that serve the members' goals, such the Iraqi militias' attempts to cause US forces to withdraw from Iraq. At the same time, axis activities serve Iran's interests by diverting Israeli, US, and allied militaries and intelligence services from focusing on or attacking Iran.[98] Following the outbreak of the Israel-Hamas War in October 2023, Iran further stressed the members' independence as it tried to distance itself from the front's operations against US forces and interests.[99]

The IRGC-QF greatly overshadows the MOIS in this arena, despite the latter's early role after its founding in maintaining contacts with militants within the Shia populations of the Gulf Arab states.[100] Over the years, the US government regularly included the MOIS in its charges of Iranian support to terrorism in the Middle East and Latin America, primarily in reference to Hezbollah and some Palestinian militant activities.[101] In 2012 the Treasury Department charged the MOIS with providing support to Hezbollah as well as participating in multiple joint computer-hacking projects with the group.[102] The extent of MOIS cooperation with Sunni Palestinian groups also is unknown, but in February

1999 Palestinian police discovered documents that indicated a MOIS transfer of $35 million to Hamas, allegedly to finance terrorist activities against Israeli targets.[103] The United States subsequently sanctioned the ministry for supporting the group.[104] The MOIS role with the axis probably involves intelligence sharing, specialized training, and technical support the IRGC-QF does not or cannot provide. The latest Israel-Hamas conflict seems likely to increase the axis members' demands for funding and rearming, which may cause Tehran to call on the MOIS to do more in support of the rebuilding.

MOIS contacts with al-Qaeda appear limited to supervising group members living in Iran. Going back to the early 2000s, collaboration between the Islamic Republic and al-Qaeda appeared to vacillate between periods of hostility and cautious tactical accommodation.[105] The regime detained many al-Qaeda members fleeing Afghanistan in late 2001 and later extradited some to their home countries while keeping or allowing others to remain in Iran.[106] Approximately three hundred declassified documents captured from Osama bin Laden's compound in Abbottabad, Pakistan, in 2011 indicated that al-Qaeda viewed Iran as hostile but used the country to smuggle people and money clandestinely.[107]

Tehran apparently struck a deal where al-Qaeda members in Iran refrained from conducting operations in Iranian territory and kept regime authorities informed of their activities.[108] In return, the regime allowed the members to plan and direct operations outside Iran and gave them and their families the freedom of uninhibited travel. In February 2012 the US Treasury Department sanctioned the Ministry of Intelligence for its support of al-Qaeda and its affiliate, al-Qaeda in Iraq.[109] In 2015, as part of its effort to gain the release of the kidnapped Iranian diplomat in Yemen, the regime announced another deal with al-Qaeda in which it released five of the organization's leaders, including its second-in-command, Abu Muhammad al-Masri, who was later gunned down in Tehran by Israeli operatives in 2020.[110]

The MOIS connection to al-Qaeda demonstrated some of the risks of an adversarial relationship. First, linkages to adversarial groups can harm a service's reputation. The killing of al-Masri, for example, was another blow to the ministry's reputation for protecting Iran against outside interference. Being tied to an enduring target in America's war on terrorism, meanwhile, undermined attempts by the Khatami and

Rouhani administrations to improve relations with Iran's neighbors and the West. Moreover, after al-Qaeda in Iraq transformed into ISIS, Iran's earlier tolerance appeared extremely shortsighted as the group mutated into a virulent extremist threat to Iran's security and interests. With Iran isolated from much of the world, however, the MOIS cannot be too scrupulous about where it seeks help in defending against the regime's foes.

Notes

1. "Agency Outlines Iran's Intelligence Units, Duties."
2. US Treasury Department Office of Public Affairs, *Fact Sheet: Sanctions on Iranian Government and Affiliates*, November 8, 2012, https://www.treasury.gov/press-center/press-releases/.
3. "Iran Unveils 'Structural Changes' to Police Force," BBC Monitoring Middle East [IRNA, Mehr News in Persian], December 8, 2021, ProQuest; Amir Toumaj, "Iran's Law Enforcement Shuffle Reflects Concern about Protests," Washington Institute for Near East Policy, January 5, 2022, https://www.washingtoninstitute.org/policy-analysis/irans-law-enforcement-shuffle-reflects-concern-about-protests.
4. Information on the existence of an AFGS intelligence counterpart to the IRGC and Artesh intelligence organizations appears limited to some media mentions that IRGC major general Mohammad Hossein Bagheri, now the AFGS chief, had previously served as AFGS deputy commander for intelligence and operations.
5. "Iran Seeks to Expand Military Cooperation with China," Cihan News Agency, October 14, 2015, ProQuest; Farzin Nadimi, "Who Is Iran's New Armed Forces Chief of Staff?" Washington Institute for Near East Policy, PolicyWatch no. 2,642, July 5, 2016, https://www.washingtoninstitute.org/policy-analysis/who-irans-new-armed-forces-chief-staff.
6. 1983 Ministry of Intelligence Establishment Law.
7. 1983 Ministry of Intelligence Establishment Law.
8. "Agency Outlines Iran's Intelligence Units, Duties"; "Iran Intelligence Revelations: How Khamenei Wields Power," *IranWire*, October 17, 2014, https://iranwire.com/en/features/660; "Rouhani's Intelligence Ministry and Khamenei's IRGC Widen Crackdown ahead of Election"; Buchta, *Who Rules Iran?*, 164.
9. "Agency Outlines Iran's Intelligence Units, Duties."
10. "Covert Terror."
11. "Iran Intelligence Revelations."
12. "Iran Intelligence Revelations."
13. "Iran Press: Politicians Comment on Plans for Intelligence Body Supervision," BBC Monitoring Middle East [Aftab-e Yazd in Persian], September 2, 2005, ProQuest; Bill Samii, "Iran: Who Watches the Watchers?" Radio Free Europe / Radio Liberty, September 6, 2005, https://www.rferl.org/a/1061181.html.
14. "Iran Press: Politicians Comment"; Samii, "Iran: Who Watches the Watchers?"
15. "Iran Press: Politicians Comment."
16. Peterson, "In Iran, a Hardline Hunt"; "Iran: Former Minister Elaborates"; "Iran

Ex-Commander Reveals His Account of Ahmadinezhad's Reaction to 2009 'Sedition,'" BBC Monitoring Middle East [Sharq in Persian], September 2, 2015, ProQuest.

17. Peterson, "In Iran, a Hardline Hunt."
18. "Iran Intelligence Revelations."
19. Sahimi, "Who's Who of Iranian Players"; Khoshnood, "Iran's Killing Machine," 8; "Covert Terror."
20. Sahimi, "Who's Who of Iranian Players."
21. Banerjea, "Revolutionary Intelligence," 99; Toumaj, "Iran's Law Enforcement Shuffle."
22. Saeid Golkar and Kasra Aarabi, "Why Iran's Ali Khamenei Removed Hossein Taeb from the IRGC," *Foreign Policy*, July 8, 2022, https://foreignpolicy.com/20 22/07/08/iran-irgc-khamenei-hossein-taeb-removal-power/.
23. Boroujerdi and Rahimkhani, *Postrevolutionary Iran*, 760; Zimmt, "Intelligence Organization of IRGC," 17–18.
24. Golkar, "Iran's Intelligence Organizations and Transnational Suppression."
25. Zimmt, "Intelligence Organization of IRGC," 3, 28.
26. Zimmt, 13; Randolph, "Iranian IRGC Consolidates Primacy."
27. Peterson, "In Iran, a Hardline Hunt"; Insikt Group, "Despite Infighting and Volatility," 12.
28. "Iran: Official Says Spy Cases."
29. Banerjea, "Revolutionary Intelligence," 97.
30. Arango et al., "Iran Cables."
31. Zimmt, "Intelligence Organization of IRGC," 12–13.
32. Zimmt, 15–16.
33. "Iran: Article Details Petrol Unrest"; "Intel Min. Releases Docs"; "Iran Busts Kurdish 'Terror Cell' ahead of Quds Day Rallies," BBC Monitoring Middle East [Tasnim in Persian], April 29, 2022, ProQuest; "Iran Thwarts Plots against Sunni Clerics, IRGC Officers," Fars News Agency, September 29, 2023, ProQuest.
34. Muhammad Sahimi, "Pro-reform Candidates Did Surprisingly Well at the Ballot Box," *National Interest*, March 3, 2016, http://nationalinterest.org/feature/irans-de ep-state-suffers-stinging-defeat-15382.
35. "Iran Intelligence Ministry Criticises Weekly."
36. "Daily Questions Performance."
37. "Iran Intelligence Ministry Criticises Weekly."
38. "Iran Reformist Daily Slams Outgoing Parliament's New Law as 'Last Sabotage,'" BBC Monitoring Middle East [Sharq in Persian], May 31, 2016, ProQuest.
39. Zimmt, "Intelligence Organization of IRGC," 14.
40. Khoshnood, "Iran Might Purge."
41. Peterson, "In Iran, Assassination Shock"; "Commentary Says Security Issues in Iran Stem from Lack of Coordination," BBC Monitoring Middle East [Etemad in Persian], February 18, 2021, ProQuest.
42. "Commentary Says Security Issues"; Randolph, "Iranian IRGC Consolidates Primacy."
43. "The Shocking Statements of Khatami's Minister of Information: Mossad Has Penetrated in Different Parts of the Country; Officials Should Be Worried about Their Lives," Aftab News, ca. June 2021, https://aftabnews.ir/fa/news/715834/اط

ه%E2%80%8Cدهنده-وزیر-اطلاعات-دولت-خاتمی-موساد-در-بخش%E2%80%8Cهارات-تکان
.ای-مختلف-کشور-نفوذ-کرده-است-مسئولان-نگران-جانشان-باشند

44. Toumaj, "Iran's Law Enforcement Shuffle"; "Iran Unveils 'Structural Changes.'"
45. "Ministry Has Close Relationship with Intelligence Community—Iran Minister," BBC Monitoring Middle East [Voice of the Islamic Republic of Iran in Persian], November 26, 2008, Proquest.
46. "Iranian Intelligence Minister Presents Programs."
47. Zimmt, "Intelligence Organization of IRGC," 16.
48. "Iran Intelligence Minister Discusses Security with New IRGC Chief," BBC Monitoring Middle East [Rajanews in Persian], May 7, 2019, ProQuest.
49. "Iran: Official Says Spy Cases"; "Iran: Hardline Daily Slams Ex-Minister's Remarks on Mossad Infiltration," BBC Monitoring Middle East [Kayhan and Jamaran in Persian], July 1, 2021, ProQuest.
50. "Iran's Rival Intelligence Agencies Seek to 'Boost Synergy,'" BBC Monitoring Middle East [ISNA in Persian], January 31, 2022, ProQuest; "Raisi Urges 'Convergence' among Iran's Intelligence Agencies," BBC Monitoring Middle East [president.ir website in Persian], February 7, 2022, ProQuest.
51. "BBCM Iran Watchlist for 23 June," BBC Monitoring Middle East, June 23, 2022, ProQuest; David S. Cloud and Aresu Eqbal, "Iran's Revolutionary Guard Names New Intelligence Chief amid Suspicious Deaths," *Wall Street Journal*, June 23, 2022, https://www.wsj.com/articles/irans-revolutionary-guard-names-new-intelli gence-chief-amid-suspicious-deaths-11656014544.
52. "BBCM Iran Watchlist for 24 June," BBC Monitoring Middle East, June 24, 2022, ProQuest; Cora Engelbrecht and Farnaz Fassihi, "Iran Dismisses Powerful Intelligence Chief, *New York Times*, June 24, 2022; Zvi Bar'el, "The Iranian Octopus' Arms Are More Important Than Its Head," *Haaretz*, June 24, 2022, ProQuest.
53. Annika Ganzeveld, Amin Soltani, Ashka Jhaveri, Andie Parry, and Nicholas Carl, "Iran Update," AEI Critical Threats Project, June 22, 2023, https://www.criticalth reats.org/analysis/iran-update-june-22-2023.
54. "BBCM Iran Watchlist for 23 June," BBC Monitoring Middle East, June 23, 2023, ProQuest.
55. "BBCM Iran Watchlist for 23 June."
56. On types of intelligence relationships, see Jennifer E. Sims, "Foreign Intelligence Liaisons: Devils, Deals, and Details," *International Journal of Intelligence and CounterIntelligence* 19, no. 2 (2006): 197–200, https:www.tandfonline.com/loi /ujic20.
57. Sims, "Foreign Intelligence Liaisons," 203.
58. Dina Esfandiary and Ariane Tabatabai, *Triple-Axis: Iran's Relations with Russia and China* (London: I. B. Taurus, 2018), 136.
59. "Iranian Intelligence Minister Presents Programs."
60. "Mole Hunt."
61. "Iran Dismantles Large US Cyber Espionage Network: Top Security Official," Mehr News Agency, June 17, 2019, ProQuest.
62. "Hardline Daily Says Iran Infiltrates"; "Iran Dismantles Espionage Network."
63. Wege, "Iran's Intelligence Establishment," 40.
64. "Iran, Russia Discuss Intelligence Sharing," BBC Monitoring Middle East [IRNA in English], September 5, 2008, ProQuest; "Iran, Russia Agree on Intelligence

Sharing," Islamic Republic News Agency, September 5, 2008, at Global Security Intelligence News Archive, https://www.globalsecurity.org/intell/library/news/2008/intell-080905-irna01.htm.

65. Michael R. Gordon, "U.S. Scrambles as Russia Surprises with Mideast Pact," *New York Times International Edition*, September 29, 2015, ProQuest; "Iran/Iraq: Iran Offers to Develop Quadrilateral Baghdad Intelligence Sharing Center to Int'l Coalition," *Asia News Monitor*, December 16, 2015, ProQuest.

66. Esfandiary and Tabatabai, *Triple-Axis*, 134.

67. "Russia, Iran Discuss War on Terror," *Tehran Times*, December 11, 2019, https://www.tehrantimes.com/news/442944/Russia-Iran-discuss-war-on-terror.

68. Farnaz Fassihi and Ronen Bergman, "The Double Life of Britain's Spy in Iran's Regime," *New York Times*, May 1, 2023; "Alireza Akbari Executed over Spying for British Intelligence Agency," Press TV, January 14, 2023, ProQuest.

69. "Iran, Russia Sign Cyber Security Agreement," BBC Monitoring Middle East [IRNA in Persian], January 26, 2021, ProQuest.

70. Morgan Demboski, "Analysis of Iranian Cyber Attack Landscape," IronNet, April 26, 2021, https://www.ironnet.com/blog/iranian-cyber-attack-updates.

71. Demboski. See also Khoshnood, "Russia and Iran Sign Intelligence Pact."

72. "Iran Calls for 'Strategic Plan' with Russia to Overcome Sanctions," BBC Monitoring Middle East [ISNA in Persian], May 27, 2022, ProQuest.

73. Nasser Karimi and Vladimir Isachenkov, "Putin, in Tehran, Gets Strong Support from Iran over Ukraine," *Washington Post*, July 19, 2022, https://www.washingtonpost.com/world/putin-heads-to-tehran-for-talks-with-leaders-of-iran-turkey/2022/07/19/dce243da-0722-11ed-80b6-43f2bfcc6662_story.html.

74. Hadi Semati, "Iran in 2022: Protests, Politics & Russian Alliance," USIP Iran Primer, December 21, 2022, https://iranprimer.usip.org/blog/2022/dec/21/iran-2022-protests-politics-russian-alliance; Courtney Kube and Carol E. Lee, "Russia Is Providing 'Unprecedented' Military Support to Iran in Exchange for Drones, Officials Say," NBC News, December 9, 2022, https://www.nbcnews.com/politics/russia-providing-unprecedented-military-support-iran-exchange-drones-o-rcna60921.

75. Esfandiary and Tabatabai, *Triple-Axis*, 134.

76. Peterson, "Behind Iran Spy Drama."

77. Dorfman and McLaughlin, "CIA's Communications Suffered."

78. Dorfman and McLaughlin.

79. Demboski, "Analysis of Iranian Cyber Attack Landscape"; Arvin Khoshnood and Ardavan Khoshnood, "Security Implications of the Iran-China Deal," BESA Center Perspectives Paper no. 2,019, May 10, 2021, https://besacenter.org/iran-china-deal-security-implications.

80. Karim Sadjadpour, "Iran's Unwavering Support to Assad's Syria," *CTC Sentinel* 6, no. 8 (August 2013): 12–13.

81. "Official Says USA Formed 'Intelligence NATO.'"

82. US Treasury Department, Office of Foreign Assets Control, "Designation of One Entity Pursuant to Executive Order 13572 of April 29, 2011, 'Blocking Property of Certain Persons with Respect to Human Rights Abuses in Syria,'" February 13, 2012, https://plus.cq.com/doc/fedreg-4034208.

83. "MOIS Head: We're Monitoring Terrorists' Bases in Syria," AEI Critical Threats

Project, March 15, 2017, https://www.criticalthreats.org/briefs/iran-news-round
-up/iran-news-round-up-march-15-2017.

84. "Alavi: The Cooperation of the Region's Intelligence Services Is Essential for the
    Security of Economic Transactions," Jamaran, February 22, 2015, https://www.ja
    maran.news/fa/tiny/news-75612.

85. "Iran, Uzbekistan Agree to Set Up 'Joint Security Commission,'" BBC Monitor-
    ing Middle East [Mehr News Agency in Persian], March 9, 2022, ProQuest.

86. Karen Zraick, "Leaked Iran Cables: Key Findings from Secret Documents," *New
    York Times*, November 18, 2019, https://www.nytimes.com/2019/11/18/world/mid
    dleeast/iran-iraq-cables.html.

87. "Iran Intelligence Minister Meets Top Iraqi Officials in Baghdad," Press TV, May
    15, 2016, ProQuest.

88. "MOIS Apprehends Tehran Terrorist Attack 'Mastermind' outside of Iran," AEI
    Critical Threats Project, June 13, 2017, https://www.criticalthreats.org/briefs/iran
    -news-round-up/iran-news-round-up-june-13-2017.

89. "UN Welcomes Iran, Afghanistan, Pakistan Joint Anti-Drug Trafficking Efforts,"
    Moj News Agency, December 19, 2012, ProQuest.

90. "Iran, Pakistan to Enhance Anti-Terror Cooperation," Moj News Agency, Septem-
    ber 4, 2010, ProQuest.

91. Frances Mao, Caroline Davies, and Paul Adams, "Pakistan Launches Retaliatory
    Strikes into Iran, Killing Nine People," BBC, January 18, 2024, https://www.bbc
    .com/news/world-asia-68014882.

92. Shabnam von Hein, "Iran and the Taliban: Counterterrorism Cooperation?" Deut-
    sche Welle, September 20, 2023, https://www.dw.com/en/iran-and-the-taliban
    -counterterrorism-cooperation/a-66866895.

93. "Iranian Intelligence Minister Visits Saudi Arabia," Moj News Agency, December
    13, 2011, ProQuest.

94. "Narration of Proposed Minister of Intelligence."

95. "Intelligence Minister: Arab Nations Unable to Buy Security through Normaliza-
    tion with Israel," Fars News Agency, February 26, 2023, ProQuest.

96. "Iran's Intelligence Minister Vows Harsh Revenge Awaiting Israel over Gaza Car-
    nage," Fars News Agency, October 22, 2023, ProQuest.

97. One other state, Bashar Assad's Syria, joins Iran in the Axis of Resistance.

98. For more details on the militants' and Iran's actions, see Sina Toossi, "How Iran
    Really Sees the Israel-Hamas War," *Foreign Policy*, November 2, 2023, https://
    foreignpolicy.com/2023/11/02/how-iran-really-sees-the-israel-hamas-war; Narges
    Bajoghli and Vali Nasr, "How the War in Gaza Revived the Axis of Resistance,"
    Foreign Affairs, January 17, 2024, https://www.foreignaffairs.com/united-states
    /how-war-gaza-revived-axis-resistance; Alissa J. Rubin, "How Closely Does Iran
    Control Its Proxy Forces? It Depends," *New York Times*, February 2, 2024, https://
    www.nytimes.com/2024/02/02/world/middleeast/iran-militias-israel.html; "Proxy
    Attacks: Iraq, Syria and Yemen," USIP Iran Primer, December 14, 2023, http://iran
    primer.usip.org/blog/2023/dec/14/proxy-attacks-iraq-syria-yemen.

99. Leily Nikounazar, "Iran's Supreme Leader Issues Tehran's Latest Denial of In-
    volvement in Israel Attacks," *New York Times*, October 10, 2023, https://www
    .nytimes.com/2023/10/10/world/middleeast/iran-israel-hamas-attacks.html;
    "Spokesman: Iran Not Ordering Regional Resistance Groups," Fars News Agency,

December 7, 2023, ProQuest; Cassandra Vinograd, "Iran Denies Ordering Drone Strike as Biden Weighs a Response," *New York Times*, January 29, 2024, https://www.nytimes.com/2024/01/29/world/middleeast/iran-us-troops-jordan.html; Toossi, "How Iran Really Sees the Israel-Hamas War"; Rubin, "How Closely Does Iran Control?"

100. For example, the CIA wrote about Iranian networks among the Shia populations in the 1980s in CIA Directorate of Intelligence, *Iranian Threats to Persian Gulf States*, NESA M-87-20067, June 29, 1987, https://www.cia.gov/readingroom/document/cia-rdp90t00114r000700390001-9.

101. For example, see US State Department, *Country Reports on Terrorism 2012*, May 30, 2013, https://2009-2017.state.gov/j/ct/rls/crt/2012/index.htm; and "Designation of One Entity Pursuant to Executive Order 13572."

102. US Department of the Treasury, "Treasury Designates Iranian Ministry."

103. US Congress, Senate Foreign Relations Committee, Subcommittee on Near Eastern and South and Central Asian Affairs, 112th Cong., 2nd Sess., July 25, 2012 (Matthew Levitt testimony).

104. US Department of the Treasury, "Treasury Designates Iranian Ministry."

105. See Bryce Loidolt, "Al-Qaeda's Iran Dilemma: Evidence from the Abbottabad Records," *Studies in Conflict & Terrorism* (July 16, 2020): 1–28; and Assaf Moghadam, "Marriage of Convenience: The Evolution of Iran and al-Qa'ida's Tactical Cooperation," *CTC Sentinel* 10, no. 4 (April 2017): 12–18.

106. "Iran Says It Made Al Qaeda Arrests; Rank of Suspects Is Still Unknown," *Washington Post*, May 27, 2003; Faye Bowers, "Iran Holds Al Qaeda's Top Leaders," *Christian Science Monitor*, July 28, 2003, 1; Douglas Farah and Dana Priest, "Bin Laden's Son Plays Key Role in Al Qaeda," *Washington Post*, October 14, 2003.

107. Loidolt, "Al-Qaeda's Iran Dilemma," 3.

108. Moghadam, "Marriage of Convenience," 15. See also Helen Cooper, "Treasury Dept., Citing Six People as Operatives, Accuses Iran of Aiding Al Qaeda," *New York Times*, July 29, 2011.

109. US Department of the Treasury "Treasury Designates Iranian Ministry."

110. Adam Goldman, Eric Schmitt, Franaz Fassihi, and Ronen Bergman, "Al Qaeda's No. 2, Accused in U.S. Embassy Attacks, Was Killed in Iran," *New York Times*, November 13, 2020, https://www.nytimes.com/2020/11/13/world/middleeast/al-masri-abdullah-qaeda-dead.html.

6

Cultural Representations

Chapter 3 provided a discussion of the ministry's organizational culture and the values, practices, and goals that guide routine MOIS activities. This chapter examines the service's cultural representation to the country and the wider world. This refers to MOIS efforts to use media, entertainment, and other forms of popular culture to present itself as it wants to be seen and, secondarily, to distort and marginalize the perceptions of regime opponents. Drawing on a legacy that predates the establishment of the Islamic Republic, the Ministry of Intelligence has been active for decades in using media to burnish its reputation, advance national security goals, and counter negative portrayals of its work.

The Iranian revolutionaries of the late 1970s understood the value of presenting themselves as representatives of Iran's true culture and aspirations. Their large public protests in Iran and Western capitals showed a sophisticated understanding of the impact of television and other media. In particular, a significant opposition demonstration in Washington in November 1977 that disrupted a state visit by the shah seemed to harm his standing as a leader. When tear gas fired at the protestors wafted over the welcoming ceremony on the White House lawn, the scene created a perception of a weakened monarch, who along with the US president publicly wiped away tears.[1] Similarly, the group Muslim Student Followers of the Imam's Line used various media effectively from late 1979 to early 1981 to broadcast their political message and instill national pride during the 444-day US hostage crisis.[2] Subsequently, regime leaders gave media an important role in their state-building project, using it to avert what Khomeini and Khamenei believed were Western attempts to wield culture as a means to influence Iran's population.[3]

The ministry appears to view soft war—the combination of perceived Western information and psychological operations; popular Western culture; and Persian-language satellite-television programs, movies, and Internet content—as a genuine threat. Khamenei's use of the term seems intentionally linked to American political scientist Joseph S. Nye's use of the term "soft power" to describe the importance of the attractiveness of a country's culture, political ideals, and policies in advancing its foreign policy objectives.[4] To counter the perceived soft power threat, the leader's office has given media production supported by the regime a privileged platform since the late 2000s as Khamenei has repeatedly discussed the need to "vaccinate" society against soft war.[5]

The regime has been working in a difficult environment because Iranians are exposed to and expect a wide variety of engaging media. For example, starting in the 1990s Iranian cinema became recognized as one of the world's most innovative and exciting as filmmakers, politicized by regime restrictions, mastered ambiguity to present immensely popular works that provided a social critique not otherwise available in Iran.[6] Over this same time frame, Persian has become one of the most used languages on the Internet, which, although heavily censored in Iran, was used by an estimated fifty-seven million Iranians in 2021.[7] Moreover, in recent years, social media platforms have become ubiquitous in Iran, while Iranians watch dozens of diaspora Persian-language television stations via widely available but technically illegal satellite dishes.

Aware of cinema's power, the regime under Khomeini made a concerted but ultimately failed attempt to dominate film using the Ministry of Culture and Art. It showed its hand when it later recast this bureaucracy as the Ministry of Culture and Islamic Guidance and began to subject movies and other media to a process of Islamization.[8] In the 2000s Khamenei's soft war concept incorporated the idea of "cultural invasion," which became the hard-line conservatives' ideological tool for discrediting their leftist opponents and suppressing domestic calls for more freedom for the arts and media.[9] By 2006 Khamenei had highlighted the potential danger posed to the regime by the media when he

commented to filmmakers, "Your influence is many times as much as
. . . that of a clergyman or a preacher or a writer."[10] Concern about the
media remained unabated through the late 2010s as the regime continued to demonize Western and diaspora media for waging soft war with
"fake news" and disinformation campaigns meant to sow discord among
the Iranian people.[11] Alavi, despite his reformist leanings, conveyed an
overtone of an intent to stifle criticism when he stated in 2019 that MOIS
activities sought to create security in the media and cultural arenas.[12]

The MOIS and the Media

The ministry for many of its early years appeared to remain in the background of government efforts to use television programs, movies, and
other broadcast media to influence domestic audiences and disseminate
its propaganda. It cooperated with Islamic Republic of Iran Broadcasting (IRIB), a state-controlled television and radio organization whose
head is appointed by the supreme leader, on disinformation campaigns
and propaganda dissemination. In 1996, the MOIS sponsored an IRIB
television program called *Hoviyyat* (Identity), which Said Emami, before being charged with being the mastermind of the Chain Murders,
claimed in a videotaped speech to have initiated.[13] The series focused
each week on a different regime critic, particularly intellectuals and artists, and smeared them as un-Islamic foreign agents and security threats.
The program notoriously began with a shot of a $100 bill in which the
portrait of Benjamin Franklin morphed into the face of that week's featured intellectual critic, to infer that the United States was behind their
criticism. *Hoviyyat* also spliced in scenes of exiled royalists and oppositionists to imply a connection with the targeted Iranian. The series did
not last long, however, because Iranian viewers saw through its transparent fearmongering.[14]

The ministry produced and broadcast documentary films through IRIB
about successful MOIS operations, although the impact was mixed.[15] In
mid-2007, for example, Iran broadcast a likely MOIS-produced television program, *In the Name of Democracy*, that included the coerced
confessions of two Iranian American academics, Haleh Esfandiari and
Kian Tajbakhsh, along with images of the generally peaceful revolutions

of the mid-2000s in Georgia, Ukraine, and Lebanon.[16] The intent was to portray Western nongovernmental organizations and scholarly exchanges as part of a US-financed plot to undermine the regime. After her release, however, Esfandiari wrote that subsequent encounters with Iranians on the street suggested that the footage of the color revolutions had an opposite effect from the discouraging one the regime intended.[17]

After the capture of Abdulmalik Rigi in 2010, the MOIS provided unprecedented news-coverage access. Moslehi appeared on national television to explain the operation, emphasize MOIS competence, and stress America's alleged culpability for Jundallah's separatist violence. Iranian broadcasts highlighted a photograph of Rigi allegedly at a US base in Afghanistan. The presentations also included a statement by the Jundallah leader claiming that he had been promised military support by the United States.[18] Years later, in 2019, the IRGC commander praised *Second View*, an MOIS television documentary on Rigi's arrest, and credited it with changing public opinion, presumably in favor of the regime, as well as with altering "the enemy's assumptions" about Iran.[19]

Similarly, the MOIS used a 2011 television documentary, *A Diamond for Deception*, to claim that an MOIS officer, Mohammad Reza Madhi, had infiltrated an exiled opposition group and prevented a plan to create what was described as a "government in exile."[20] The documentary, which was aired just a few days before the second anniversary of the disputed 2009 reelection of President Ahmadinejad, sought to discredit the Iranian opposition movement by claiming it was supported by Western countries. Madhi, who presented himself as a disgruntled former IRGC officer when he met with oppositionists, made unsubstantiated allegations about Western funding of Iranian opposition groups and claimed to have met Vice President Joe Biden and Secretary of State Hillary Clinton, which the US government denied. Nonetheless, the documentary advanced MOIS efforts to present the ministry as an active and effective regime defender.[21]

Other MOIS programs and documentaries continued this effort with similar mixed success. In mid-2019, following the purported disruption of a CIA communication network, the ministry produced a polished video that illustrated how the CIA allegedly recruited Iranians outside the country with promises of visas and cash, provided the new assets with encrypted communication gear, and tasked them with spying on Iranian nuclear and military sites.[22] The nineteen-minute documentary, called *Hunting the Spies*, trumpeted MOIS counterespionage capabilities against US methods. In the video, Alavi boasts about infiltrating "the very source" of American attacks, which the documentary called "an undeclared war."[23]

The documentary provided various details about alleged CIA tradecraft, such as the use of "fake companies" to recruit Iranians with offers of visas and help with establishing businesses in Iran to collect information.[24] It described how assets were trained in third countries in intelligence collection and interrogation resistance and included audio from purported wiretaps of communications with CIA assets in multiple countries. In one scene, a young Iranian woman described how she was recruited by the CIA in Sweden. In another, a "spy" detailed how he followed email instructions and picked up a secure communication device hidden in a brick under a tree. The broadcast also featured an unidentified blonde woman in Dubai speaking Persian with an American accent who credited MOIS effectiveness, saying that her location was "dangerous" because Iranian intelligence was "spread everywhere."[25]

To validate MOIS claims and possibly embarrass Washington, the documentary was supplemented by Iranian media reports that published photographs of alleged American handlers along with documents, business cards, and other details.[26] Apparently as part of the ministry's popular intelligence public-education approach, MOIS officials in these press reports described and denigrated alleged CIA recruitment and agent-running procedures with the goal of helping Iranians avoid traps.[27] They also discussed how they gained knowledge of purported CIA agent–exfiltration routes out of Iran to intercept and arrest some of the suspects.[28] The documentary and newspaper reports pressed the themes of MOIS competence and seeming omnipresence with depictions of its adversary's deceitfulness, unreliability, and defeat.

Other documentaries meant to promote MOIS effectiveness and discredit the MEK have cast the ministry in a bad light. In 2012 Iran convicted and executed confessed assassin Majid Jamali-Fashi for his role in an Israeli-directed killing of a nuclear scientist. Anonymous sources in Israeli intelligence and American diplomatic circles later conveyed to Western media that Israel was behind the assassinations and Fashi had given a generally true confession.[29] IRIB broadcast an MOIS-provided television program on other alleged conspirators, titled *Bash-gah-e Terror* (The terror club).[30] The IRIB program focused on MEK members and sympathizers allegedly recruited by Mossad and rounded up by the MOIS. These Iranians confessed to having received forty-five days of training in Israel before operating in multicell teams to surveil their victims, determine routines, and then execute the instructions given by their Israeli handlers.[31]

The broadcast confessions apparently meant to create a sense of national unity among Iranians, rally them against Israeli and Western interference, and discredit politicians seeking better relations with the West.[32] However, in 2019 Maziar Ebrahimi, one of the alleged conspirators, appeared in a BBC documentary claiming the confessions were largely obtained under torture after the MOIS misidentified and arrested the wrong suspects.[33] In the IRIB broadcast, Ebrahimi had confessed to being in command of operations to assassinate two nuclear scientists. Later, after an IRGC interrogation determined Ebrahimi was innocent, he was released and left Iran for Germany.[34] In an example of MOIS accountability to the legislature, Alavi went before the Majles's National Security and Foreign Policy Committee in September 2019 to answer questions about the affair, even though it occurred during the previous administration.[35] The MOIS still probably suffered some reputational damage from the confirmation of popular views of the ministry's brutality while reinforcing establishment views that by allowing Ebrahimi's release it had been too lenient.

Popular Intelligence in Film and Television

While nominally fact-based MOIS documentaries seek to highlight the competence of ministry operations and discredit the regime's domestic and foreign foes, other MOIS media seem to focus on educating Iranians about security threats and encouraging their support for the regime and ministry. In February 2021 Alavi revealed that the ministry played a substantial role in the production of films and television shows, confirming what had long been suspected by regime opponents.[36] Saying that the productions were intended to "educate the public" and "protect society against espionage," Alavi attributed several films and television series to his ministry, although some film producers disputed his claim.[37] Among these productions, the Rigi case and foreign threats against Iran's nuclear program were popular subjects. Moreover, some MOIS-supported films and shows presented the theme that the MEK, Saudi Arabia, Israel, and the United States were responsible for the Green Movement. They also presented MOIS personnel as effective spy hunters who embody the dedication, honesty, and courage desired of Iranian intelligence officers.[38]

Cyanur (Cyanide) is one of the films described as MOIS-supported that attempted to discredit the MEK.[39] The 2015 film appeals to audiences by telling a love story involving two MEK members as it recounts the group's prerevolution development. Part of this evolution involves the split between Marxist and Islamist MEK factions. The film highlights the conflicts between key early MEK figures, some of whom would form the Mujahedin of the Islamic Revolution, which was a foundation of the Revolutionary Guard. The film's name comes from its tragic ending when one of the lovers must choose to take cyanide to avoid interrogation or risk putting the other in danger.

That same year, the MOIS helped to produce *Rubah* (The fox), a typical spy thriller.[40] In the film, MOIS officers are in a race against time to prevent the murder of a nuclear scientist by a Mossad agent and trained assassin, who, in a slap at one of the regime's main antagonists, is presented as the brother of the then Israeli prime minister Benjamin Netanyahu. The MOIS also supported the 2016 anti-MEK drama *Emkan-e Mina* (Mina's choice).[41] This movie is about the happily married Mina and Mehran, whose lives are disrupted when Mina is recruited into the MEK. As his wife becomes absorbed in the group's violent activities, Mehran becomes suspicious, and the marriage unravels over their differences.

In 2019 the ministry supported two well-regarded movies about the Rigi case.[42] *Shabi ke Mah Kamel Shod* (The night of the full moon) is based on the true story of Faezeh Mansouri, a young woman from Tehran, who falls in love with and marries Abdul Hamid Rigi, the brother of the Jundallah leader.[43] Faezeh slowly becomes aware of the rebellious actions of some of her husband's family members. She and Abdul

Hamid try to escape to Pakistan but are intercepted by Abdulmalik Rigi, who involves them in Jundallah operations until the MOIS captures the two Rigi brothers. The second film, *Ruz-e Sefr* (Day zero) depicts the MOIS operation that resulted in Rigi's arrest.[44]

In his 2021 comments, Alavi singled out the television series *Khane-ye Amn* (Safe house) as a ministry production.[45] *Khane-ye Amn* is a thriller that first aired in 2016 in which MOIS officers hunt spies, terrorists, and traitors. In one storyline, MOIS counterterrorist and anticorruption teams unwind complex terrorist and economic situations to track down ISIS terrorists and prevent an attack in Tehran. Another episode that aired in 2020 presented the case of exiled dissident Jamshid Sharmahd, whom the regime abducted from Dubai in July 2020. By the fall of 2020 fifty episodes of *Khane-ye Amn* had aired, nearly all of which, according to a human rights organization, portrayed real cases involving detainees facing politically motivated charges.[46] Other television series associated with the ministry include *Paazel* (Puzzle), which apparently debuted in 2014 as *Amel-e-Savvom* (The third agent), and *Saregh-e Ruh* (The soul thief). In one of the former program's episodes, MOIS officers discover that spies have gained entry into Iran's nuclear energy program and must try to stop their plans to use sabotage to humiliate Iran in front of foreign guests and journalists.[47]

The IRGC Approach to Cultural Representation

By trying to accentuate a quiet competence, MOIS representation differs from that of the IRGC Intelligence Organization, which has taken a more political and self-aggrandizing approach to its cultural representations. Guard cultural producers recognized in the mid-2000s that entertainment needed to connect with Iran's increasingly young population and move away from what they called "the 'propaganda' of the 1980s and 1990s."[48] Common tropes in subsequent proregime films and television programs incorporated banned pop songs from Iranian diaspora singers and the use of irreligious and immoral characters who learn to believe in the revolution from pious IRGC and Basij role models.[49]

Films likely produced under IRGC auspices included the 2015 production *Film-e-Natamami Bara-ye Dokhtaram Somayyeh* (An unfinished film for my daughter Somayeh) and the 2011 documentary *Gorgha*

Figure 6.1: MOIS television program and film posters (clockwise from top left): *Cyanur, Rubah, Khane-ye Amn, Shabi ke Mah Kamel Shod.*

(The wolves), both of which denigrated the MEK. The former told the story of Iranian refugees who suffer various crimes and misfortunes after joining the MEK at a camp in Iraq. The film's intent to discourage frustrated Iranian youth from joining any opposition movement was partially camouflaged by negative portrayals of the Islamic Republic that made it difficult to detect the regime's hand in its production.[50] *Gorgha*, meanwhile, used Iraqi film and documentation captured after the US removal of Saddam Hussein's regime in 2003 to show the MEK's connection to Iran's foreign enemies. In 2014 it was placed into Iran's high school curriculum.[51]

The IRGC-IO apparently was behind *Gando*, one of the more popular proregime television series.[52] It was an expensive and slickly produced spy thriller that portrayed the IRGC as virtually invincible (a gando being a small, agile crocodile indigenous to southeastern Iran that is renowned for its patience, tenacity, and cunning in hunting). Unlike the more apolitical MOIS productions, the show actively supported hard-line conservative political positions. Several episodes portrayed President Rouhani's administration, particularly the Foreign Ministry, as infiltrated by foreign spies during the negotiations that led to the JCPOA deal.[53]

In addition to this apparent attempt to turn public opinion against the administration's support for dialogue and relations with the West, the show attacked opposition activists and Western journalists as enemies of the state while depicting pragmatic Iranian politicians as sellouts to America and Israel.[54] The show's first season centered on a fictional representation of Jason Rezaian, the *Washington Post* correspondent arrested on espionage charges by the Guard in 2014 and freed in a January 2016 prisoner swap deal.[55] Another *Gando* storyline featured Ruhollah Zam, the Iranian opposition activist whom the IRGC lured to Baghdad in 2019 and then captured, tried, and executed.[56] *Gando* was produced by the Shahid Avini Cultural and Artistic Institute, which was close to the IRGC and Basij and had Mehdi Taeb, the brother of former longtime IRGC-IO chief Hossein Taeb, as its vice chairman.[57]

The IRGC produced another highly popular television series about the judiciary, called *Aghazadeh* (The highborn).[58] "Aghazadeh" usually is an unflattering term for the spoiled rich children of Iran's elite. Its connotations of nepotism and corruption undoubtedly appeal to Iranian audiences, who would be eager to see the show's aghazadeh villain face justice. The show, described by one human rights group as the "most-watched" in Iran, used sensationalist and sexually charged plots to attract audiences while whitewashing the mistreatment of dissidents.[59] To temper any antiregime implications, the show's hero was an aghazadeh who had embraced revolutionary values. One of the series' apparent goals was to attack the integrity of Iran's defense attorneys to undermine legal challenges to state practices and justify the repression of nonviolent dissent.

Super Spies versus Secret Police

As recently as late 2019, according to Iranian press reports, another controversial documentary revealed a struggle between the MOIS and the IRGC over the use of media to influence the populace and enhance the intelligence services' status.[60] In November one of Iran's main television networks began a broadcast of *Maznoonin-e Hamishegi* (Permanent suspects), a revealingly paranoid title for a documentary on Kavus Seyyed-Emami, an Iranian Canadian professor and environmentalist who died in prison in 2018, and other environmental activists arrested by the IRGC. The TV network, however, halted the show after only three minutes, which it blamed on technical problems. Iranian media instead suggested that complaints about airing the program before the activists had been convicted played a role in a decision by government officials to end the broadcast.[61] The regime possibly intervened to avoid a repeat of the embarrassing documentary *Bashgah-e Terror*, which had been discredited just a few months earlier.

   Such controversies probably represent only one type of major challenge facing the Ministry of Intelligence should it continue trying to improve its standing with the Iranian people. Its claimed counterespionage victories at home are overshadowed by the security services' repeated failures to prevent assassinations and major sabotage incidents. Professions of the ministry's piety and professionalism are undermined by MOIS and parallel intelligence organization abuses of the judicial process and their resort to torture and harsh interrogation methods. Past mistaken arrests and the broadcasting of false confessions almost certainly create serious credibility problems for the ministry's image making.

Gauging the ministry's overall reputation, however, is difficult. Beyond occasional anecdotal reporting on popular Iranian views, data is absent on the effectiveness of MOIS efforts to represent itself as it wants to be seen. As one of many arms of a repressive regime, the ministry does not appear to have a positive standing within Iran. Its claims to some successes against Iran's enemies and to being less harsh and slightly more law-abiding than the IRGC and other security organizations do little to mitigate the negative aspects of its reputation. Beyond Iran's borders, views of the MOIS are likely to remain focused on its human rights abuses, involvement in lethal external operations, and occasional ineptitude in overseas operations.

Notes

1. Paul W. Valentine, "2 Iran Factions Clash; 124 Hurt at White House," *Washington Post*, November 16, 1977, ProQuest.
2. Mark Bowden, *Guests of the Ayatollah: The First Battle in America's War with Militant Islam* (New York: Atlantic Monthly Press, 2006), 190.
3. Narges Bajoghli, "*The Outcasts*: The Start of 'New Entertainment' in Pro-Regime Filmmaking in the Islamic Republic of Iran," *Middle East Critique* 26, no. 1 (2017): 66. The widely popular 2007 movie *Ekhrajiha* (The outcasts) was a slapstick comedy that featured a group of hoodlums who, to impress their girlfriends and wives, journey to the Iran-Iraq warfront with no intention to fight. Over the course of the film, a kind Basij soldier helps the group and transforms them into men worthy of their comrades and, by extension, the Islamic Republic.
4. Bajoghli, 66. On soft power, see Joseph S. Nye, "Soft Power and American Foreign Policy," *Political Science Quarterly* 119, no. 2 (2004): 255–70.
5. Narges Bajoghli, *Iran Reframed: Anxieties of Power in the Islamic Republic* (Stanford, CA: Stanford University Press, 2019), 39; Bajoghli, "*The Outcasts*," 66.
6. Ziba Mir-Hosseini, "Iranian Cinema," *Middle East Report*, no. 219 (2001), https://merip.org/2001/06/iranian-cinema/.
7. Bajoghli, "*The Outcasts*," 65; Holly Dagres, "Iranians on #Social Media," Atlantic Council, December 15, 2021, 4, https://www.atlanticcouncil.org/in-depth-research-reports/report/iranians-on-socialmedia/.
8. Mir-Hosseini, "Iranian Cinema."
9. Mir-Hosseini.
10. Peterson, *Let the Swords Encircle Me*, 421.
11. Bajoghli, *Iran Reframed*, 44; "West Seeks to Sow Seeds of Discords between Iranian People, Officials—Ministry," BBC Monitoring Middle East [IRNA in English], June 21, 2012, ProQuest.

12. "Iran Security Official Claims."

13. Elaine Sciolino, *Persian Mirrors: The Elusive Face of Iran* (New York: Free Press, 2000), 242; Afshin Valinejad, "Students Defy Iranian Authorities," Associated Press, November 30, 1999, https://apnews.com/article/22805d48e2245db6bc e1bc3a63ae1d4f.

14. Sciolino, *Persian Mirrors*, 242; Abrahamian, *Tortured Confessions*, 222.

15. Library of Congress, *Iran's Ministry of Intelligence and Security*, 41–42.

16. Peterson, *Let the Swords Encircle Me*, 418–20.

17. Peterson, 422.

18. Library of Congress, *Iran's Ministry of Intelligence and Security*, 42; Margaret Coker, "A Foreign Hand in Protests? Iranians See Proof in Their History," *New York Times*, January 4, 2018, ProQuest.

19. "Iran Intelligence Minister Discusses Security."

20. Golnaz Esfandiari, "Alleged Iranian Agent Who Infiltrated Opposition Claims He Met with Hillary Clinton," Radio Free Europe / Radio Liberty, June 10, 2011, https://www.rferl.org/a/iran_agent_opposition_clinton_intelligence_minis try/24231353.html.

21. Esfandiari.

22. "Iran Documentary Alleges 'Shattering Blow' to CIA Spy Network," BBC Monitoring Middle East [Press TV in English], July 21, 2019, ProQuest; Peterson, "Behind Iran Spy Drama."

23. "Iran Documentary Alleges 'Shattering Blow.'"

24. "Iran Documentary Alleges 'Shattering Blow.'"

25. Peterson, "Behind Iran Spy Drama."

26. "Mole Hunt"; "Iran Documentary Alleges 'Shattering Blow'"; "Director-General of the Ministry of Intelligence Counter-Espionage"; "Ministry of Intelligence's Second Strike against CIA," Fars News Agency, July 22, 2019, https://www.fars news.ir/news/13980431000263.

27. "Mole Hunt"; "Iran Documentary Alleges 'Shattering Blow.'"

28. "Director-General of the Ministry of Intelligence Counter-Espionage"; "Ministry of Intelligence's Second Strike."

29. Karl Vick, "Mossad Cutting Back on Covert Operations inside Iran, Officials Say," *Time*, March 30, 2012, http://world.time.com/2012/03/30/mossad-cutting-back-on-covert-operations-inside-iran-officials-say/; Roblin, "Israel Tried to 'Eliminate' Iran's Nuclear Program by Killing Scientists."

30. Paul Mutter, "Media Watch: 'Terror Club': Iranian TV's Prime-Time Assassination 'Confessions,'" Tehran Bureau, August 9, 2012, https://www.pbs.org/wgbh /pages/frontline/tehranbureau/2012/08/media-watch-terror-club-iranian-tvs-prime -time-assassination-confessions.html; Roblin, "Israel Tried to 'Eliminate.'"

31. Roblin.

32. Library of Congress, *Iran's Ministry of Intelligence and Security*, 44.

33. "Article Calls on Iran's Intelligence to Clarify Claims by Former Prisoner," BBC Monitoring Middle East [Alef in Persian], August 8, 2019, ProQuest; "Iran Report on Intelligence Ministry Lawsuit."

34. "Article Calls on Iran's Intelligence."

35. "Iran Report on Intelligence Ministry Lawsuit."

36. "Iran's Intelligence Establishment Is Spreading Propaganda through Films and TV," Center for Human Rights in Iran, March 31, 2021, https://iranhumanrights .org/2021/03/irans-intelligence-establishment-is-spreading-propaganda -through-film-and-tv/; Shahriar Kia, "Iranian Intelligence Minister's Statement Unwittingly Invites International Scrutiny," National Council of Resistance of Iran, February 12, 2021, https://www.ncr-iran.org/en/news/iran-resistance/iranian -intelligence-ministers-statement-unwittingly-invites-international-scrutiny/.

37. Kia, "Iranian Intelligence Minister's Statement." Producers' disagreements covered in "Commentary Says Security Issues."

38. Bajoghli, *Iran Reframed*, 85.

39. Kia, "Iranian Intelligence Minister's Statement." Except where noted, the descriptions of these MOIS-produced films were taken from promotional material in Persian and English from film and streaming websites, such as www.imdb.com and https://en.ifilmtv.ir.

40. "Director Says Film on Iran's Slain Nuclear Scientists Box Office Failure," BBC Monitoring Middle East [ISNA in Persian], April 16, 2015, ProQuest; Kia, "Iranian Intelligence Minister's Statement."

41. Kia, "Iranian Intelligence Minister's Statement."

42. Kia.

43. "'When the Moon Was Full' ('Shabi Ke Maah Kamel Shod'): Film Review," *Hollywood Reporter*, April 30, 2019, https://www.hollywoodreporter.com/movies /movie-reviews/moon-was-full-shabi-ke-maah-kamel-shod-review-fajr-2019-120 6112/.

44. "Record-Holder Titles with Most Awards at 38th Fajr Film Festival," *Iran Daily*, February 12, 2020, ProQuest; Kia, "Iranian Intelligence Minister's Statement."

45. "Iran's Intelligence Establishment Spreading Propaganda."

46. "Iran's Intelligence Establishment Spreading Propaganda"; "Films and Series Made with the Help of the Ministry of Intelligence," Khabar Online, February 14, 2021, https://www.khabaronline.ir /news/1486122.

47. Kia, "Iranian Intelligence Minister's Statement."

48. Bajoghli, "*The Outcasts*," 62.

49. Bajoghli, 62.

50. Bajoghli, 87–91.

51. Bajoghli, 95–96.

52. Ramin Mostaghim and Nabih Bulos, "How Iran Parlayed Its Answer to 'Homeland' into Must-See TV," *Los Angeles Times*, July 22, 2019, ProQuest.

53. Sina Toossi, "Iran's Hardliners Are Using a TV Thriller to Undermine Their Rivals," *Foreign Policy*, April 28, 2021, https://foreignpolicy.com/2021/04/28/iran -irgc-zarif-tv-spy-thriller-undermine-moderate-rivals/.

54. Scott Peterson, "Iran Attacked: Is Revolutionary Guard Looking the Wrong Way?" *Christian Science Monitor*, May 11, 2021, https://www.csmonitor.com/World /Middle-East/2021/0511/Iran-attacked-Is-Revolutionary-Guard-looking-the -wrong-way#.

55. "Iran's Intelligence Establishment Spreading Propaganda."

56. Toossi, "Iran's Hardliners Using TV Thriller."

57. Toossi.

58. "Iran's Intelligence Establishment Spreading Propaganda."

59. "Iran's Intelligence Establishment Spreading Propaganda."

60. "Iran: Paper Highlights 'Distorted Facts' in TV Documentary on Detained Activists," BBC Monitoring Middle East [Etemad in Persian], November 14, 2019, ProQuest.

61. "Iran: Paper Highlights 'Distorted Facts.'"

7

Legacy and Outlook

As the Ministry of Intelligence completes its fourth decade, it faces an ever more complex and challenging operating environment for safeguarding Iran's clerical establishment and Iranian national security interests. While no longer the primary "fist of the regime," the MOIS has established a legacy as an oppressive force against Iranians seeking political change. The ministry remains fearsome, intimidating, and generally unpopular as it plays its diminished but still critical role in protecting the government against all challengers. Concurrently, MOIS actions abroad add to regional tensions as it supports Iranian policies for confronting exiled dissident groups and rival countries. Under Esmail Khatib's leadership, the ministry has seemed more willing to use repression to support a regime dependent on a shrinking political base of support. Such a shift likely will undermine MOIS efforts to improve its social status and reputation as a professional and accountable agency.

The MOIS will continue to serve a nation beset by multiple external threats and numerous domestic problems. The nezam—and the MOIS—seem likely to remain under duress because Tehran faced troubled relations with the United States and its allies and partners even before the outbreak of the Israel-Hamas War in October 2023. Iranian leaders also have been unable to relieve their fears of externally inspired sedition and ethnic unrest. Battered by severe international economic sanctions, Iran's mismanaged and slumping economy had spawned sporadic yet significant antiregime protests throughout the early 2020s that focused on the people's economic despair. Responding in a series of speeches in mid-2022, Supreme Leader Khamenei explicitly threatened a harsh crackdown on political and other dissidents. Harking back to the violence surrounding the 1981 IRP bombing, he blamed the protests on "the enemy's soft war on the Iranian people" and the "enemy objectives of provoking the nation."[1]

Already restive during the summer of 2022, Iranians were ready to take to the streets when prospects for economic relief from US sanctions disappeared as negotiations between the United States and Iran over reinstituting the JCPOA nuclear agreement faltered in early September. On September 16, 2022, the death in custody of twenty-two-year-old Mahsa (Jina) Amini sparked a monthslong series of antigovernment protests as Iranians across the country proclaimed their frustrations with a range of social, economic, and political grievances. The regime's morality police, an arm of Iran's judiciary, had detained Amini, a Kurdish Iranian woman, on the nebulous charge of "improper hijab," part of Iran's strict dress code forbidding the exposure of too much hair, wearing excessive makeup, and other minor infractions. The subsequent countrywide women-led demonstrations coalesced around the slogan "*Zan, zendegi, azadi* [Woman, life, freedom]," and by year's end the protests had eclipsed the size and duration of the 2009 Green Movement and included pockets of violent militancy.[2]

The MOIS shared responsibility for suppressing the protests with the IRGC-IO, LEC, and Basij. The ministry and IRGC-IO split the missions of identifying and arresting individuals, placing activists under house arrest, and intimidating the media. Plainclothes officers, primarily Basij but also MOIS, IRGC, and LEC, were active in trying to disrupt protests and arrest demonstrators.[3] From the outset, Khatib threatened protesting Iranians with prosecution.[4] Khamenei's first response, repeatedly echoed by other officials, was to justify the regime's brutal response by blaming the United States, the United Kingdom, Israel, Saudi Arabia, and other countries for fomenting the unrest.[5]

In December 2022 the US intelligence community judged that the regime did not perceive the sustained protests as an imminent threat to stability but that Iran faced a greater risk of unrest and instability over time.[6] Similar concerns in Tehran that external and domestic problems could wear down the regime seemed to have arisen among Iran's security forces following the start of the Raisi administration. An early 2022 leak of the purported minutes of a November 2021 meeting of representatives from the IRGC, Basij, Tehran Prosecutor's Office, and other intelligence bodies, presumably including the MOIS, revealed the establishment's concerns over potential social unrest due to the deteriorating economy.[7] In June 2022 the regime launched a crackdown on dissent, arresting prominent protestors, reformist politicians, family members of Iranians killed in demonstrations, and even acclaimed film directors.[8] At a ceremony introducing Kazemi as his new intelligence chief, IRGC commander Salami warned that the "war of intelligence has today turned into the most consistent and the most real war."[9] Regime leaders seem likely to continue to press the MOIS and other security services to expand efforts to quash the unrest, counter subversion, and target exiled dissidents.[10]

Factors Shaping the MOIS

The MOIS response to future challenges domestically, internationally, and in the cyber domain will depend on a number of political and security developments over the coming years. One of the most important factors likely will be the consequences of Khamenei's consolidation of hard-line conservative power over the government's elected and unelected policymaking bodies. If sustained, this portends a potential shift in the ministry's relationship with and accountability to the executive and legislative branches. Another critical driver probably will be the MOIS-judiciary relationship and the extent of the ministry's adherence to its ideals of popular intelligence and observance of constitutional protections. Two other potential key factors involve the hostile relationship between Iran and the United States and its allies plus the ongoing shadow war with Israel. Finally, the MOIS is almost certain to be shaped by an alternately collaborative and competitive relationship with the Revolutionary Guard's intelligence bodies.

Khamenei's Consolidation of Conservative Power

Over the past two decades, the MOIS generally maintained its political neutrality as Khamenei and his hard-line conservative supporters consolidated their control of the legislative, judicial, and executive branches.[11] Khamenei, meanwhile, groomed Ebrahim Raisi as his handpicked choice for Iran's chief executive, in large part, to end the competition for influence between the Office of the Supreme Leader and the presidency.[12] Raisi's four presidential predecessors—Khamenei's revolutionary peer Rafsanjani, the reformist Khatami, the populist Ahmadinejad, and the pragmatist Rouhani—all tried to advance policy agendas that challenged some of the supreme leader's preferences and goals. Raisi, in contrast, came to office parroting many of the leader's goals and promising to unite Iran's political factions.[13]

Given Raisi's earlier work with the Ministry of Intelligence and his past association with Khatib, his administration may restore some of the MOIS's institutional influence by reviving hard-liner trust and acceptance. In an address to MOIS officers in March 2022, Raisi advanced conservative interests by calling for the ministry's transformation to preserve and protect the system and the Islamic Revolution.[14] Implicitly criticizing the ministry's performance under his predecessor, the president enumerated as fundamental steps a change in MOIS approaches to its missions and the transformation of its processes. He did not elaborate on the transformation's end goal but stressed the importance of "religious people" and "trust in the administrative system and its efficiency."[15] Raisi warned that the MOIS needed to be protected against its enemies' influence, (political) deviations, and corruption. He also emphasized the need for cooperation among the intelligence agencies, possibly indicating a desire for the MOIS to take the lead in achieving this.[16]

Upon being nominated as minister, Khatib promised a transformation program focused on providing improved "surveillance and protection for national security."[17] The MOIS under Khatib may seek such improvement by showing even less deference to the law as it works to defend the revolutionary values seen by the hard-liners as a cornerstone of national security. Moreover, at least while the reformists and pragmatists remain politically sidelined, the leader may shift his favor toward a trusted MOIS to help stifle differences among the conservatives and to monitor potential political challenges from within the establishment.

Judiciary Ties Could Add Clout

Another potential institutional advantage and driver of change in the ministry is the rise of former MOIS head Mohseni-Ejei to the powerful position of Iran's chief justice. Mohseni-Ejei reportedly became a close friend to Raisi during the period 2014–21 when he served alongside the future president in the judiciary.[18] Moreover, Khatib's tenure as head of the Judiciary Protection and Intelligence Center from 2012 to 2019 overlapped with Mohseni-Ejei's judiciary assignments, raising the likelihood of a sustained working relationship between the two. The potentially powerful linkage between the presidency, judiciary, and Ministry of Intelligence through these three men and potential conservative successors might give the MOIS a larger role in and more latitude for enforcing Iran's vague national security laws and combating soft cultural threats.

As discussed in previous chapters, by the end of the Rouhani administration, the MOIS was participating in a security clampdown to prevent feared cultural invasion, sedition, and infiltration. As early as the start of Rouhani's second term of office in late 2017, the judiciary was asserting its ultimate responsibility over the MOIS for determining the status and final disposition of espionage cases.[19] Similarly, Alavi's touting of the ministry's approach to protect people's lives, assets, and reputations for raising the service's popular appeal seems to have left judiciary and other establishment leaders unimpressed.[20] By mid-2022 Mohseni-Ejei was enlisting Khatib's MOIS in protecting religious and cultural values, setting the fuse for the unrest that followed Mahsa Amini's death. After accusing Iran's enemies of promoting immorality in society, the chief justice called on the country's intelligence bodies to take strong action against groups campaigning against the mandatory wearing of the hijab for women.[21] In July the MOIS deputy minister for political, cultural, and social affairs publicly urged more regime actions to promote religious observations and regulate social media, which he called a "homewrecking calamity" that weakened religion in society.[22]

The same deputy minister warned that Iran's enemies were looking "to transform economic difficulties into social and security-related ones."[23] Economic insecurity affecting nearly all Iranians had been overshadowing civil and political rights as a motive for unrest. By 2022 it was combining with broader popular grievances to present greater challenges to the intelligence and security services. The deputy encouraged Iran's political elite to close ranks and help the current government undertake overdue economic reforms. The regime's reaction, however, was encapsulated in Khamenei's mid-2022 threats to return to the harsh internal security measures of the 1980s to confront rising social discontent, more frequent and larger demonstrations, and shaken public trust in the conservative establishment.[24]

As a sop to Iranians dissatisfied with the economy, the regime seems likely to continue publicizing MOIS efforts to target corruption that affects economic growth, as Raisi directed in his March 2022 speech.[25] Based on past anticorruption efforts, however, new campaigns are unlikely to touch some of the worst perpetrators within the regime's establishment, primarily the Revolutionary Guard. Iran's so-called resistance economy, initiated in the early 2010s to withstand sanctions, and the conservatives' attempts to grasp all levers of power have fueled an expansion of the IRGC's already pervasive involvement in the economy. According to some estimates, the Guard controls as much as one-sixth of Iran's declared gross domestic product through its activities in the construction, oil and gas, financial and banking, and telecommunication sectors.[26] Popular belief in entrenched IRGC corruption, a regular topic in the Iranian press, probably was boosted in early 2022 when the US-funded Radio Farda (Tomorrow) broadcast a leaked audio recording of two former senior IRGC officers in the late 2010s discussing corruption within their service. The audio revealed that high-ranking regime members and military commanders—including then IRGC-IO chief Taeb—were aware of practices that eventually resulted in a lower-level IRGC commander and a Tehran deputy mayor being sentenced to lengthy prison sentences in March 2021.[27]

These connections to the leader, presidency, and judiciary, if matched with increased conservative satisfaction with the ministry's demonstrated loyalty to the nezam, may result in the regime's willingness to strengthen the MOIS. Given the IRGC's growing power and influence, the clerical leadership in Tehran may desire an intelligence service robust enough to prevent IRGC intelligence organs from concentrating potentially regime-threatening power. As a result, the MOIS under Khatib could be well positioned to find a higher and more appropriate stature within the regime. In turn, it may be better able to maintain at least some of its long-standing characteristics and culture as well as recover its putative role as head of Iran's intelligence community. However, an expanded role focused on popular unrest, corruption, and political deviation among other regime elements is likely to come at the expense of MOIS attention to genuine foreign intelligence threats inside and beyond Iran.

Continued Iranian-Western Hostility

The need for MOIS external operations seems likely to grow as part of Iran's efforts to expand its power and influence, Western responses to these efforts, and the rounds of retaliation in the sporadic hybrid war between the United States and Axis of Resistance members in Iraq, Syria, and Yemen. The continued relevance of Iran's revolutionary ideology to its security policies can be seen in the regime's recurring narratives about resistance, anti-imperialism, and nationalism,[28] especially following the start of the latest Israel-Hamas war. As long as Supreme Leader Khamenei is head of government and works to maintain the anti-Western values and other principles of the revolution, his ideological preferences, stated in multiple speeches and pronouncements, will influence foreign, security, and other policies that guide MOIS operations. The fear of and hostility toward Western influence also drives the regime's repression of cultural, social, and personal freedoms, which keeps Iranian security services, including the MOIS, focused on forestalling popular reactions and protests.

Iran has shown little willingness to diminish its hybrid warfare activities in the region or its anti-Israel and anti-American positions as it confronts persistent military and economic pressure.[29] In March 2022 congressional testimony, the four-star general leading US forces in the Middle East judged that the threat posed by Iran was graver than ever as it fomented conflict, in Washington's view, in an arc tracing from Yemen through the Arabian Peninsula across Iraq and Syria into Lebanon and to the borders of Israel.[30] Despite the fact that Iran and US-led coalition forces in Iraq and Syria faced a common enemy in the Sunni extremists in ISIS and other groups, the general also noted that Iranian-allied militias in Iraq and Syria persisted in a low-level campaign of indirect fire and drone attacks against US and coalition forces to drive them from the region. While this situation persists, the MOIS, as suggested by the Iran Cables, will make intelligence collection against US diplomatic efforts and military forces in the region a high priority.[31]

Escalating US-Iranian tension since the 2020 assassination of IRGC-QF commander Qassem Soleimani will keep the MOIS engaged across the region, if only in support of Revolutionary Guard attempts to take revenge and deter future actions against Iran.[32] In 2021 Iran indicted thirty-six individuals in connection with the assassination, among them former president Trump, his secretaries of state and defense, and the former head of US Central Command.[33] These retaliatory threats gained credence when, at the start of 2022, the Biden administration publicly warned Iran against threatening US persons and extended diplomatic security details for former Trump administration officials.[34] Iran's history of taking years to kill exiled opponents such as Shahpour Bakhtiar and Mohammad Reza Kolahi Samadi suggests that its promised revenge will be a threat to and potential spark for escalation with the United States for many years.

Plagued by concerns about sedition and separatism, Iran's intelligence services, primarily the IRGC-QF, stepped up efforts through 2023 to kidnap and kill government officials, activists, and journalists around the world, including in the United States, according to government documents and interviews with officials in Washington, Europe, and the Middle East.[35] Iranian intelligence threats to dual nationals, in particular, have intensified in recent years and worsened Iran's relations with Western Europe. Tehran does not recognize dual nationality, and over the past two decades the MOIS and IRGC-IO have detained dozens of Iranians with European citizenship on suspicion of espionage, denying them consular services and adequate representation. In 2023 Iran heightened tensions by executing MOIS-captured British and Swedish dual nationals Alireza Akbari and Habib Chaab. Iran's Supreme Court in April also upheld the death sentence for German Iranian Jamshid Sharmahd, kidnapped in the United Arab Emirates by the MOIS in 2020.[36]

While the Western-based MEK is no longer a true danger to the regime—it is despised by most Iranians—its cooperation with Israel and networks inside Iran feed Tehran's desire to remove this persistent threat. The Raisi administration in early 2022 condemned Western countries for turning a blind eye to MEK involvement in assassinations and terrorist attacks inside Iran and for providing haven and immunity to the group.[37] Iran urged the United Nations and the European Union to prevent the free movement of MEK members and to hold them accountable for their crimes. The MEK will maintain its standing as a priority MOIS target as long as it remains involved in Israeli operations against Tehran and launches occasional cyber operations such as its claimed mid-2022 hack that temporarily controlled Tehran city government websites and thousands of the capital's surveillance cameras.[38] The MOIS almost certainly will continue to work with IRGC cyber units on influence operations targeting the MEK and other Iranian dissident groups, like the 2020 attack aimed at the annual online conference of the MEK-led National Council of Resistance of Iran.[39]

In the summer of 2022 Iran's anti-MEK activities included cyberattacks that targeted Albanian public services, state records, and government intranet communications. In response, Albania, which hosted approximately three thousand MEK members resettled from Iraq, cut ties with Tehran, while Washington sanctioned Khatib and the MOIS for these and other cyber activities.[40] Iranian diplomatic pressure and continued MOIS cyber activities in Albania, however, apparently caused Albanian authorities in June 2023 to raid an MEK camp and seize 150 computers allegedly linked to prohibited political activities.[41] The MOIS hailed the Albanian police for acting against the camp, which the ministry alleged provided training and funding to MEK terrorists in Iran.[42]

The ministry's cyber capabilities to strike against enemies outside Iran seem likely to grow. For example, shortly after Turkey foiled the kidnapping of a former Iranian military officer in late 2021, Iran escalated a long-standing cyber campaign against Ankara using the cyberespionage group MuddyWater, which US Cyber Command in early 2022 connected to the MOIS. This APT organization, also known as Static Kitten, had attacked government networks across North America, Europe, the Middle East, and South Asia to remove state information and steal valuable intellectual property. MuddyWater also targeted foreign computer networks with ransomware and destructive malware.[43] In the

spring of 2023 the group attempted to use a standard ransomware campaign to cover efforts against Israeli and other Middle Eastern entities to
destroy and disrupt on-premises devices and cloud resources, including
server farms, virtual machines, storage accounts, and virtual networks.[44]
MOIS-affiliated hackers probably will keep pace with other groups in
using generative artificial intelligence to disseminate convincing "deep-
fake" text, voice, and images online to support offensive cyber and psychological operations.

The Israeli Threat

Israel is another source of likely continued pressure on Iran and a driver
of future MOIS external operations, especially in the aftermath of the
most recent Israel-Hamas war. For decades Iran and Israel have fought a
shadow conflict featuring an intelligence war, proxy attacks, air strikes,
and naval operations. Since 1979 the Islamic Republic's ideological
stance has stoked criticism of prerevolution Israeli cooperation with the
shah's security services, Israel's 1982 invasion and lengthy occupation
of Shia-dominated parts of Lebanon, and its ongoing treatment of Palestinians and confiscation of Palestinian land in the occupied territories.
The regime also has sought to deter persistent Israeli attacks and sabotage with efforts to expand the Iranian military's reach and retaliatory
actions by the Axis of Resistance. In turn, Israeli officials cite Iranian
leaders' outspoken antipathy toward Israel, Tehran's support of violent
Palestinian militants and Hezbollah, and the threat from Iranian ballistic
missiles and suspected pursuit of nuclear weapons as justification for a
"campaign between the wars" strategy.[45]

Begun in 2013, this campaign refers to Israel's overt and covert efforts to prevent Iran and its allies from developing the capabilities to
change the regional balance of power and undermine Israeli deterrence.
Israeli operations have included air and drone strikes in Syria and Iraq
to restrict the flow of Iranian arms to Hezbollah and deter Iran from
maintaining a military presence near Israel's border. The Israeli military
claims to have carried out hundreds of air strikes in Syria and other parts
of the Middle East that killed hundreds of Iranians, Syrians, Iraqis, and
others from 2017 to mid-2023.[46] Tehran usually absorbed these Israeli

strikes and, despite IRGC casualties, only sporadically attempted to retaliate.[47]

At the start of 2022 the low-intensity conflict began to involve the MOIS more when it entered a new stage under the "Octopus Doctrine" of then Israeli prime minister Naftali Bennett.[48] The strategy targeted Iran directly rather than through Hezbollah and other Iranian-supported groups in a bid to exhaust Tehran's power using a range of diplomatic, financial, cyber, covert, and preemptory military actions. In February 2022 an Iranian air base that housed significant numbers of Iranian unmanned aerial vehicles in the western province of Kermanshah was severely damaged by what Iran alleged was a large Israeli drone attack.[49] The IRGC retaliated in March by firing missiles at alleged Mossad operational bases in Erbil, Iraq, which Iranian broadcasters referred to as a "wake-up call" for countries that gave Israel an operational platform against Iran.[50]

The conflict escalated a few weeks later in May when, in a style of attack that echoed previous Israeli and MEK operations,[51] two assassins on motorcycles in Tehran killed IRGC-QF colonel Hassan Sayyad Khodai, who allegedly was behind a series of plots against Israeli businesspeople and diplomats in various countries.[52] Following Khodai's death, two Iranian scientists working with the military died in separate poisoning incidents, and an IRGC officer fell suspiciously to his death from a balcony. Subsequently, quadcopter drones launched from inside Iran attacked the highly sensitive Parchin military complex in Tehran, which resulted in the death of a young defense ministry engineer. A similar quadcopter drone attack then damaged a centrifuge production facility in Karaj.[53]

In a February 2022 speech that followed the announcement of Israel's Octopus Doctrine, Khamenei tasked his government to match Iran's enemies' "hybrid warfare" with similar offensive actions in the intelligence, security, media, and economic realms.[54] The MOIS has been involved in the response by countering Mossad actions inside Iran. For example, Iranian officials announced that the ministry in April 2022 had disrupted a suspected Mossad-linked cell that was plotting to assassinate Iranian nuclear scientists and, in another operation, arrested alleged Mossad-linked agents in a Baluch-dominated province in eastern Iran.[55]

The ministry claimed in late July that it had arrested a team of suspected Israeli operatives just hours before they carried out a major "terrorist" bombing against a sensitive military site near Esfahan.[56] Among the equipment and weapons purportedly confiscated by the MOIS officers were bombs hidden in pieces of furniture, pistols with silencers, and special technical tools for disrupting control systems and remote detonation. The MOIS claimed the group had entered Iran through the Kurdish region of Iraq and were members of the Marxist Kurdish separatist group Komala.[57]

In December 2022 Benjamin Netanyahu replaced Bennett as Israeli prime minister and formed a radically conservative government with even more pronounced hawkish views on Iran. Israel continued its campaign between the wars into 2023, as evidenced by continued MOIS claims of multiple Israeli-linked plots inside Iran.[58] Ongoing Israeli attacks on Iranian bases in Syria and US retaliatory strikes against aggressive IRGC-QF–backed Iraqi and Syrian Shia militias kept regional tensions high. Meanwhile, Israeli-Palestinian violence in the West Bank and domestic turmoil in Israel created a volatile situation in the months before the Israelis faced their next major war.

On October 7, 2023, Palestinian fighters led by Hamas stunned Israel by breaching roughly thirty points along the Gazan border, capturing military posts, attacking towns, killing approximately twelve hundred civilians and soldiers, and taking more than two hundred as hostages. The attack provoked massive Israeli air bombardment of Gaza followed by a ground offensive intended to root out and destroy the Hamas militias. Iranian leaders appeared caught off guard by the attack,[59] but, having supplied and helped train Hamas, Tehran almost certainly was aware of the group's capabilities and objectives. Under Iran's leadership, the Axis of Resistance remained unified and began coordinating responses against Israel on all fronts for the first time.[60]

Although details are limited, the Ministry of Intelligence continued espionage, counterespionage, and cyber activities against Israel during the war.[61] The Iranian regime, meanwhile, tried to avoid widening the conflict even as it benefited from axis-member actions that distracted Israeli forces, hurt Israel and the world economically by threatening maritime traffic in the Red Sea, undermined the US positions in Iraq and Syria with drone and rocket attacks, and diminished the popularity of Arab governments viewed as doing too little for the Palestinians.[62] In anticipation of the conflict's end leading to the transition to Israel's next campaign between the wars, the MOIS probably began to prepare for an undiminished intelligence war for the foreseeable future. As mentioned in chapter 5, the MOIS may be called to support efforts to rebuild Hamas or its successor and help strengthen the other axis members. In a likely atmosphere of heightened postconflict hostility, MOIS influence operations and film and television programs are almost certain to continue to denigrate Israel while boasting about Iran's and its allies' capabilities to confront their Israeli nemesis.

Impact of Relationship with the IRGC on MOIS Culture

Under Khatib the ministry's standing relative to the IRGC-IO and IRGC-QF seems poised for a rebound. But, barring changes as described above, the rise may be limited. To compete with the Revolutionary Guard, the MOIS may have to abandon any remaining adherence to the ideals set by Khatami, Rouhani, Yunesi, and Alavi. In 2019 President Rouhani told MOIS officers that acting religiously, legally, and reputably were the three key pillars of the ministry's mission. He cited the decisions made in 1983 in establishing the MOIS to highlight the ministry's acceptance of legal accountability and emphasized the importance of Iranians "with different social tastes" believing in the ministry's integrity, authority, and protection.[63] In the absence of an institutional champion for Alavi's belief in accountability, citizen rights, obedience to the law, and the creation of a domestic security environment that strengthened confidence in the MOIS and regime, these already weakened ideals seem likely to diminish over the coming years.[64]

As their mix of competition and collaboration with the Revolutionary Guard continues, MOIS officers may alter their desired characteristics in the direction of the IRGC's more ideological traits. In this case, the ministry's historical commitment to the leader's authority could trend toward a subservience less accountable to the executive and legislative branches. At the same time, the officers' required devotion to Iran's laws and Islamic ethical standards may come to mimic the IRGC's political-ideological dogmatism. Given the Raisi administration's stated preference for strong approaches to security, the apparent MOIS turn away from attempting to earn public trust and confidence under Khatib seems likely to affect its "less bad cop" reputation negatively.

Should MOIS officers adopt IRGC practices of politicizing security issues, they could make the ministry vulnerable to the same criticisms lodged at the Revolutionary Guard. Foremost among them is the charge that the IRGC's focus on relatively innocuous groups distracts it from defeating actual security threats. Meanwhile, accusations of foreign intelligence penetrations of the Guard, such as those by Ahmadinejad and Alavi, seem to be politically motivated responses to IRGC interventions in politics and government operations.[65] These allegations probably undermine trust and cooperation among the members of Iran's intelligence community, and similar charges against the MOIS would cause further harm. Perhaps aware of these potential problems, Raisi told MOIS officers in early 2022 that, while thinking and acting in a revolutionary manner, they should not be influenced by politicians.[66] Still, in an address to IRGC commanders in late August 2023, Khatib asserted that their joint successes came from the synergy created between the institutions and obedience to Khamenei's instructions and orders.[67]

Dutiful Soldiers

Khatib's transformation plan promised a focus on improving the production of intelligence information. To date, it is unclear whether the regime will devote the resources for training and procedures, as Rouhani once proposed, to enable the Ministry of Intelligence to "discover the facts in the digital world and provide strategic and future-related information and analysis."[68] Instead, the ministry under Khatib and future ministers may be more susceptible to serving the establishment's ongoing efforts to boost conformity and national unity rather than applying objective analysis and dispassionate approaches to basic intelligence missions. It remains to be seen whether the MOIS can meaningfully sustain efforts started under the Rouhani administration to become a more professional and ethical agency.

Since its founding in 1979, the Islamic Republic has endured against unfavorable global forces and regular domestic challenges to its political system. For all of the regime's emphasis on ideology, its attention to the structural development of its intelligence and security apparatus accounts for much of the nezam's resilience. This success can be credited, in part, to the revolution's ability to abolish the shah's order while retaining elements, such as SAVAK's professionals, necessary to secure the replacement of political and social institutions the revolutionaries established. More than forty years after the Islamic Revolution, the regime is dominated by political and security leaders who are veterans of the antishah movement, the battles to establish the Islamic Republic, and the Iran-Iraq War. Shaped by these experiences, Iran's leaders, even when divided by different factional outlooks, have remained dutifully bound to maintaining the political order they brought to life.

The conservative elites of the Islamic Republic probably can expect greater consensus on Iranian national security policies over the rest of the 2020s. While men like Khamenei may soon pass from the scene, others such as Mohseni-Ejei and Khatib, both in their sixties, are likely to remain active in government for many years to come. Challenges like the protests at the end of 2022 suggest that Tehran will continue to value the surveillance and security capabilities of the Ministry of Intelligence to prevent and suppress further dissent. Prioritizing the nezam's survival seems likely to remain a key driver of the activities at home and abroad of the dutiful unknown soldiers.

Notes

1. "Iran's Supreme Leader Threatened Protesters. But Iranians Aren't Listening," Atlantic Council Iran Source, July 8, 2022, https://www.atlanticcouncil.org/blogs/iran source/irans-supreme-leader-threatened-protesters-but-iranians-arent-listening.

2. For a brief assessment of this period, see Hadi Semati, "Iran in 2022: Protests, Politics and Russian Alliance," USIP Iran Primer, December 21, 2022, https://iran primer.usip.org/blog/2022/dec/21/iran-2022-protests-politics-russian-alliance. See also Azadeh Moaveni, "'It's like a War out There.' Iran's Women Haven't Been This Angry in a Generation," *New York Times*, October 7, 2022, https://www.ny times.com/2022/10/07/opinion/iran-women-protests.html; and "Women Lead the Way: Iran's Ruling Ayatollahs Are Hanging On," *Economist*, September 22, 2022, https://www.economist.com/middle-east-and-africa/2022/09/29/irans-ruling-ayatol lahs-are-hanging-on.

3. Ehsan Mehrabi, "Explainer: The Islamic Republic of Iran's Architecture of Suppression," IranWire, September 25, 2022, https://iranwire.com/en/society/107906 -explainer-the-islamic-republic-of-irans-architecture-of-suppression/.

4. "Intelligence Ministry Warns Iranians against Taking Part in Protests," BBC Monitoring Middle East [Press TV in English], September 23, 2022, ProQuest.

5. Maziar Motamedi, "Iran's Khamenei Blames Israel, US in First Comments on Protests,"

Al Jazeera, October 3, 2022, https://www.aljazeera.com/news/2022/10/3/irans
-khamenei-blames-israel-us-in-first-comments-on-protests.

6. Laura Rozen, "US Intel Chief: Iran Protests 'Not Imminent Threat' to Regime, but
Portend 'Greater Risk of Unrest and Instability over Time,'" Diplomatic, December
5, 2022, https://diplomatic.substack.com/p/us-intel-chief-iran-protests-not.

7. James Dorsey, "Israel Expands Its Iran Strategy amid Potential Social Unrest in
the Islamic Republic," Modern Diplomacy, February 7, 2022, https://moderndiplo
macy.eu/2022/02/07/israel-expands-its-iran-strategy-amid-potential-social-unrest
-in-the-islamic-republic/; Golnaz Esfandiari, "Radio Farda's Exclusive from the
'Very Secret' Document of Sarollah Camp: 'Society Is in a State of Subcutaneous
Explosion,'" Radio Farda, February 2, 2022, https://www.radiofarda.com/a/radio
-farda-exclusive-report-protests-iran/31682008.html.

8. Mehrdad Khonsari, "'Deep State' in Iran Arrests Prominent Critics to Create Fear," IranWire, July 11, 2022, https://iranwire.com/en/guest-blogger/10
5608-guest-post-irans-deep-state-arrests-more-prominent-critics; "Dozen
Arrested after 'Supreme Leader' Threatens Repeat of 1980s Violent Repression," Iran Human Rights, July 11, 2022, https://iranhumanrights.org/2022/07
/heightened-reign-of-terror-in-iran-under-new-intelligence-chief/.

9. Najmeh Bozorgmehr, "Israeli Attacks Feed Distrust and Fear in Iran," *Financial
Times*, July 19, 2022, Gale General OneFile.

10. "Rights Monitor: More Than 500 Killed since Iran Protests Began," Voice of
America News, December 19, 2022, https://www.voanews.com/a/rights-monitor
-more-than-500-killed-since-iran-protests-began/6882138.html; "Iran Monthly
Protests Report: December 2022," BBC Monitoring Middle East, January 5, 2023,
ProQuest.

11. Farnaz Fassihi, "A New President Takes Office in Iran, Solidifying Hard-Line Control," *New York Times*, August 5, 2021, https://www.nytimes.com/2021/08/05/world
/middleeast/iran-president-raisi-inaugurated.html; "Iran's New Parliament Heralds
Conservative Consolidation," International Crisis Group, June 12, 2020, https://
www.crisisgroup.org/middle-east-north-africa/gulf-and-arabian-peninsula/iran
/irans-new-parliament-heralds-conservative-consolidation. See also Mohammad
Ayatollahi Tabaar, "Iran's War Within," *Foreign Affairs* 100, no. 5 (September/
October 2021): 155–68.

12. For a useful overview of relations between Raisi and Khamenei, see Sahimi,
"Who's Who of Iranian Players."

13. Fassihi, "New President Takes Office."

14. "Raisi Urges Intelligence Apparatus to Fight Injustice, Counter Corrupters and
Profiteers," *Iran News*, March 14, 2022, Gale General OneFile.

15. "Raisi Urges Intelligence Apparatus."

16. "Raisi Urges Intelligence Apparatus."

17. "Promises of the Minister of Information for Transformation in Ministry," Khabar
Online, August 29, 2021, https://www.khabaronline.ir/news/1549535.

18. "Who Iran's New Judiciary Chief Is," *Tehran Times*, July 2, 2021, Gale General
OneFile.

19. Randolph, "IRGC Consolidates Primacy," 6.

20. "Iran's Intelligence Agency Enjoys"; "Iran Security Official Claims."

21. "Judiciary Chief Calls for Strong Action against Anti-Hijab Campaigners in Iran,"

BBC Monitoring Middle East [Fars News Agency in Persian], July 11, 2022, ProQuest.

22. "Senior Iranian Intelligence Official Urges."
23. "Senior Iranian Intelligence Official Urges."
24. "Iran's Supreme Leader Threatened Protesters."
25. "Raisi Urges Intelligence Apparatus."
26. Hesam Forozan and Afshin Shahi, "The Military and the State in Iran: The Economic Rise of the Revolutionary Guards," *Middle East Journal* 71, no. 1 (Winter 2017): 67–68, ProQuest. See also Amir Toumaj, *Iran's Economy of Resistance: Implications for Future Sanctions* (Washington, DC: Critical Threats Project of the American Enterprise Institute, November 2014), 7–8, https://www.criticalthreats .org/wp-content/uploads/2016/07/imce-imagesToumajA_Irans-Resistance-Econo my-Implications_november2014-1.pdf.
27. Golnaz Esfandiari, "Radio Farda Exposé on IRGC Corruption, Infighting Raises Ire of Iranian Authorities," RFE / RL Radio Farda, February 18, 2022, https:// www.rferl.org/a/farda-leaked-conversation-corruption-irgc/31710316.html; "Iran's IRGC Confirms Leaked Audio of Former Head Discussing Corruption," Al-Monitor, February 14, 2022, https://www.al-monitor.com/originals/2022/02/irans -irgc-confirms-leaked-audio-former-head-discussing-corruption; "Briefing: Iranian Conservatives Downplay Leaked Guards Corps Audio," BBC Monitoring Middle East [Fars News Agency, Tasnim in Persian], February 14, 2022, ProQuest.
28. See Olivia Glombitza, "Islamic Revolutionary Ideology and Its Narratives: The Continued Relevance of the Islamic Republic's Ideology," *Third World Quarterly* 43, no. 5 (May 2022): 1156–75.
29. On Iranian threat perceptions, see Defense Intelligence Agency, *Iran Military Power*, 12.
30. US Central Command, "Senate Armed Services Committee Hearing on the Posture of United States Central Command and United States Africa Command, March 15, 2022," March 16, 2022, https://www.centcom.mil/MEDIA/Transcripts/Article/296 8166/senate-armed-services-committee-hearing-on-the-posture-of-united-states-ce ntral/.
31. Arango et al., "Iran Cables."
32. "Iranian President Calls for Carrying on Soleimani's Legacy," BBC Monitoring Middle East [Islamic Republic of Iran News Network in Persian], January 3, 2022, ProQuest; "Top Iranian Commanders Vow Revenge for Slain Officer," BBC Monitoring Middle East [ISNA in Persian], May 24, 2022, ProQuest.
33. "Senior Cleric: World Security Restored by Anti-Terror Commander General Soleimani," Fars News Agency, December 24, 2021, ProQuest.
34. White House, "Statement by National Security Advisor Jake Sullivan on Iranian Threats and Provocations against American Citizens," January 9, 2022, https:// www.whitehouse.gov/briefing-room/statements-releases/2022/01/09/statement-by -national-security-advisor-jake-sullivan-on-iranian-threats-and-provocations-agai nst-american-citizens/; Margaret Brennan, "U.S. Intelligence Shows Iran Threats on U.S. Soil, but Blinken and Schiff Say This Shouldn't Derail New Nuclear Deal," CBS News, March 12, 2022, https://www.cbsnews.com/news/iran-threats-pompeo -nuclear-deal/.
35. Shane Harris, Souad Mekhennet, and Yeganeh Torbati, "Rise in Iranian Assassination,

Kidnapping Plots Alarms Western Officials," *Washington Post*, December 1, 2022, https://www.washingtonpost.com/world/2022/12/01/iran-kidnapping-assass ination-plots/; US Department of the Treasury, "Treasury Designates Perpetrators of Human Rights Abuse"; "Iran Is Targeting Its Opponents in Britain," *Economist*, February 9, 2024, https://www.economist.com/britain/2024/02/08/iran-is-targeting -its-opponents-in-britain.

36. Tom Spender, "Habib Chaab: Iran Executes Swedish-Iranian for Alleged Terrorism," BBC News, May 6, 2023, https://www.bbc.com/news/world-middle-east -65507083; Patrick Wintour, "UN Inquiry into Rights in Iran Urged to Look at Detention of Dual Nationals," *Guardian*, September 20, 2023, ProQuest; "Who Are the Dual Nationals Jailed in Iran?" BBC, September 19, 2023, https:// www.bbc.com/news/uk-41974185.

37. "Iran Raps Western States' Blind Eye to MKO Crimes," Fars News Agency, March 9, 2022, ProQuest.

38. "Exiled Iran Group Claims Tehran Hacking Attack," Security Week, June 2, 2022, https://www.securityweek.com/exiled-iran-group-claims-tehran-hacking-attack/.

39. "Treadstone 71 Releases Intelligence Advisory on Iranian Influence Operations," PR Newswire, December 10, 2020, Gale General OneFile.

40. "Albania Cuts Iran Ties over Cyberattack; U.S. Vows Further Action," Reuters, September 7, 2022, https://www.reuters.com/world/albania-cuts-iran-ties-orde rs-diplomats-go-after-cyber-attack-pm-says-2022-09-07/; US Department of the Treasury, "Treasury Sanctions Iranian Ministry of Intelligence and Minister for Malign Cyber Activities," September 9, 2022, https://home.treasury.gov/news/press-re leases/jy0941.

41. Andrew Higgins, "A NATO Minnow Reels from Cyberattacks Linked to Iran," *New York Times*, February 25, 2023, https://www.nytimes.com/2023/02/25/world /europe/albania-iran-nato-cyberattacks.html; Llazar Semini, "Police Raid Iranian Opposition Camp in Albania, Seize Computers," Associated Press, June 20, 2023, https://apnews.com/article/albania-mek-iranian-opposition-police-raid -851dcb5fc32cd6bc60206e342eea7b16.

42. "Iran Intel. Ministry Hails Albanian Police Act against MKO," Mehr News, July 2, 2023, ProQuest.

43. "Iran-Linked Hacker Group Targets Turkey's Cyber Network," ICT Monitor Worldwide, February 18, 2022, Gale General OneFile; "US Military Links Prolific Hacking Group to Iranian Intelligence," CNN Wire, January 12, 2022, Gale General OneFile.

44. Ravie Lakshmanan, "Iran-Based Hackers Caught Carrying Out Destructive Attacks under Ransomware Guise," Hacker News, April 8, 2023, https://thehackernews .com/2023/04/iran-based-hackers-caught-carrying-out.html.

45. For an example of Iranian antipathy, see "Iran Guards Chief Warns Israel of Imminent 'Destruction,'" BBC Monitoring Middle East [Islamic Republic of Iran News Network in Persian], April 29, 2022, ProQuest; Daniel Avis, "Understanding the Shadow War between Israel and Iran," Bloomberg.com, August 4, 2021, https://www.bloomberg.com/news/articles/2021-08-04/understanding -the-shadow-war-between-israel-and-iran-quicktake; Benjamin Kerstein, "Israeli Expert: Destruction of Iran-Connected Sites in Iraq 'No Coincidence,'" *Algemeiner*, August 21, 2019, https://www.algemeiner.com/2019/08/21/israeli -expert-destruction-of-iran-connected-sites-in-iraq-no-coincidence/; Seth J.

Frantzman, "Iran and Hezbollah Analyze Israel's 'War between the Wars,'" *Jerusalem Post*, November 14, 2021, https://www.jpost.com/middle-east/iran-and -hezbollah-analyze-israels-war-between-the-wars-684950.

46. Dion Nissenbaum, "Israel's 'War between the Wars' with Iran Expands across Middle East," *Wall Street Journal* (online), April 10, 2022, ProQuest; Jonathan Spyer, "The 'War between Wars,'" *Jerusalem Post*, August 11, 2023, ProQuest. See also Ofer Shelah and Carmit Valensi, "The Campaign between Wars at a Crossroads: CBW, 2013-2023: What Lies Ahead?" Institute for National Security Studies Memorandum 227, November 2023, https://www.inss.org.il/publication/the -war-between-the-wars/.

47. Nissenbaum, "Israel's 'War between the Wars'"; Hadas Gold, Mostafa Salem, Oren Liebermann, and Jack Guy, "Israel Accuses Iran of Drone Attack on Oil Tanker off Oman Coast," CNN, November 16, 2022, https://www.cnn.com/2022/11/16/middl eeast/oil-tanker-oman-projectile-intl/index.html.

48. Dorsey, "Israel Expands Its Iran Strategy"; "Iran's Khamenei Appears to Respond to Israel with Call for 'Hybrid' Offensive," *Times of Israel*, February 8, 2022, https://www.timesofisrael.com/liveblog_entry/irans-khamenei-appears-to-respond -to-israel-with-call-for-hybrid-offensive/; "Bolder Abroad, Embattled at Home," *Economist*, June 8, 2022, https://www.economist.com/middle-east-and-africa/20 22/06/08/israels-prime-minister-explains-his-new-approach-to-iran.

49. Ben Caspit, "Israel-Iran Conflict Escalates to Drone War," Al-Monitor, March 15, 2022, https://www.al-monitor.com/originals/2022/03/israel-iran-conflict-escalates -drone-war.

50. Nissenbaum, "Israel's 'War between the Wars.'"

51. The MEK's failed assassination of Tehran judiciary head Ali Razini in January 1999 was the first such attack, conducted by two motorcyclists who attached explosives to the victim's car. See also box 4.1.

52. Farnaz Fassihi and Adam Nossiter, "A Senior Member of Iran's Revolutionary Guard Is Killed in Tehran," *New York Times*, May 22, 2022, https://www.nytimes .com/2022/05/22/world/asia/iran-revolutionary-guard-killed.html; "Weekly Iran Watch: 19–25 May 2022," BBC Monitoring Middle East, May 25, 2002, ProQuest; "Slain Iranian Officer Said to Have Planned Attacks against Israelis, Jews Worldwide," *Times of Israel*, May 22, 2022, https://www.timesofisrael.com/slain -iranian-officer-said-to-have-planned-attacks-against-israelis-jews-worldwide/; "More Details on Razini's Assassination," *Tehran Times*, January 26, 1999, https:// www.tehrantimes.com/news/27893/More-Details-on-Razini-s-Assassination.

53. Farnaz Fassihi and Ronen Bergman, "Iran Suspects Israel Poisoned Two Scientists to Death," *New York Times*, June 13, 2022, https://www.nytimes.com/2022/06/13 /world/middleeast/israel-poison-iranian-scientists.html.

54. On Iran's national security and hybrid warfare strategies, see Defense Intelligence Agency, *Iran Military Power*, 12–13, 22–23; and "Briefing: Speculation on Iran Leader's Call for 'Hybrid Warfare,'" BBC Monitoring Middle East [Kayhan and Javan in Persian], February 9, 2022, ProQuest.

55. Maziar Motamedi, "Iran Says Suspected Israel Cell Members Planning Attack Arrested," Al Jazeera, July 24, 2022, https://www.aljazeera.com/news/2022/7/24/iran -says-suspected-israel-cell-members-planning-attack-arrested.

56. "Iran Says Arrested Israel-Linked Agents Were Kurdish Rebels," Agence France-Presse, July 27, 2022, https://www.al-monitor.com/originals/ 2022/07/iran-says-ar

rested-israel-linked-agents-were-kurdish-rebels; "Intelligence Min. Reveals New Info on Detained Mossad Spies," Mehr News, July 27, 2022, ProQuest; "Intelligence Minister: Several Successful Operations Carried Out against Israel in Recent Months," Fars News Agency, July 27, 2022, ProQuest.

57. "Intelligence Min. Reveals New Info on Detained Mossad Spies."
58. For an assessment of the shadow war from early 2023, see Dalia Dassa Kaye, "Israel's Dangerous Shadow War with Iran: Why the Risk of Escalation Is Growing," *Foreign Affairs*, February 27, 2023, https://www.foreignaffairs.com/israel/israels-dangerous-shadow-war-iran.
59. Adam Entous, Julian E. Barnes, and Jonathan Swan, "Early Intelligence Shows Hamas Attack Surprised Iranian Leaders, US Says," *New York Times*, October 11, 2023, https://www.nytimes.com/2023/10/11/us/politics/iran-israel-gaza-hamas-us-intelligence.html.
60. Clayton Thomas, "Iran-Supported Groups in the Middle East and U.S. Policy," Congressional Research Service in Focus, IF12587, February 7, 2024, https://crsreports.congress.gov/product/pdf/IF/IF12587.
61. For example, see Amir Bohbot, "Iran Recruited Israeli Civilians for Spying, Intelligence Missions," *Jerusalem Post*, December 22, 2023, ProQuest; Kevin Poireault, "Iranian Hackers Target Israel and US to Sway Public Opinion in Hamas Conflict," *InfoSecurity Magazine*, February 14, 2024, https://www.infosecurity-magazine.com/news/iran-target-israel-sway-public/.
62. Scott Peterson, "US Confronts 'Axis': Who Are Iran's Allies? Can They Be Deterred?" *Christian Science Monitor*, February 6, 2024, https://www.csmonitor.com/World/Middle-East/2024/0206/US-confronts-Axis-Who-are-Iran-s-allies-Can-they-be-deterred; "Iran Does Not Want Israel-Hamas Conflict to Spread, Foreign Minister Says," Reuters, October 29, 2023, https://www.reuters.com/world/middle-east/iran-does-not-want-israel-hamas-conflict-spread-foreign-minister-2023-10-29/; Farnaz Fassihi, "Iran Tries to Avoid War with U.S. after Stoking Mideast Conflicts," *New York Times*, February 1, 2024, https://www.nytimes.com/2024/02/01/world/middleeast/iran-us-war.html.
63. "Dr Rouhani in a Meeting with Intelligence Minister, DY Ministers Senior Executives," States News Service, October 8, 2019, Gale General OneFile.
64. "Rouhani's Intelligence Ministry and Khamenei's IRGC Widen Crackdown ahead of Election," Center for Human Rights in Iran, March 16, 2017, https://www.iranhumanrights.org/2017/03/increase-arrest-by-ministry-of-intelligence; "Iranian Intelligence Minister Presents Programs."
65. Scott Peterson, "Why Iran Nuclear Talks Are Moving Ahead, Despite Israeli Attack," *Christian Science Monitor*, April 19, 2021, https://www.csmonitor.com/layout/set/print/World/Middle-East/2021/0419/Why-Iran-nuclear-talks-are-moving-ahead-despite-Israeli-attack#; Peterson, "In Iran, Assassination Shock"; "Ahmadinejad Accuses 'Ring' in Iran Intelligence of Espionage," Al-Monitor, July 22, 2021, https://www.al-monitor.com/originals/2021/07/ahmadinejad-accuses-ring-iran-intelligence-espionage.
66. "Raisi Urges Intelligence Apparatus."
67. "Iran Detained Spies from France, Sweden, UK: Intel. Min," Mehr News, August 20, 2023, ProQuest.
68. "Dr Rouhani in a Meeting"; "Promises of the Minister of Information."

Selected Bibliography

Books and Articles

Abrahamian, Ervand. "The Guerrilla Movement in Iran, 1963–1977." *Middle East Review* 86 (March/April 1980). http://www.merip.org/mer/mer86/guerrilla-mo vement-iran-1963-1977.

———. *A History of Modern Iran*. Cambridge: Cambridge University Press, 2008.

———. *The Iranian Mojahedin*. New Haven, CT: Yale University Press, 1989.

———. *Tortured Confessions: Prisons and Public Recantations in Modern Iran*. Berkeley: University of California Press, 1999.

Alfoneh, Ali. *Iran Unveiled: How the Revolutionary Guards Is Turning Theocracy into Military Dictatorship*. Washington, DC: AEI Press, 2013.

———. "The Revolutionary Guards' Role in Iranian Politics." *Middle East Quarterly* 15, no. 4 (2008): 3–14. http://www.meforum.org/1979/the-revolutionary-guards -role-in-iranian-politics.

Axworthy, Michael. *Revolutionary Iran: A History of the Islamic Republic*. New York: Oxford University Press, 2013.

Bajoghli, Narges. *Iran Reframed: Anxieties of Power in the Islamic Republic*. Stan ford, CA: Stanford University Press, 2019.

———. "*The Outcasts*: The Start of 'New Entertainment' in Pro-Regime Filmmaking in the Islamic Republic of Iran." *Middle East Critique* 26, no. 1 (2017): 61–77.

Bajoghli, Narges, and Vali Nasr. "How the War in Gaza Revived the Axis of Resis tance." *Foreign Affairs*, January 17, 2024. https://www.foreignaffairs.com/united -states/how-war-gaza-revived-axis-resistance.

Bakhash, Shaul. *The Reign of the Ayatollahs: Iran and the Islamic Revolution*. Lon don: I. B. Tauris, 1985.

Banerjea, Udit. "Revolutionary Intelligence: The Expanding Intelligence Role of the Iranian Revolutionary Guard Corps." *Journal of Strategic Security* 8, no. 3 (2015): 93–106. https://scholarcommons.usf.edu/jss/vol8/iss3/6.

Behravesh, Maysam. "Iran Is Starting to Want the Bomb." *Foreign Policy*, March 10, 2021. https://foreignpolicy.com/2021/03/10/iran-is-starting-to-want-the-bomb.
———. "Iran's Spies Are at War with Each Other." *Foreign Policy*, August 9, 2019. https://foreignpolicy.com/2019/08/09/irans-spies-are-at-war-with-each-other/.
Boroujerdi, Mehrzad, and Kourosh Rahimkhani. *Postrevolutionary Iran: A Political Handbook*. Syracuse, NY: Syracuse University Press, 2018.
Bowden, Mark. *Guests of the Ayatollah: The First Battle in America's War with Militant Islam*. New York: Atlantic Monthly Press, 2006.
Buchan, James. *Days of God: The Revolution in Iran and Its Consequences*. New York: Simon & Schuster, 2012.
Buchta, Wilfried. *Who Rules Iran? The Structure of Power in the Islamic Republic*. Washington, DC: Washington Institute for Near East Policy, 2000.
Cohen, Ronen A. *The Rise and Fall of the Mojhahedin Khalq, 1987–1997*. Brighton, UK: Sussex Academic Press, 2009.
"Covert Terror: Iran's Parallel Intelligence Apparatus." *Iran Human Rights Documentation Center*, February 3, 2011. https://iranhrdc.org/covert-terror-irans-parallel-in telligence-apparatus/.
Dasgupta, Sunil. "Internal Security and Military Reorganization: The Rise of Paramilitaries in Developing Societies." PhD diss., University of Illinois at Urbana-Champaign, 2003. ProQuest.
Defense Intelligence Agency. *Iran Military Power: Ensuring Regime Survival and Securing Regional Dominance* (Washington, DC: DIA, 2019). https://www.dia .mil/Portals/110/Images/News/Military_Powers_Publications/Iran_Military_Po wer_LR.pdf.
Director General to IAEA Board of Governors. "Final Assessment on Past and Present Outstanding Issues Regarding Iran's Nuclear Programme." GOV/2015/68. December 2, 2015. https://www.iaea.org/sites/default/files/gov-2015-68.pdf.
Ebadi, Shirin, with Azadeh Moaveni. *Iran Awakening: One Woman's Journey to Reclaim Her Life and Country*. New York: Random House, 2006.
Esfandiair, Haleh. *My Prison, My Home: One Woman's Story of Captivity in Iran*. New York: Ecco, 2009.
Esfandiary, Dina, and Ariane Tabatabai. *Triple-Axis: Iran's Relations with Russia and China*. London: I. B. Taurus, 2018.
Fard, Erfan. "Iran's Intelligence Minister Sends a Clear Signal to the Biden Administration." BESA Center Perspectives Paper no. 1,929. February 12, 2021. https:// besacenter.org/iran-intelligence-minister/.
Forozan, Hesam, and Afshin Shahi. "The Military and the State in Iran: The Economic Rise of the Revolutionary Guards." *Middle East Journal* 71, no. 1 (Winter 2017): 67–86. ProQuest.
Gasiorowski, Mark J. *Mohammad Mosaddeq and the 1953 Coup in Iran*. Syracuse, NY: Syracuse University Press, 2004.
———. "The Nuzhih Plot and Iranian Politics." *International Journal of Middle East Studies* 34, no. 4 (2002): 645–66.
Ghazvinian, John. *America and Iran: A History, 1720 to the Present*. New York: Alfred A. Knopf, 2021.
Glombitza, Olivia. "Islamic Revolutionary Ideology and Its Narratives: The Continued

Relevance of the Islamic Republic's Ideology." *Third World Quarterly* 43, no. 5 (May 2022): 1156–75.

Golkar, Saeid. *Captive Society: The Basij Militia and Social Control in Iran*. Washington, DC: Woodrow Wilson Center Press, 2015.

———. "Iran's Intelligence Organizations and Transnational Suppression." Washington Institute for Near East Policy, PolicyWatch no. 3,517 (August 5, 2021). https://www.washingtoninstitute.org/policy-analysis/irans-intelligence-organiz ations-and-transnational-suppression.

Kaye, Dalia Dassa. "Israel's Dangerous Shadow War with Iran: Why the Risk of Escalation Is Growing." *Foreign Affairs*, February 27, 2023. https://www.foreignaff airs.com/israel/israels-dangerous-shadow-war-iran.

Khoshnood, Ardavan. "Iran Might Purge Its Intelligence and Counterintelligence Community." BESA Center Perspectives paper no. 2,025 (May 13, 2021). https://besacenter.org/iran-intelligence-purge.

———. "Iran's Killing Machine: Political Assassinations by the Islamic Regime." BESA Center Mideast Security and Policy Studies paper no. 185 (December 2020). https://besacenter.org/iran-political-assassinations/.

———. "Russia and Iran Sign an Intelligence Pact." BESA Center Perspectives paper no. 1,948 (March 4, 2021). https://besacenter.org/russia-iran-intelligence-pact.

Khoshnood, Arvin, and Ardavan Khoshnood. "Security Implications of the Iran-China Deal." BESA Center Perspectives paper no. 2,019 (May 10, 2021). https://besacen ter.org/iran-china-deal-security-implications.

Kinzer, Stephen. *All the Shah's Men: An American Coup and the Roots of Middle East Terror*. Hoboken, NJ: John Wiley & Sons, 2003.

Levitt, Matthew. *Hezbollah: The Global Footprint of Lebanon's Party of God*. Washington, DC: Georgetown University Press, 2013.

Library of Congress, Federal Research Division. *Iran's Ministry of Intelligence and Security: A Profile*. Washington, DC: Library of Congress, December 2012.

Loidolt, Bryce. "Al-Qaeda's Iran Dilemma: Evidence from the Abbottabad Records." *Studies in Conflict & Terrorism* (July 16, 2020): 1–28.

Majidyar, Ahmad. "Latest Crackdown in Iran Points to I.R.G.C.'s Meddling in Elections." Middle East Institute (March 20, 2017). https://www.mei.edu/publications /latest-crackdown-iran-points-irgcs-meddling-elections.

Maloney, Suzanne. *Iran's Long Reach: Iran as a Pivotal State in the Muslim World*. Washington, DC: United States Institute of Peace Press, 2008.

Mir-Hosseini, Ziba. "Iranian Cinema." *Middle East Report*, no. 219 (2001). https://merip.org/2001/06/iranian-cinema/.

Nye, Joseph S. "Soft Power and American Foreign Policy." *Political Science Quarterly* 119, no. 2 (2004): 255–70.

Office of the Director of National Intelligence (ODNI). *Annual Threat Assessment of the US Intelligence Community*. Washington, DC: ODNI, February 7, 2022. https://www.hsdl.org/c/2022-annual-threat-assessment-released/.

———. *Annual Threat Assessment of the US Intelligence Community*. Washington, DC: ODNI, February 6, 2023. https://www.dni.gov/index.php/newsroom/reports -publications/reports-publications-2023/3676-2023-annual-threat-assessment-of -the-u-s-intelligence-community.

Office of the Director of National Intelligence, National Intelligence Council. *Iran: Nuclear Intentions and Capabilities*. November 2007. https://www.dni.gov/files /documents/Newsroom/Reports%20and%20Pubs/20071203_release.pdf.

Ostovar, Afshon. *Vanguard of the Imam: Religion, Politics, and Iran's Revolutionary Guards*. New York: Oxford University Press, 2016.

Peterson, Scott. *Let the Swords Encircle Me: Iran—A Journey behind the Headlines*. New York: Simon & Schuster, 2010.

Posch, Walter. "Ideology and Strategy in the Middle East: The Case of Iran." *Survival* 59, no. 5 (October/November 2017): 69–98.

Ramazani, Rouhollah K. "Constitution of the Islamic Republic of Iran." *Middle East Journal* 34, no. 2 (Spring 1980): 181–204.

———. "Ideology and Pragmatism in Iran's Foreign Policy." *Middle East Journal* 58, no. 4 (Autumn 2004): 549–59.

Randolph, Eric. "Iranian IRGC Consolidates Primacy in Intelligence Operations." *Jane's Intelligence Review* (August 19, 2020). https://www.janes.com/defence-ne ws/news-detail/iranian-irgc-consolidates-primacy-in-intelligence-operations.

Rodier, Alain. "Iranian Intelligence Services." French Intelligence Research Center News Note no. 200 (January 2010). https://cf2r.org/actualite/les-services-de-ren seignement-iraniens/.

Saberi, Roxana. *Between Two Worlds: My Life and Captivity in Iran*. New York: Harper, 2010.

Samii, A. William. "Factionalism in Iran's Domestic Security Forces." *Middle East Intelligence Bulletin* 4, no. 2 (February 2002). https://www.meforum.org/meib/ar ticles/0202_me2.htm.

Shelah, Ofer, and Carmit Valensi. *The Campaign between Wars at a Crossroads: CBW, 2013–2023; What Lies Ahead?* Ramat Aviv, Israel: Institute for National Security Studies, 2023. https://www.inss.org.il/publication/the-war-between-the-wars/.

Shires, James, and Michael McGetrick. *Rational Not Reactive: Re-evaluating Iranian Cyber Strategy*. Cambridge, MA: Belfer Center for Science and International Affairs, 2021.

Sims, Jennifer E. "Foreign Intelligence Liaisons: Devils, Deals, and Details." *International Journal of Intelligence and CounterIntelligence* 19, no. 2 (2006): 195–217. https:www.tandfonline.com/loi/ujic20.

Sullivan, Mark P., and June S. Beittel. *Latin America: Terrorism Issues*. Report for Congress no. RS21049. Washington, DC: Congressional Research Service, 2013.

Tabaar, Mohammad Ayatollai. "Factional Politics in the Iran-Iraq War." *Journal of Strategic Studies* 42, nos. 3–4 (June 2019): 480–506.

———. "Iran's War Within." *Foreign Affairs* 100, no. 5 (September/October 2021): 155–68.

Taremi, Kamran. "Iranian Strategic Culture: The Impact of Ayatollah Khomeini's Interpretation of Shiite Islam." *Contemporary Security Policy* 35, no. 1 (2014): 3–25.

Thaler, David E., Alireza Nader, Shahram Chubin, Jerrold D. Green, Charlotte Lynch, and Frederic Wehrey. *Mullahs, Guards, and Bonyads: An Exploration of Iranian Leadership Dynamics*. Santa Monica, CA: RAND National Defense Research Institute, 2010.

Theohary, Catherine A. "Iranian Offensive Cyber Attack Capabilities." Congressional

Research Service in Focus, IF11406 (January 13, 2020). https://crsreports.congr ess.gov.

Thomas, Clayton. "Iran-Supported Groups in the Middle East and U.S. Policy." Congressional Research Service in Focus, IF12587 (February 7, 2024). https://crsre ports.congress.gov/product/pdf/IF/IF12587.

Toossi, Sina. "How Iran Really Sees the Israel-Hamas War." *Foreign Policy*, November 2, 2023. https://foreignpolicy.com/2023/11/02/how-iran-really-sees-the-israel -hamas-war.

———. "Iran's Hardliners Are Using a TV Thriller to Undermine Their Rivals." *Foreign Policy*, April 28, 2021. https://foreignpolicy.com/2021/04/28/iran-irgc-za rif-tv-spy-thriller-undermine-moderate-rivals/.

Toumaj, Amir. *Iran's Economy of Resistance: Implications for Future Sanctions.* Washington, DC: Critical Threats Project of the American Enterprise Institute, November 2014. https://www.criticalthreats.org/wp-content/uploads/2016/07 /imce-imagesToumajA_Irans-Resistance-Economy-Implications_november2014 -1.pdf.

US Department of Justice. "Iranian Intelligence Services Allegedly Plotted to Kidnap a U.S. Journalist and Human Rights Activist from New York City for Rendition to Iran." July 13, 2021. https://www.justice.gov/opa/pr/iranian-intelligence-officials -indicted-kidnapping-conspiracy-charges.

US Department of Justice, Office of Public Affairs. "One Iranian and Two Canadian Nationals Indicted in Murder-for-Hire Scheme," January 29, 2024. https://www .justice.gov/opa/pr/one-iranian-and-two-canadian-nationals-indicted-murder-hire -scheme.

US Department of State, Office of the Coordinator for Counterterrorism. "Patterns of Global Terrorism, 1993." April 1993. https://www.hsdl.org/?abstract&did=48 1510.

US Department of the Treasury. "Treasury Designates Former President of Iran." September 18, 2023. https://home.treasury.gov/news/press-releases/jy1739.

———. "Treasury Designates Iranian Ministry of Intelligence and Security for Human Rights Abuses and Support for Terrorism." February 16, 2012. https://www .treasury.gov/press-center/press-releases/Pages/tg1424.aspx.

———. "Treasury Designates Perpetrators of Human Rights Abuse and Commemorates the 75th Anniversary of the Universal Declaration of Human Rights." December 8, 2023. https://home.treasury.gov/news/press-releases/jy1972.

———. "Treasury Sanctions Iranian Ministry of Intelligence and Minister for Malign Cyber Activities." September 9, 2022. https://home.treasury.gov/news/press-re leases/jy0941.

———. "The United States and United Kingdom Target Iranian Transnational Assassinations Network." January 29, 2024. https://home.treasury.gov/news/press-re leases/jy2052.

US Department of the Treasury, Office of Foreign Assets Control. "Designation of One Entity Pursuant to Executive Order 13572 of April 29, 2011, 'Blocking Property of Certain Persons with Respect to Human Rights Abuses in Syria.'" February 13, 2012. https://plus.cq.com/doc/fedreg-4034208.

US Treasury Department, Office of Public Affairs. "Fact Sheet: Sanctions on Iranian

Government and Affiliates." November 8, 2012. https://www.treasury.gov/press
-center/press-releases/.

Utchel, Donald M. "The Parallel Security Apparatus: Examining the Cases of Baathist
Iraq, Syria, and Iran." PhD diss., University of Nevada, Las Vegas, 2019. ProQuest.

Ward, Steven R. *Immortal: A Military History of Iran and Its Armed Forces*. Washington, DC: Georgetown University Press, 2009.

Wege, Carl Anthony. "Iran's Intelligence Establishment." *Intelligencer: Journal of
U.S. Intelligence Studies* 21, no. 2 (Summer 2015): 63–67.

———. "Iranian Counterintelligence." *International Journal of Intelligence and
CounterIntelligence* 32, no. 2 (2019): 272–94.

Zabih, Sepehr. *The Iranian Military in Revolution and War*. London: Routledge, 1988.

Zimmt, Raz. "The Intelligence Organization of the IRGC: A Major Iranian Intelligence
Apparatus." Meir Amit Intelligence and Terrorism Information Center, November
5, 2020. https://www.terrorism-info.org.il/en/the-intelligence-organization-of-the
-irgc-a-major-iranian-intelligence-apparatus.

Selected Iranian and Other Related Persian- and English-Language Websites

Aftab-e Yazd (https://aftabyazdonline.ir): a reformist-affiliated Persian-language daily
newspaper.

Aftab News (https://aftabnews.ir/fa/news): a moderate semiofficial Persian-language
news agency once associated with former president Ali Akbar Hashemi Rafsanjani.

Al-Alam (https://fa.alalam.ir/news): the IRIB's Arabic-language satellite channel,
which has an accompanying website with posts in multiple languages.

Donya-e-Eqtesad (https://www.donya-e-eqtesad.com/fa): a private daily newspaper
in Iran that publishes in Persian on business, economic, and political news.

Eghtesad News (https://www.eghtesadnews.com/fa): a private Persian-language
economic news organization.

Entekhab (https://www.entekhab.ir): a semiofficial Persian-language news website.

Etemad Online (https://www.etemadonline.com/fa): a Persian-language reformist
news website.

Fars News Agency (https://www.farsnews.ir): an IRGC-affiliated news website that
publishes in Persian and English.

Hamshahri (https://www.hamshahrionline.ir): a reformist Persian-language newspaper.

Iran Daily (https://newspaper.irandaily.ir): an English-language newspaper published
by the Islamic Republic News Agency.

Iran News (available at ProQuest and Gale Online): an English-language daily published in Tehran by the proregime Sokhan Gostar Institute.

Iran Student Correspondents Association (https://www.iscanews.ir): a Persian-
language news website affiliated with Islamic Azad University, a private university
system with campuses throughout Iran.

Iranian Labour News Agency (https://www.ilna.ir): reformist-leaning news agency
owned by a labor union controlled by the government.

Iranian Students News Agency (https://www.isna.ir/news): a semiofficial Persian- and
English-language news organization run by university students.

Islamic Republic News Agency (https://www.irna.ir/news): the official state news agency of Iran, which operates under the Ministry of Culture and Islamic Guidance.

Jamaran (https://www.jamaran.news/fa): a Persian- and English-language history website dedicated to Grand Ayatollah Khomeini.

Javan (https://www.javanonline.ir): IRGC-affiliated Persian-language conservative daily newspaper.

Jomhuri-ye Eslami (https://telegram.me/jenewspaper): a conservative Persian-language daily newspaper started in 1979 by the Islamic Republican Party.

Kayhan (https://kayhan.ir): a hard-line conservative Persian-language daily newspaper.

Khabar Online (https://www.khabaronline.ir): an independent reformist news website.

Mashregh News (https://www.mashreghnews.ir): an allegedly IRGC-IO–affiliated Persian-language news website.

Mehr News (https://www.mehrnews.com): a Persian- and multiple-language news agency directed by the regime's Islamic Propagation Organization (aka the Islamic Development Organization).

Press TV (https://www.presstv.ir): the IRIB's English-language satellite channel.

Shargh Daily (https://www.sharghdaily.com): a reformist-affiliated news website.

Tabnak (https://www.tabnak.ir/fa/news): a conservative Persian-language news service.

Tarikh Irani (http://tarikhirani.ir/fa/news): a Persian-language history website that republishes news stories, book excerpts, and illustrated history from other media.

Tasnim (www.tasnimnews.com): an IRGC-affiliated Persian-language news organization.

Tehran Times (https://www.tehrantimes.com): a state-run, progovernment, English-language newspaper published by the Mehr News Agency under the direction of the Islamic Propagation Organization.

Young Journalists Club (https://www.yjc.news/fa): a student news website affiliated with the state-run IRIB television network.

Antiregime Persian- and English-Language Websites

Iran International (https://iranintl.com): an anti–Islamic Republic of Iran Persian- and English-language news website based in Washington, DC, that is partially owned by Saudi investors.

IranWire (https://iranwire.com/en/): a news website published in the United Kingdom in Persian, English, and other languages, founded by Maziar Bahari and run by exiled Iranian journalists.

Payvand (http://www.payvand.com): a Persian-and English-language news website run by Iranian exiles.

Radio Farda (https://www.radiofarda.com): the Persian-language service of the US government's Radio Free Europe / Radio Liberty broadcast network.

Index

About the Author

Steven R. Ward worked as an intelligence officer for nearly thirty years with the Central Intelligence Agency, covering Middle Eastern, South Asian, and related national security issues. He served as a deputy national intelligence officer for the Near East and South Asia on the National Intelligence Council (2005–6) and as a director of intelligence programs for the National Security Council (1998–99). Ward is a retired US Army Reserve lieutenant colonel and a United States Military Academy graduate. He also is the author of *Immortal: A Military History of Iran and Its Armed Forces* (Georgetown University Press, 2nd ed. 2014).